Wilderness Survival

2nd Edition

by John Haslett and Cameron M. Smith

for **dummies**®

A Wiley Brand

Wilderness Survival For Dummies®, 2nd Edition

Published by: **John Wiley & Sons, Inc.**, 111 River Street, Hoboken, NJ 07030-5774, www.wiley.com

Copyright © 2023 by John Wiley & Sons, Inc., Hoboken, New Jersey

Media and software compilation copyright © 2023 by John Wiley & Sons, Inc. All rights reserved.

Published simultaneously in Canada

For general information on our other products and services, please contact our Customer Care Department within the U.S. at 877-762-2974, outside the U.S. at 317-572-3993, or fax 317-572-4002. For technical support, please visit https://hub.wiley.com/community/support/dummies.

Wiley publishes in a variety of print and electronic formats and by print-on-demand. Some material included with standard print versions of this book may not be included in e-books or in print-on-demand. If this book refers to media such as a CD or DVD that is not included in the version you purchased, you may download this material at http://booksupport.wiley.com. For more information about Wiley products, visit www.wiley.com.

Library of Congress Control Number: 2023931496

ISBN 978-1-394-15988-8 (pbk); ISBN 978-1-394-15989-5 (ebk); 978-1-394-15990-1 (ebk)

SKY10042723_021323

Contents at a Glance

Table of Contents

Introduction

Welcome to the realm of the extraordinary. Survival situations can bring out greatness in some people — but they can also bring out foolishness, terror, radical changes in perspective, and sometimes, just enormous gratitude for being alive. We, your friendly authors, have crawled like fleas in the face of enormous winds and waves, and we, too, have experienced these extraordinary states of mind — and many more.

But more often than not, survival situations aren't so romantic: You're on a day hike, five miles from a major city — but hopelessly lost — and even though you can hear and see signs of civilization, you're still in danger of dying from hypothermia in the next hour. This situation can kill you just as readily as being lost on an expedition to the North Pole. Well, we wrote this book with sympathy for *both* — those involved in exotic adventures and those who just got a little turned around while taking pictures.

You may worry that wilderness survival requires you to bite off the heads of snakes or maybe leap from a cliff into a raging river. But really, most survival skills are much more mundane. For example, you can extend the life of batteries by taking them out of your flashlight and putting them inside your shirt, against your skin. Keeping batteries warm preserves their charge in cold conditions. There. That wasn't so bad, was it? You picked up a basic survival skill and you didn't have to shiver or go hungry. You're already rolling.

About This Book

This book is designed to thoroughly cover the basics of wilderness survival. To compile the information, we've selectively researched many tried-and-true sources, such as *The U.S. Army Survival Manual* (U.S. Govt. Printing Office FM21-76) and *Essentials of Sea Survival* (Human Kinetics Press), but we've called upon our own practical experiences and those of many field experts.

Throughout this book, we use the word *we* when we, Cameron and John, both want to say something personal to you, our reader. This book comes from the combined experiences of two people who've been through a lot of misadventures over decades across the globe, and who are very close friends. We've been in enough trouble — and scared enough — that we think alike, basically, and therefore we speak with the same voice.

We define the *wilderness* as just about any place out-of-doors. We know from bitter experience that it's easy to freeze to death in places that a geographer wouldn't necessarily think of as "wilderness areas." With that in mind, you should know that this isn't a camping or 'bushcraft' book; it's a book for anyone at risk of perishing from exposure to the elements, whether camping or off on a "harmless" stroll.

We try to keep the language simple and direct; when we do offer new vocabulary, we *italicize* and define it.

We hope you enjoy reading every word that we've written, but if you just want the bare essentials of surviving in the wild, feel free to skip the sidebars that appear in the gray shaded boxes. This is additional information, purely for the curious. We hope you read them, but if you don't, you won't miss any vital information.

To make the content more accessible, we divided it into five parts:

>> Part 1, Stayin' Alive: Basic Wilderness Survival Principles

>> Part 2, Exploring Advanced Survival Techniques

>> Part 3, Surviving in Extreme Land Environments

>> Part 4, Surviving on the Seas, Oceans, and Great Lakes

>> Part 5, The Part of Tens

Foolish Assumptions

Although we know that you don't fit every description in this list of assumptions we make about you, we do assume that you have at least a few of the following characteristics:

>> You're someone who enjoys nature and being outdoors.

>> You want a basic survival book that gives clear, practical instructions for surviving in the wild, including how to find your way back to civilization or signal a search and rescue team.

>> You may be exploring solo or out with a group.

>> You're interested in safety while being outdoors for extended periods, such as backpacking trips, prolonged sailing trips, or camping trips.

>> You prefer your advice served warm and friendly, not cold and dry like other survival manuals you may have tried.

>> You want a survival manual that you can throw in your car or backpack (or carry-on luggage) or download to your phone for greater portability, just in case.

>> You've seen survival shows on television and they intrigue you.

Icons Used in This Book

Icons, little pictures in the margins, are placed next to some of the paragraphs that we feel need extra emphasis.

TIP

This symbol indicates additional information to make something easier to do or understand, and sometimes suggests alternatives.

REMEMBER

This symbol flags important information or actions that you should squirrel away in your brain for quick recall later.

WARNING

This symbol means danger. We use it to emphasize some aspect of a survival situation that can really get you into trouble.

Beyond the Book

In addition to the abundance of information and guidance related to wilderness survival that we provide in this book, you get access to even more help and information online at *Dummies.com*. Check out this book's online Cheat Sheet. Just go to *www.dummies.com* and search for "Wilderness Survival For Dummies Cheat Sheet."

Where to Go From Here

Feel free to start reading this book anywhere you like. The five parts are completely modular, so you don't have to read them in order. However, Chapter 1 is certainly a good place to start because it tells you exactly what to do first if you find yourself lost outdoors.

Part 1 is a great place to get a good foundation for all things wilderness survival. If you're planning on a trip to an extreme environment, you may want to start with Part 3. On the other hand, if you're looking for adventures on the sea, you can go straight to Part 4.

Of course, when you're in a survival situation, you can check out the index or table of contents and simply flip to the information you need. If you're bleeding, or if you've twisted your ankle, or if you've been bitten by a snake, check out Chapter 13. Or if your ship has gone under and you find yourself in a life raft, go to Chapter 19.

1

Stayin' Alive: Basic Wilderness Survival Principles

Chapter **1**

Staying Safe in the Great Outdoors

K nowing the threats you face in the wilderness and the wisest courses of action to take to counter those threats can go a long way toward keeping you alive in a bad situation. If you find yourself lost or adrift, this prior knowledge allows you to start working on your survival priorities immediately, changing you from victim to survivor.

This chapter is a jumping-off point to wilderness survival. We give you a prioritized overview of the basics you need to know in practically any wilderness survival situation. We describe the main threats to survival and how to take care of them in the right order. Finally, we show you how so many people go wrong and how you can prevent your situation from getting worse — or perhaps how to stay out of trouble altogether!

Being Prepared and Proactive

Preparation gives you the knowledge to extend your life, and it may even give you what you need to avoid a crisis. Chapter 2 discusses what you can do and bring to be prepared in any wilderness.

Being *proactive* usually means stopping and getting control — such as slowing your swimming stroke or even floating to conserve your energy. If you suddenly feel lost, don't react and don't speed up; stop, sit, and think carefully about your situation. This is the beginning of taking control of the situation before it takes control of you.

Keeping the Right Attitude

Real survival situations feel enormously unfair — it's as though the world is conspiring against you or the odds are simply beyond your abilities. To survive this situation, you must accept the situation and keep a positive outlook; Chapter 3 covers survival psychology. To cultivate a positive attitude, begin by accepting the situation and taking it all in. Many people perish simply because they can't master disbelief.

The following suggestions can help you keep your spirits up:

>> **Be resourceful and creative.** Resources and options that you've never considered are available to you. Use rocks as hammers, nails as fishhooks, and belt buckles as reflectors for signaling. Then think of new options and work out more plans. Think of a way.

>> **Be patient.** Consider that being rescued or working your way out of the problem may take time, but never assume that no one will come looking for you.

>> **Never say die.** Misery and fear can fool you into thinking you're finished. Don't let your mind play tricks on you. You can keep going long after you feel like you can't. A *lot* longer. Don't give up. Keep a positive attitude, or grit your teeth in grim determination. If you slip into a negative attitude, you'll melt like a candle.

Applying Survival Basics

After accepting the situation, your next survival priority is to address your survival needs in the order they appear in this section.

You may also face a medical situation, which may take precedence over the ones we mention here, depending on its severity. For first aid procedures, see Chapter 13.

Regulating body temperature

Thermoregulation is the management of your body temperature. It's the highest priority because being too cold *(hypothermia)* or being too hot *(hyperthermia)* are the fastest killers in the wilderness. Here's how to manage your body temperature:

>> **Cold environments:** Stay dry — be careful near streams and rivers, shelter yourself from rain, and keep sweating to a minimum. If night is coming, realize that hypothermia is a dire threat and make a fire and a shelter.

>> **Hot environments:** If you are getting uncomfortably hot, take action by finding shelter and taking a rest. Waiting too long is the biggest contributor to heat exhaustion. It's especially important to stay hydrated in hot environments, so drink water if you have it, or start thinking about where you are going to get it.

The four components that govern thermoregulation are clothing, fire, shelter, and your own actions. Use these things to keep your body at a healthy temperature.

Your first line of defense: Clothing

In a survival situation outdoors you will probably have different daytime and nighttime temperatures, and your activity level will differ at these times as well. The best way to manage these temperature differences is dress in layers, improvised if needed. The key is to add or subtract clothing layers depending on temperature. For more on clothing, see Chapter 4.

REMEMBER

In many survival situations, people discard clothing that they don't think they need. Never discard any clothing, under any circumstances. If you take off a shirt or jacket, tie it around your waist or jam it in your belt; you'll want it again some time, guaranteed!

If you're in a cold environment and working hard, strip off layers of clothing to prevent sweat from soaking your clothes (wet clothes lose insulating capacity). If you're facing a cold night, add insulating layers by stuffing grass, leaves, or moss inside your clothing, creating a 'dead air' layer that helps to keep you warm.

In all environments, cover your head. If you don't have a hat, improvise one that covers your head and neck thoroughly. In the cold, a head and neck covering deters hypothermia, especially if you've fallen into cold water, and in the sun, it deters heat stroke.

Warming up to the fire

A fire helps prevent hypothermia and boosts morale. Its light can be seen by night and its smoke by day. Carefully prepare your fire in a survival situation — don't rush things. Plan it out and have lots of backups to keep the flame going after it ignites. For info on how to make fire, see Chapter 5.

Taking shelter

Even the crudest shelter can also keep you warm and improve morale. We cover shelter basics in Chapter 6, and provide specific tips for different environments in Part 3.

Regulating your temperature in the water

If you're in a water environment, thermoregulation is especially important because you are much more susceptible to hypothermia when wet. Take the following measures to stay warm:

>> **Stay as still as you possibly can.** Don't tread water if you can help it; that just depletes energy, which will eventually make you colder.

>> **Cover your head.** Use anything you can to insulate your head, because the scalp dissipates a lot of body heat.

>> **Try to keep your armpits closed by holding your elbows at your sides, and keep your crotch closed by crossing your legs.** These areas also leak a lot of body heat.

Check out Chapter 18 for information about staying warm at sea.

Signaling for rescue

After you address body temperature management, think about how to make yourself 'findable' by rescuers. Don't ever believe that no one will come for you — someone usually does.

The main principle of signaling for rescue is to stand out from the natural environment. Visual signals should be large and bright and contrast with nature. Lay out tarps, sleeping bags, and other materials so your location is easier to see from a helicopter, for instance. You can use reflective surfaces and fire to gain attention day and night. Shouting is fine if that's all you can do, but human voice doesn't travel very far, and shouting is exhausting; better to carry a whistle in your survival kit. Chapter 12 gives you a lot more information on signaling for help.

Avoiding dehydration

With body temperature under control and a signaling plan underway, next address hydration. In a hot environment, water can become a life-threatening problem within hours, but in most temperate environments, you usually have roughly three days before the lack of water completely incapacitates you. The minute you think you're in trouble, start practicing *water discipline*, which means minimizing water usage. Here are some useful water discipline methods:

>> **Stop consuming diuretics immediately.** These are liquids that make you urinate a lot, like coffee, tea, soda, and alcohol.

>> **Minimize your physical exertion if you can.** Even if you can't feel it, you're losing water through perspiration and heavy breathing.

>> **Don't eat or smoke.** These activities use up your body's water reserves. Try to enforce this measure as long as possible.

>> **Limit your water intake as much as you can.** If you're in temperate conditions or at sea, don't drink anything for the first 24 hours — you'll just lose it through urination. The only exception to this rule is if you're in very hot conditions on land. In these conditions, you have to drink as soon as you feel yourself becoming incapacitated.

Check out Chapter 7 for a thorough discussion of catching water, finding water, treating water, and drinking water in the wilderness.

Staying nourished

Food is the last priority on the list because, in most cases, you're rescued before it becomes a real factor. You can go a week or more before a lack of food begins to incapacitate you. Nevertheless, finding and eating something can really boost your energy and morale.

Many plants and animals are poisonous. If you're in any way uncertain about a food source, don't eat it — becoming incapacitated is the worst thing that can happen to you in the wild. For more on finding food in the wilderness, see Chapter 8.

Navigating in the Wild

While in most cases it's best for you to stay put and wait for rescue, in some cases the grave decision to move must be made. Rather than just wandering aimlessly, this requires *navigation*, the art of consciously-directed travel. The fundamental rule of navigation is to know where you are and to update that information any time that you move.

Many methods make wilderness navigation possible and survivable, but any time you move, there is the potential for getting even more lost than you were before. To avoid this, in Chapter 11 we further explore methods for navigating, rather than wandering, in wilderness situations, using basic tools including the sun and stars as direction-finders.

Relying on tools to navigate

You may find this astounding, but many people are rescued every year even though they have a map and GPS in their hands. Satellite navigation and modern map making haven't taken *all* the challenge out of the wilderness — indeed, they give many people a false sense of confidence. Always know how your navigation instruments (compass, GPS unit, and/or cellphone) work, and be sure you have current maps. Chapter 9 provides in-depth coverage on using these tools to help you navigate in the wilderness.

Looking to the heavens

Finding direction with the use of the sun and stars is really quite easy. You can start with the sun — it rises in the east and sets in the west, and if you're anywhere in North America, Europe, or Northern Asia, it's due south of you at midday. Check out Chapter 10 for lots of other ways to use the sun and stars to find your way.

Surviving Injury

Staying healthy and injury-free can go a long way toward surviving in the outdoors. To do so, keep the following tips in mind, and for more on first aid, check out Chapter 13.

>> **Always be on guard for hypothermia and hyperthermia.**
Even if you don't feel the symptoms, someone in your party may be becoming incapacitated, and unfortunately, people don't necessarily cry out when they're afflicted by hypothermia — they just lie down.

>> **Treat trauma immediately.** If a member of your party has suffered a trauma, start by ensuring their circulation, airway, and breathing are okay, and be prepared to administer *cardiopulmonary resuscitation* (CPR).

- **Circulation:** Make sure they have a pulse.

- **Airway:** Check to make sure nothing is interfering with the person's airway (food or vomit in the windpipe or *trachea*).

- **Breathing:** Make sure the subject is breathing.

 If you've checked these signs and the subject is fine, put them in the *recovery position*, which means lying on their side with their head on an arm.

>> **Stop bleeding.** Address bleeding by applying direct pressure to larger wounds for 10 to 15 minutes; in many cases, this allows the blood to coagulate and stop up the wound.

Avoiding Common Causes of Survival Situations

This section introduces some of the most common reasons people end up lost in the wild to help prevent you from ending up in the same situation.

Making errors in judgment

A leading cause of crises in the wilderness is *errors in judgment*. This is a broad term, but a few examples show how people commit errors in judgment in the wilderness:

>> **Not watching out for potential falls:** Be especially careful whenever you're near cliffs or when traveling at night or in low visibility conditions. Watch for ledges and earthen trails that can give way.

>> **Letting yourself become dehydrated:** You only have to dehydrate by about 5 percent to become physically and mentally impaired by 20 percent. When you add dehydration on top of fatigue and hypothermia, you end up incapacitated. Carry a good supply of water and drink when you are thirsty.

>> **Trying to walk too far:** Anytime you or one of your party isn't physically fit, you need to be prudent in estimating how far you can go. If you've missed a meal or have been through an excessively exhausting event within the previous 24 hours, don't push it.

>> **Continuing to walk long after you're lost:** Doing so just gets you more lost.

>> **Wearing inadequate clothing:** You should know that wet cold is vastly more dangerous than dry cold. Anytime you face wet cold, take extra precautions. Chapter 4 discusses important clothing information.

>> **Carrying inadequate gear:** Not carrying warm clothing and footgear, or the tools to start a fire, are the prerequisites for a deadly hypothermia scenario. Chapter 2 identifies the equipment to take.

>> **Relying too much on GPS or cellphones to carry you through unknown conditions:** Not watching your maps because you have GPS or ignoring a deteriorating situation because you think you can always call for help is a recipe for disaster. Take a look at Chapter 11 for more on this.

Book knowledge is obviously useful, but learning good outdoor judgment takes experience. Making mistakes is natural and, in fact, okay if you're careful to analyze and learn from them.

Losing it: Behaviors that help you get lost

In addition to making poor decisions — which can happen to even the most experienced outdoorspeople on occasion — it's possible to become lost in the wild for an infinite number of reasons. Still, there are some well-known ways that people most commonly get lost, and they're worth knowing in advance:

>> **Leaving the trail to take a shortcut:** An inordinate number of people get lost every year because they leave the trail to try a shortcut. Stick to the trail, especially if you're in unknown territory.

>> **Letting your awareness lapse:** You pass through a tunnel in the foliage, or you're concentrating on your photography or on seeing a particular species of bird, and suddenly you're not exactly sure where you are.

>> **Walking downslope from a trail:** Whenever you walk down from a trail (descend), you break your line of sight with the trail.

>> **Being overconfident in wilderness areas that you haven't been in for a while:** You can easily get lost when going back to your old stomping grounds.

>> **Turning onto false trails:** Keep in mind that the world's wilderness areas are constantly in flux. One good rain can wash away enough earth to make it appear as though there's a new trail.

>> **Forging ahead:** Many people get lost because they reach a point where the trail fades or is poorly marked and they continue on but can't pick up the trail again. Be on guard for this, and make sure you leave behind your own markers in these areas.

>> **Going farther than you normally go when hunting, hiking, bird-watching, shooting outdoor photography, or berry- or mushroom-picking:** You leave your normal stomping grounds — you push a little farther, and then when you turn around to come back, you get turned around.

>> **Falling behind the group:** Parties of friends or social groups get spread out, or one particular person begins to straggle.

>> **Getting separated from the group:** This can happen whenever you're transported to a remote area, such as when you're taken to a dive site or a location in the desert. If you go off exploring on your own, let someone in the main group know.

Chapter 11 provides a lot more information on what to do to prevent getting lost, and what to do when it happens.

Chapter 2

Preparing Yourself for a Survival Situation

Errors in judgment cause more emergencies in the wild than just about anything else. High on that list of mistakes is being ill-equipped for the environment. Properly judging what you're getting into — and carrying the right gear for the environment — can go a very long way toward staying out of survival situations.

Because increasing your survivability means making preparations, you need to understand how to properly assess the weather and stock your survival kit. So in this chapter, we give you some practical suggestions for predicting bad weather and knowing how to handle it, and we show you a practical survival kit and how to carry it.

Being Weather Aware

By knowing what weather to expect, you can take precautions in deciding what clothing to wear (see Chapter 4) and when and where to venture. This section helps you get a firm grasp on weather-related issues.

Using weather forecasts

Before you head out into the field — and until you build up enough expertise to read clouds and wind — your best bet for knowing what kind of weather to expect is to use the forecasts available to you. Try the following resources:

>> **The local news:** It can give you very detailed, specific info that nationwide forecasts can't.

>> **The Internet:** You can find dozens of good weather websites. National weather service forecasts are usually reliable, but their websites can be challenging to use. So we suggest the following sites for most of the U.S.:

- **For traveling on land:** A great place to start if you're going to travel on land in the U.S. is the National Weather Service site: (https://www.weather.gov/). On this site, you can enter the zip code or closest town to your planned area of travel and get short, medium, and (less reliable) long-term forecasts. National weather services for other countries and regions exist, but you should get acquainted with them before traveling.

- **For traveling on or near coastal waters:** If you're going to coastal areas or plan to travel on them, the National Weather Service's Marine weather site (https://www.weather.gov/marine/mttservices). can give you forecasts of such variables as wind speed and direction, wave height, and so on for your selected region.

- **For traveling on or near the Great Lakes:** For various reasons, the Great Lakes often create their own weather, so be sure to check out the forecast at https://www.weather.gov/greatlakes/.

- **NOAA Storm Prediction Center:** The site brings up a large, easily digested map of current and near-term predicted severe weather (www.spc.noaa.gov/).

- **Commercial sources:** Other good sources are AccuWeather (www.accuweather.com), Intellicast (www.intellicast.com also known as the Weather Underground), and The Weather Channel (www.weather.com). These sites have advisory sections listing watches and warnings of bad weather throughout the world.

A great resource for all kinds of weather-related safety information is at www.weather.gov/safety/. Here you can get basic information on such topics as flooding, thunderstorms, winds, and much more. You can also get specific forecasts for fog, riptide, thunderstorms, and many other hazards.

>> **Weather radios:** If you plan to be out more than a few days, consider carrying a NOAA radio receiver. These inexpensive radios receive weather alerts and forecasts. The hand-crank models don't need batteries.

Keep in mind that a *weather watch* is simply the weather service's way of telling you that ideal conditions exist for a certain type of weather — tornadoes, floods, storms, and so on. A *weather warning* means that the weather phenomenon is known to be occurring at this moment. For example, a tornado warning means that someone actually saw a tornado nearby.

Before setting out for your adventure, know these three main pieces of weather information:

>> **The 24-hour temperature range:** This one piece of information prepares you more than just about anything else because it tells you how to dress and what gear you need to take. If you get lost, delayed, or injured, you may end up having to endure the entire temperature range — from the lowest to the highest.

If you're planning on leaving your base, such as a road or a campsite, for any length of time, take the estimated temperature range, add 10 degrees to the high and subtract 10 degrees from the low, and prepare accordingly. Also consider wind and precipitation in your preparations.

>> **The short-term forecast:** The three-day forecast is usually the most reliable. Be sure to watch for predicted precipitation.

>> **The air pressure trend:** *Barometric pressure* is simply a measurement of how much air is sitting on top of the area you're in. On weather maps and televised forecasts, you will often see large L's indicating low pressure air masses and H's

indicating high pressure air masses, generally moving from west to east. The pressure tells you one of two things:

- If the pressure is low or dropping, the atmosphere around you is becoming unstable. This means that the weather is probably going to deteriorate.

- If the pressure is high or rising, the atmosphere around you is stabilizing. Rising or steady pressure usually means good weather or a continuation of the weather you already have.

Some outdoor watches and other tools have a barometer that indicates the atmospheric pressure. After using these for a little while you can use them to identify the pressure trend — but remember that you need to have several observations over several hours to be sure of a trend. These tools can't tell you that a storm is imminent, only that things are developing in a higher- or lower-pressure direction. If you're familiar with the pressures in your travel area, this can be invaluable.

Watching for weather signs from wind and clouds

When you're in the field, you usually don't have a chance to check the Internet. However, you can watch out for signs of approaching weather — especially changes that weren't predicted or that had a low chance of occurring. Pay attention to the winds and clouds to help you make weather predictions.

Considering the winds

It's a good practice to always have a general feel for the wind speed and direction when you're outdoors. After some practice, you almost subconsciously keep track of these. If the wind significantly increases or changes direction, conditions around you are changing. If the wind changes radically, that usually means a substantial change in the weather is imminent and you may need to take cover.

TIP

To gauge the possible effect of wind that you *don't* feel (but might come up), try to size up the terrain around you and then estimate what a big wind would do if it were to come upon you suddenly. Here's what wind can do in various terrains:

>> If you're on an exposed mountainside, a hard wind can cause a drastic drop in temperature.

>> If you have open plains around you, remember that wide open spaces are nature's speedway for high winds.

>> If you're near an exposed cliff, the wind may come in, explode against that cliff, and cause havoc, with both updrafts and downdrafts at the cliff face.

>> In forested terrain, consider the dangers of trees being blown over or (more likely) branches falling from trees.

>> In desert or plains terrain, consider the possibility of sandstorms or dust storms.

>> On open water, such as a lake, remember that wind creates waves and that even a little wind can push around a small craft like a canoe or kayak.

Consulting the clouds

Two types of clouds signify the coming of rain within a few hours or minutes. Here are the *nimbus* (rain) clouds:

>> **Any dark, low, heavily laden clouds:** Rain's obviously coming, right? These gray, blanket-like clouds are *nimbostratus* clouds.

>> **Tall, dense, fluffy clouds:** Though less obvious, this second type of rain cloud indicates heavy rain and thunderstorms. An anvil head (a *cumulonimbus* cloud) is usually tall, dense (like a large island or column in the sky), and as puffy as cotton. If, during the day, you see this type of cloud grow very tall in the sky, you're seeing a potential thunderstorm (see Figure 2-1) These storm clouds usually bring rain, lightning, high winds, and sometimes hail. When the top of the cloud is being blown sideways, the thunderstorm is in its dissipating phase, which is good news. Plus, most thunderstorms last just a few hours, and many are followed by clear, good weather. So, no need to panic — just hunker down and wait it out. The storm will end.

TIP

If you've received a forecast of 20 percent chance of rain and an anvil head or low, gray clouds are nearby, feel free to increase the chance of rain to 50 percent (or more), all by yourself.

FIGURE 2-1: An anvil head storm cloud indicating the rain and strong winds will end soon

Carrying Survival Equipment

Always carry a survival kit (not just a first aid kit) in the wilderness. If you spend enough time in the dark and in trouble, as we've done, you find that one little item is almost always what saves you. Being prepared and carrying a survival kit can often turn a bad situation into at least a tolerable one.

In this section, we discuss different types of kits. Each list of equipment is slightly more elaborate than the previous one. Sometimes we list a piece of equipment twice because to be fully prepared, having two types of a particular item is ideal.

REMEMBER

Top priorities in a survival situation are to maintain a healthy body temperature, secure water and food, and prepare to signal for rescue. The items you carry in a survival kit should be selected to at least help with these basics. Depending on where you are going, you may need to tailor your kit a little, for example, for switching up what you used for desert travel to better accommodate river travel.

Keeping five essential items on hand

You need to always have five basic items with you, even if others in your party have them, too. Without these items, you're utterly defenseless — naked, in fact. The good news is that they shouldn't weigh you down — you can put three of these items on a keychain, and four out of the five can fit in one pocket.

If you're flying, be ready to check your survival kit with luggage or prepare to restock forbidden items (matches, knives, and so on) when you arrive at your travel area.

A reliable light source

You need light to perform complicated tasks in the dark and also so you can signal for help at night. Many times, especially when you have plenty of moonlight, you should try to do everything with your natural night vision; however, you may not have time to adjust to darkness, or you may have to perform a critical task, such as map reading in a dense forest on a moonless night. Luckily, your light options are plentiful, advanced, and relatively inexpensive:

>> **LED keychain flashlights:** The bare minimum, these tiny flashlights (they might be just the size of a large coin or a pencil) fit on your keychain or in your pocket, and they use LEDs, or *light-emitting diodes,* that don't break if they're dropped. Because LEDs use only a tiny amount of energy, these lights last a long time on a single battery.

>> **LED headlamp:** Excellent, lightweight LED headlamps are available; these leave your hands free to do things, and they are often very bright.

Try to buy an LED light with multiple bulbs, as opposed to a single bulb. They give off a lot of light for their size.

Fire maker and tinder

Being able to make fire is crucial because it provides heat, light, and improves morale at night. A fire maker, such as a lighter or magnesium bar, is essential. Also keep a small supply of *tinder* or (dry, highly flammable material for fire-starting) in your kit and you'll radically increase your chances of success.

In most cases, hypothermia poses an even greater threat than dehydration. Dying of dehydration takes anywhere from one to ten days, but you can die of hypothermia in less than 90 minutes.

We discuss fire makers in more detail in the section titled "Building the basic survival kit," later in this chapter. But, fire makers work only if you know how to build a fire. For more on fire, check out Chapter 5.

Penknife, pocketknife, or multitool

You don't have to have a big, impressive knife in the wild (although it sure helps), but you do need to have some kind of durable, metal blade. Your three main options — all of which have blades that fold down — are:

>> **Penknife:** The smallest knife, the penknife, fits on a keychain. This little item may be the best purchase you ever make — even if you never set foot in the outdoors — allowing you to cut, scrape, pry, and puncture.

>> **Pocketknife:** The next step up from the penknife is the small pocketknife. You can choose from infinite varieties. Regardless of which type you buy, it should have a hole at one end for a *lanyard,* a string that runs from the knife to your wrist, so you don't lose your blade when you're working. A 5-inch long folding pocketknife with a sturdy lanyard on it is a lifesaver.

>> **Multipurpose knife or multitool:** The next step up is the multipurpose pocketknife, such as the Swiss Army knife, which has a variety of tools folded into one case (see Figure 2-2e, later in this chapter).

Some multitools are over-designed and clumsy to use; do some research before buying. The best ones have durable blades, screwdriver heads, and needle-nose pliers.

Water container

Staying hydrated is essential for keeping you strong and running at your peak. Carrying a good container gives you the ability to refill it easily.

Keep in mind the following ideas when buying a water container:

>> **Durability and versatility:** Overall the best survival water containers are metal because you can disinfect water in them by boiling. An army-style canteen is great because it's durable and has a wide mouth, making filling in a river or lake easier. If a canteen is too bulky, consider carrying a

collapsible water container, but remember these are vulnerable to puncture. Whatever the container type, it should be about a liter (¼ gallon) in size.

>> **Convenience in carrying:** Many times, unbelievably, people who are lost discard equipment, clothing, water bottles, and so on — you don't want that temptation, so be sure to pick a water container that you don't mind carrying long distances.

Instruments, electronics, and power sources

Survival instruments include GPS receivers, personal tracking devices, and compasses (Figure 2-2m). And just about everyone carries a smartphone outdoors these days. For whatever of these you are carrying, be sure you are starting with charged or new batteries, and carry alternate or backup power sources, such as spare batteries and solar charging panels. For more on these types of equipment and how they can help you navigate, check out Chapter 9.

Building the basic survival kit

Good wilderness survival kits are available on the market, but we strongly suggest you make your own because you can be sure of the quality of the components and that they are appropriate to your outdoor activity. (It's also fun!) The basic kit we discuss in this section weighs only a few pounds and you can assemble it in a day. You can see a fully assembled survival kit in the section titled "Building the complete kit" later in this chapter.

REMEMBER

If you're going to be in some kind of watercraft, a life jacket (also known as a *personal flotation device* or PFD) should be considered part of the basic survival kit. Also, always carry a spare propulsion device such as an extra paddle or oar. Check with your outfitter or the U.S. Coast Guard to see what's required by law to be aboard any vessel you rent. To understand which type of PFD works for your unique situation, check out the sidebar, "Finding the right flotation device."

FINDING THE RIGHT FLOTATION DEVICE

If you plan to be near water, a personal flotation device (PFD) is a must, but you have a lot of options to choose from that suit specific needs. Because PFDs are categorized by type, this list explains your options so that you carry the correct one:

- **Type I:** These life jackets are the best overall. They keep you afloat in heavy seas, and they turn you right-side-up if you've been knocked unconscious.

- **Type II:** These vests are for near-shore activities, and they don't turn you right-side-up if you're knocked unconscious.

- **Type III:** These floatation aids are used when water-skiing or duck hunting. Don't use these in the ocean.

- **Type IV:** These are life rings and seat cushions, and they're designed to be thrown to someone in peril.

- **Type V:** These are work vests, and they usually look like a harness. They're designed to inflate in time of emergency.

A waterproof container

We like to brag that you can fit this little kit into a large zipper-lock bag, but we suggest you find a sturdier container. Look for a container around your house, use an ammunition pouch from a surplus store, or your best bet, get a *dry bag*, a completely waterproof vinyl bag that you can order online or get from a boating or outdoor store. When you have the container you want, take a permanent marker and write your name and WILDERNESS SURVIVAL KIT in large letters on the container.

A complete fire-making kit

Your complete fire-making kit should contain *at least three* fire-making instruments and some tinder. Good fire-making instruments include the following:

>> **Lighters:** Butane cigarette lighters (Figure 2-2s) are good, but saltwater causes them to malfunction within just a few days. Long-nosed fireplace lighters, which are usually red and

black in color, last much longer under corrosive conditions, and they're generally superior to just about any other lighter. Some high-tech lighters claim to work in any conditions, but we take that claim with a grain of salt.

Some of our colleagues swear by Zippo-type lighters, which are metal lighters that burn liquid fuel on a wick and give you a couple hundred lights. Butane lighters will give about five times more lights, but the metal types are more durable. If you prefer, it's easy enough to carry one of each. If you carry a Zippo-type, also carry spare flints and wicks.

>> **Matches:** Carry two types — plain, wooden, strike-anywhere matches and wooden waterproof matches that you can get online or at a boating supply store (Figure 2-2t). The waterproof matches are a little more expensive, but they're invaluable to have in wet conditions.

>> **Magnesium bar (metal match):** This is a tiny rod of metal that, when you shave it forcefully with a knife, produces a small pile of magnesium, which ignites under any conditions — even when wet! On top of the bar is flint, which produces a shower of white-hot sparks when you scrape it with a knife, igniting the magnesium (Figure 2-2i).

>> **Magnifying glass:** Get a flat, flexible plastic magnifying glass, about the size of a credit card, to focus the sun's rays on your tinder (Figure 2-2r).

Tinder is the highly flammable stuff you carry that starts a fire on the first try — even in wet conditions. A film canister or small zippered baggie filled with lint from your clothes dryer and treated with a couple of drops of lighter fluid or gasoline is good (Figure 2-2b), as is rolled newspaper dipped in paraffin wax. Some people like to stuff paper egg cartons with straw, pour in wax, and then separate each little pocket to create a set of fire starters. Although these are a little bulky, the wax and straw burn for as long as 10 minutes, giving you time to get your kindling started. You can also buy prepackaged tinder, but we think it's better to make and pack your own, so you know it better.

Pack your fire–making instruments and tinder in separate water–proof containers so if you lose some, you don't lose them all.

Items for clean water, shelter, and sun protection

Pack the following items to help you take care of your basic needs for clean water and protection from the elements:

» **Water purification chemicals:** These are normally packaged chemical tablets used to disinfect water gathered outdoors from a stream, lake, or river. You can buy them online and at most outdoor stores. Follow the directions on the packaging and expect to have to wait an hour or two for purified water (Figure 2-2w).

» **Steel cup:** A small metal cup is invaluable because you can boil water in it — which is still the very best way to disinfect water in the wild (Figure 2-2k).

» **High-SPF sun block:** Get the highest rating you can find in the smallest container you can, or transfer some into a separate, clean miniature bottle. Put this in a plastic zipper storage bag so it doesn't leak on everything else (Figure 2-2x).

» **Plastic painter's tarp:** In an emergency, you can build a waterproof shelter with this tarp, or you can use it as a ground cloth or a water catcher (Figure 2-2a).

» **Space blanket:** A space blanket is a large and very thin sheet of plastic, coated with a reflective material that traps body heat (Figure 2-2q). These blankets can be invaluable on a cold night, and you can spread the bright, mirror-like surface out on the ground as a signaling device. We suggest putting two in your survival kit because they're small and lightweight.

Tools for making other things

Wilderness survival usually involves a fair amount of improvisation. You may have to make your own shelter, clothing, or weapons for hunting. Pack the following tools so you can cut, tie, cover, tape, and light your way to safety:

» **A second knife:** Even if you already have a small knife or multitool (refer to the "Keeping five essential items on hand" section, earlier in this chapter), a large knife is indispensable in a real survival situation (see Figure 2-2d). If you get into a serious situation, you have to use this knife to dig, pry, hammer, and do just about everything else, not just cut. The extra heft of a large knife makes it more durable and allows you to process denser materials (you can't chop down a sapling with a pocketknife, but you can with a heavier knife). Carry such knives on a belt clip or sheath to keep them handy and not lose them.

TIP

Look for a substantial knife that you can really punish without having it break. Consider getting a knife made from a single piece of steel (from the blade through the handle) with at least a 5-inch (13-centimeter) blade. Keep the knife sharp and learn to sharpen it outdoors on a stone; a dull knife is hard to control and will inevitably cut you.

>> **Rope and wire:** You frequently have to bind things together or make improvised repairs in the wild, so carry some cordage. Here's what to pack:

● The easiest cordage to carry is the ready-made 30-foot lengths of parachute cord (Figure 2-2j), which you can buy at outdoor stores. This is a lightweight line that has an infinite number of uses.

● A small spool of thin, 20-gauge metal wire is useful for tasks requiring more durability than cordage.

● For small jobs, such as improvised sewing, consider carrying a spool of 50-pound test monofilament fishing line or unwaxed dental floss.

>> **Plastic garbage bags:** You can use plastic bags (Figure 2-2l) as containers and as improvised rain ponchos. Get three or four bags of the heaviest gauge you can find.

>> **Duct tape and safety pins:** You can use these items when you have to bind, repair, and seal all sorts of things in a crisis (Figure 2-2y).

TIP

Reverse the batteries when you stow any electronics (lights, GPS, radio) in your kit — that way, they won't run down if the device is accidentally turned on.

REMEMBER

Take plenty of extra batteries. You never know how long you may be out there. Lithium–ion batteries are lightweight and last a lot longer than alkaline batteries.

Navigation tools

The following items can help you find your way — and eventually, your way out (for info on using navigation equipment, see Chapter 9):

>> **Compass:** Even if you've never used one, a compass can always show you the basic directions. Like your knife, your compass should have a lanyard so that you don't lose it and it's always easily in reach. If you have a choice, opt for an orienteering compass, which is molded into a baseplate (see Figure 2-2m and more in Chapter 9).

>> **Map of the area:** Any map is better than none, and practically every map is useful in some way (Figure 2-2o). If you head off into the wild, government maps are best; in North America, U.S. Geological Survey topographic maps are excellent (https://www.usgs.gov/faqs/how-do-i-find-download-or-order-topographic-maps). Almost all ranger stations have maps, and the National Park Service (www.nps.gov/carto/app/#!/parks) and National Geographic (www.natgeomaps.com/) have many available online. Bring a paper map on every outing as a backup to electronic devices.

>> **Electronic navigation tools:** Carrying a GPS unit or smartphone with basic navigation capability is always a good idea (Figure 2-2n).

Signaling tools

Use these items when the going really gets rough and you have to send a distress signal (for more on distress signals, see Chapter 12):

>> **Signal mirror:** Use a mirror to signal for help during the day. You can get a good signal mirror (Figure 2-2h) online or at an outdoor or boating store. The best of these mirrors has a sighting hole, which helps a lot in aiming your light signal (see Chapter 12). A metal mirror doesn't break as easily as glass or even plastic.

>> **Whistle:** A high-pitched whistle can be heard for at least a mile and is vastly better than using your voice. You can usually purchase a signal whistle in the same place you find signal mirrors (Figure 2-2f).

>> **A spare flashlight:** Your backup flashlight; just about any LED flashlight is fine.

The international signal for distress is three of anything; three blasts on the whistle or three light flashes, wait some seconds, three again, and so on.

Constructing the complete kit

If you have a daypack or a full backpack, or if you're traveling in a car or boat, you can carry a more complete kit (see Figure 2-2).

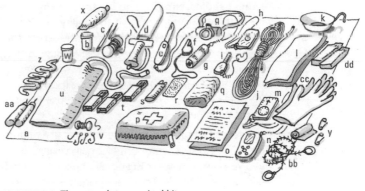

FIGURE 2-2: The complete survival kit

Here's what goes in a more complete kit. The items on this list can be added to the basic kit we discuss in the section "Building the basic survival kit" earlier in this chapter. These added tools give you a lot of staying power in the wilderness:

>> **Bivy sack (bivouac sack):** These are fabric bags that work like improvised sleeping bags/tents (see Figure 2-2q). They keep the weather off you, and though they are not insulated, they help trap body heat. Along with a space blanket or two, they can absolutely save your life in the cold. (See the "Items for clean water, shelter, and sun protection" section for more about space blankets.)

» **Heavy duty camel bag:** A *camel bag,* sometimes called a *camelback,* is a flexible/collapsible bladder that fits on your back like a backpack and has a tube that you drink from (Figure 2-2u). These are excellent water-carrying devices, though you do have to take a little care not to puncture them.

» **First aid kit with instructions:** Near last, but not least! Many premade first aid kits are available (Figure 2-2p). Good first aid kits come with pamphlets reminding you how to deal with cuts, burns, infections, broken limbs, and so on. We cover wilderness first aid in Chapters 13 and 22.

» **Maps:** Collect any map you can of the region you're visiting. Anything helps — even sightseeing or tourist maps, because each map contains different types of info. Put your maps in a zipper-lock plastic bag.

» **Sewing needles, thread, and buttons:** Being able to repair your clothing is important, as is the ability to improvise clothing from scraps of fabric, plastic, and so on. You can carry several needles in a survival kit. We suggest large, heavy needles, at least 2 inches long, with large eyes that are easy to thread with a variety of cordage (Figure 2-2c). Also carry some large buttons, which you can use to repair or improvise clothing.

» **Flexible straw/surgical tubing:** You can use tubing (Figure 2-2z) to suck water out of small crevices in rocks when you can't get water in any other way. This can be a life-saver; see Chapter 7 for important details.

» **Candles and spare wicks (Figure 2-2aa):** Before you buy candles, be sure you know how long they'll burn. Some types can burn for six hours and are favorites among mountaineers who know a thing or two about long, cold nights. You can also use them for light or to start fires.

TIP

Generally, never throw anything away in survival situations; objects are resources that may at some time help you survive. For example, keep the wax after melting a candle because you can use it as a crude adhesive or a plug for a leaky container.

>> **Wire saw:** You can buy wire saws (Figure 2-2bb) online or at outdoor stores. These saws are useful for cutting wood for any number of purposes. Put a stick through each *finger ring* or opening at either end to make using the saw more comfortable.

>> **Gloves:** Heavy-duty yard gloves (Figure 2-2cc) are useful for protecting your hands during fire-making, making stone tools, and other tasks.

>> **Food:** The body needs food and water to function. Good old-fashioned granola bars (Figure 2-2dd) can help a lot in a demoralizing situation. Other compact sources of food energy include nuts and chocolate.

>> **Mini fishing kit:** These kits (Figure 2-2v) are so lightweight and useful that you should squeeze in a couple of them if you have room. These aren't just for fishing — the hooks and the fishing line have a million and one uses.

TIP

If you have room in your pack after you assemble your complete survival kit, then we suggest including an extremely lightweight insulating pad that you can spread on cold ground to help prevent hypothermia during a long night. This is a bulky item, though, so include it only after you stock your survival kit.

Chapter **3**

The Psychology of Survival: Gaining the Upper Hand

S urvival situations usually catch you off guard; they're nothing like you expected, and the mindset that you hoped to have in a crisis suddenly seems foreign. There's no background music, like in the movies, and there's nothing heroic about the situation at all. But with a little understanding of survival psychology, perhaps you can bring that inner heroic survivor to the surface.

In this chapter, we discuss the mindset you need to get through a survival situation, what you can expect to feel when the crisis comes, and how you can expect others to act — or react — when things go wrong outdoors. We also show you how you can boost morale.

Developing a Survivor's Mindset

REMEMBER

Having the right mindset is the most important component of surviving outdoor emergencies. It's more important than training, knowledge, experience, odds, or luck. How you perceive what's happening to you dictates your ability to perform and to survive.

One startling fact when facing a survival situation is that many people succumb — they give up and perish — even before they're physically overwhelmed. They give up trying to get into a life raft after just a few tries, or they lie down on the trail after just a few hours or days of misery. Their perception, and therefore belief, is that the situation is beyond their means, or that the struggle simply isn't worth it.

Knowing how to cultivate an effective survival mentality gives you the power to hold out longer, push further, and endure more, which is the essence of survival. This section explains how to develop a survivor's mindset and how to stay focused when you're in a survival situation.

Mastering disbelief

To develop a survivor's mindset you first must master disbelief. All survival situations are extraordinary — especially when they're happening to you. Many times, the unexpected nature of the survival event leaves people so stunned with disbelief that they take action too slowly or not at all. Some of the most heartbreaking, incomprehensible stories revolve around not being able to master disbelief.

TIP

To master disbelief, you need to know that most survival situations feel unfair: You just went for a swim, and now you're 5 miles offshore, dragged out by a current. Or perhaps you're hiking in familiar territory and, although you have lots of experience, now you're lost and an unexpected cold front is coming in. The first shock you or your companions will probably feel is how unfair the situation seems.

When survival situations happen to other people, they are easy to believe, but when they happen to you, they can be virtually impossible to comprehend or internalize. Some people simply cannot get past the outrage of being put in such an extraordinary position. Don't let this happen to you. Accept that this time it's you, not someone else, and that things have gone wrong and that you have to start thinking about survival immediately. The sooner you do this, the sooner you are taking control of the situation.

REMEMBER

Keep in mind that modern ships still sink, people with GPS units still get lost, friends who are just trying to have a nice weekend hike still fall into disaster. Realize this immediately and start planning proactive procedures to save yourself and your companions.

Using SeCR or "Secure" to gain control of your situation

Once you've mastered disbelief, you may have to act immediately, such as when you are involved in the sudden sinking of a vessel, but for most other cases, your next action should be to gain psychological control of your situation. Survival situations almost invariably cloud people's judgment. All too often, your first instinct is to push harder, ignore developments around you, or, sometimes, believe that your only option is painful endurance. Taking a few moments to gain Security, Comfort, and Reassurance can, many times, prevent disaster. As shown in Figure 3-1, SeCR, or "Secure," is the progression that transforms your thinking from reactive to proactive.

"SeCR"

Security ➤ Comfort ➤ Reassurance

FIGURE 3-1: To get control of yourself and the situation, concentrate on Security, Comfort, and Reassurance

The SeCR progression is deceptively easy but incredibly effective. We, your friendly authors, have learned from bitter experience that genuine, clear-headed thought in deteriorating survival situations always pays off. Follow the three steps in the following sections to gain the upper hand.

Security

Security means getting away from immediate danger or from whatever is most distressing. For example, getting away from burning wreckage, or making or finding a shelter to escape foul weather. If the sun is setting, it can mean asking yourself, "Where is the best place to spend the night?"

The main thing is to get into a secure situation where you feel you are out of the immediate danger and able to think.

Comfort

Comfort means eliminating as much physical discomfort as you can. Get out of the wind or out of the sun. A small discomfort like a rock in your shoe or rough chafing from clothing will muddle your thinking. Simply taking your pack off, even a light daypack, can provide a little comfort so you can clear your head. Sometimes it means taking a swig of water or a bite of food.

Deciding to eat or drink has to be a judgment call. If water is scarce, don't eat (see Chapter 7 for why you shouldn't eat if you don't have water).

Reassurance

Be reassured by the knowledge that thousands of people before you have survived these same types of perilous situations. These people were probably just like you — they look like you, they talk like you — they're almost never superhuman-like people. They're just like you. And they made it. You're making progress, having arranged Security and Comfort. Now you can work on your plan for survival.

Never believe that the odds of surviving are just too low. Statistics and odds mean nothing after you go into action. If you spend enough time studying the history of human beings in impossible conditions — like the one featured in the sidebar, "Hundreds of miles from land" — you begin to see that people survive "the impossible" quite frequently.

HUNDREDS OF MILES FROM LAND

In 1995, a U.S. Marine stepped out on the deck of an aircraft carrier for a little air and promptly fell off the boat — in the middle of the Arabian Sea. The fleet sailed away into the night and there he was, with no flotation, no land for hundreds of miles, treading water — a single head in a vast, empty plain of waves. The odds of surviving were off the scale, but nonetheless, he made a flotation device by inflating his pants and then held on for 34 hours — until he was picked up by Pakistani fishermen.

UNDERSTANDING LOST PERSON BEHAVIOR

Lost Person Behavior (*LPB*) examines case histories of people who've gone lost and catalogues common denominators. Over the years, LPB has revealed some common mistakes that people make when they're lost. Most of these come from not taking a moment to go through a SeCR-type of mental transformation.

- **Speeding up:** In most cases, as soon as people suspect they're lost, they speed up. They don't exactly start running; they just start hiking much, much faster, which usually only gets them lost much, much quicker.

- **Traveling in the direction of least resistance (meandering):** When lost, many people take wrong turns on the trail intentionally because a particular part of the trail simply looks easier to walk on. Think through your trail junctions. Another path-of-least-resistance error is to go down a slope, even though it's not the way back.

- **Disbelieving instruments or maps:** This happens with compasses, GPS units, and most especially maps. Trust your instruments and the map.

- **Disrobing and discarding equipment:** Never leave anything behind. Find a way to carry it — you'll invariably end up needing it.

- **Lying down:** Sometimes the size of the wilderness simply overcomes people, and they lie down and give up.

- **Assuming no one will come looking for you:** Don't assume that no one will come looking for you. Be ready to signal.

Planning and taking action

In survival situations, confusion and bad plans can take over quickly, so make sure that you put together a thorough plan before going into action. When planning, keep the following suggestions in mind:

>> **Observe carefully.** Stressful situations can close off your powers of perception. You may have options right in front of your nose that you can't see or haven't even considered. Take time to take it all in, and never, ever assume that you see everything.

>> **Take inventory.** Get a total grip on your situation. Where are you? What are your options? How can you improve your situation? Consider taking a piece of paper and writing down the history of your situation. For example, note when and where you saw the last familiar landmark, as well as what your threats are and your options for dealing with them. Plans and escapes present themselves when you do this, and you gain strength by being proactive.

>> **Give yourself an extra choice.** In emergency situations, the either/or decision-making loop can blind you to options that are in fact right in front of you. We know that not every situation has a wide array of options, but if you have an either/or decision in front of you and both are bad, try coming up with a third — the results may shock you and even give you strength. For example, if faced with having to cross a dangerous river, one option is to look for a safer place to cross; another is to swim across aided with some flotation device, and another is to wait a few days for the water level to drop and make the crossing safer.

After you come up with a third option, continue to expand outward. View the problem from a new perspective. There may be a fourth option you haven't thought of — or maybe even a fifth. Never assume you've thought of everything.

>> **Get ready for night.** Prepare yourself for getting through the first night out. When the sun goes down, every problem you have is going to be harder to handle, even if you have flashlights. Solve as many problems as you can before the sun sets (for more on making it through cold nights, see Chapter 16).

Understanding discipline

Having the discipline to ration your food, stay put rather than succumb to the urge to start hiking back to safety, and other hard choices, is significant. Survival can be a war of attrition — a fight in which small, persistent actions allow you to succeed. The more you can conserve, the better. You're in the business of holding out, hanging on, and extending your reserves. Discipline yourself. Tell yourself that using small amounts of water, food, electrical power, and so on, is going to save your life.

GROUP DECISION-MAKING: GETTING PEOPLE IN A CRISIS TO COOPERATE

It can be challenging to get a group of people to cooperate and use discipline in stressful conditions. For many people, this may be the first time they've ever had to go on rationed food or water, and they rebel. And food and water aren't the only possible sticking points. Whenever your group has to make a decision — whether deciding when to stop for the night, coordinating your open-sea fishing team, or figuring out which way is north — you have a potential for conflict.

When working with a group, explain everything in full. Try to be as convincing as you can. One of the best ways to do this is to look at the faces around you and make a quick association with those who are cool-headed and fully functional. Try to get a majority and try to explain the wisest course of action. Remember, a cooperating group is stronger than the sum of its parts.

If you are in a leadership position, try to persuade rather than intimidate people into action. But realize that it is lonely at the top and you may have to take measures such as guarding the water, taking dangerous tools and objects away from irrational people, and even physically restraining someone who is endangering the group.

If you have people who simply won't cooperate, you may have to go it alone. Many times, groups do incredibly unwise things. You can always abstain from this; you don't have to go along with a group that's determined to destroy itself.

REMEMBER

Discipline is especially important when signaling for help. Be careful not to let excitement run away with the moment. If you're not careful, you can easily waste flares that nobody sees or run down radios that have only a limited amount of battery time. In a group setting, prepare in case you're the only one who thinks clearly in a crisis. See the sidebar, "Group decision-making: Getting people in a crisis to cooperate."

TIP

You should try to celebrate sometimes and be proud of yourself. Survival, more often than not, is a clumsy business. You get very few clean successes, and it's easy to see how imperfect your progress is. We've had times when we were making progress in the face of very grim circumstances, but because the progress was small, the pessimists among us used it to show how we were failing. Don't let this happen to you. Survival is about tiny victories. When you win, give yourself credit. It makes you stronger.

Being Aware of Your Emotions

Real survival situations often cause spontaneous reactions that you may have never considered. This section introduces some of the common emotions you and your group may feel, and how you can cope with them.

Fear

Fear is a reaction to uncertainty, and it can range from a simmering anxiety to heart-stopping terror. Fear can help us to avoid danger, but it can also paralyze us into inaction.

Before looking at how to cope with fear, it's useful to know that in surveys of lost persons, some fears tend to crop up repeatedly. None of these will come as a surprise, but knowing that others have experienced these feelings can be reassuring. Here are some top wilderness fears:

» Being alone
» Nighttime
» Suffering and pain
» The unknown
» Death
» Animal attack
» Open water

The best way to manage fear is to try to identify the specific things that are scaring you. What about the night specifically is scary? The darkness is one, you can't see what may be coming toward you. Another is the sounds you may hear, but you can't see what makes them. This unpacking of the fear allows you to think about each element and decide whether it's realistic or something of an over-reaction. If it's a realistic fear, you can work on some way to alleviate it. The point is to convert disorganized, general fear into manageable components that you can address with survival tools and techniques.

You don't have to eliminate fear to survive. It's possible to do quite incredible things even when you're afraid. One way to handle fear is to tell yourself, "I'm afraid, and now I'm going to do this." This acknowledges the sensations of fear but also lets you work toward survival.

Stress and fear, a powerful combo

After you realize you're in a survival situation, you can expect a flood of stress and fear. This is natural, and people who don't have any fear get complacent and get themselves into trouble — we know, because we've done it! What's most important is how you channel this emotional response.

You can be scared and still function. What you need is self-control; otherwise, your thinking becomes muddled. Try some of these methods to control fear and gain the upper hand:

>> **Take a deep breath and slow your heart rate.** Simply realize that your heart is racing and relax. Relax your shoulders — let them sag a bit — and then stretch your neck. Draw in a deep breath through your nose and let it out through your mouth. Your heart rate should slow down a little.

>> **Try the sandwich-making mentality.** Instead of flying into frenzied action, imagine that you're making a sandwich; just go to work addressing the components of your fears, one thing at a time. The no-nonsense body language that comes from this mentality can give you a clear head in an instant — and it has a positive effect on others around you. Frequently, when people see you act this way, they adopt this mentality for themselves. It worked when we used this technique in the middle of the night when there was panic all around us and our vessel was in trouble.

>> **Become resigned to the fact that you're in extreme peril.** Many survivors have made it through their darkest hours by resigning themselves to the moment and by taking the attitude that come what may, they're going to keep fighting.

> Many have faced deadly situations and said to themselves that they're not going to give in, and trying some course of action is better than being paralyzed by fear. This is grim business, indeed, but it has worked in many cases.

Panic

Panic is a common — and counterproductive reaction to stress. It leads to uncoordinated actions and wild, unproductive behavior. Realize that if you panic, you lose; a panicked person might not recover from the situation because they become unaware of what they are doing. An effective method of *preventing* panic is to practice self-awareness: realize which direction your emotions are taking you and reel yourself back in so that you can do organized, productive activities that will increase your chances of survival.

If you feel an enormous surge of fear rushing over you, or if you feel your body actually speeding up — such as hiking faster or shaking — immediately recognize that you're thinking in the wrong way and pull tightly on your own personal leash. Self-control may feel unnatural, but it makes you very strong in the field, and ultimately, it saves lives.

WARNING

In a survival situation, some people are going to panic and lose their heads, often lashing out and screaming, which can destabilize and demoralize a whole group of people. Unfortunately, the Hollywood cliché of someone yelling, "We're all going to die!" sometimes does come up. So: expect it, be ready for it. Some people are unstable, and they explode shrilly when stressed. Don't let their panic unnerve you or influence you into doing something stupid.

Irrationality

Frequently, people in survival situations act in completely irrational ways — ways that can astonish you. People may refuse to cooperate even though their lives depend on it, or they sometimes commit acts that put you and your party in even more danger than you're already in.

WARNING

If you have an unstable or irrational person on your hands, be ready for them to do *anything*. They might sabotage equipment, foil plans, and commit acts that can kill the whole group. Watch irrational people carefully, and never trust them with anything, even if they seem to get better. You may have to restrain them or at least assign someone to watch them.

Anger and blame

People in survival situations are often overcome by guilt for having gotten themselves into such a mess. If you find yourself feeling this way, don't despair; forgive yourself immediately. If someone else caused it, forgive them. Regret, anger, and blame only distract you from doing the things you need to do to survive, and they waste precious time and energy.

Frustration

Survival techniques often require multiple attempts to get right, such as making a fire in wet conditions. Remember that persistence and patience are key to taking positive steps forward in your survival situation. Take a break, and start over. Try new variations on what hasn't worked. Learn and progress.

Misery and fatigue

Misery and fatigue can amplify the feeling of despair to the point where it seems that you can't possibly make it. You can address major discomforts by practicing self-awareness and self-inventory. For example, be honest with yourself: You're hot, you're cold, you're hurt, you're fatigued, you're scared. Then admit that these feelings and conditions can warp your judgment and make everything seem hopeless. Once again, you are unpacking the sensations (e.g., misery) to gain some control through understanding, which leads to organized responses.

Improving Morale

TIP

The more you improve morale, the stronger you become. Even in dire situations you can give yourself an emotional boost by doing the following:

>> **Boil things down to their basics.** Ask yourself what, exactly, you are facing in your survival situation. Reduce your situation from one huge, unsurmountable problem to (hopefully) a handful of solvable problems that you can tackle one at a time.

>> **Get to work.** Taking action to address your misery, fear, frustration, and so on can improve morale. Remind yourself, "I am taking action and making progress, I am doing the things I need to survive." If you cannot tackle the largest problem right away, start small . . . but take action and make progress. Seeing that you are making progress is very good for morale.

>> **Assume a positive attitude.** Optimism and a positive attitude can turn a bad situation around in a second. Sometimes improving your outlook can be as simple as stretching a smile across your face when you don't feel like smiling at all. We've seen people use positive thinking and good humor in the field and the effect really is incredible. Many lifeboat survivors can attest to the fact that a smile and a joke — no matter how strained — can give you hope.

Although a humorous comment can alleviate stress and defuse a situation, comments that appear callous can be harmful. Sometimes you have to be sensitive. Pick and choose your moments for levity carefully.

>> **Get angry and get some contempt.** Anger can be super-potent, even in the weakest people. If you need a serious burst of strength, take a moment to get seriously angry. Refuse to accept that some small mistake is reason to lose your life. Tell nature and fear and everything else to *shove it.* Refuse to give in. Feel free to be obstinate for a little while — it works.

>> **Value life and home.** One way to get in the right mindset is to value living and value your life. In many cases, this simple idea gets lost in the moment. Realize that your life is valuable, that it's worth saving, and that you still have a lot of good living to do.

Keep in mind that people want you to return. Picturing their grief can be a powerful tool in motivating yourself to stay alive. Many survivors have done this. Know that you can cause great suffering to those back home if you don't survive and that you have a duty to them, and to your own life, to stay alive. This frame of mind can carry you through when no other can.

>> **Clean up and get organized.** Get the hair out of your eyes and wash your face. Remove as many irritants as you can. Inspect your body and look for wounds that can be treated. Take a moment to organize your equipment, no matter how meager. Cleaning up will clear your mind and give you some feeling of reassurance.

>> **Take some action to master the night.** Many times, the night is the hardest time. Take any action you can to be ready for it. Start a fire if you can, set up a watch system with your companions, or build a good shelter. For more on dealing with the night, see Chapter 4 on making insulated clothing, and Chapter 6 on building an insulated shelter.

OPTIMISM ON ICE

Perhaps the greatest expedition leader of the 20th century, Sir Ernest Shackleton, himself a survivor, always maintained a cheerful attitude no matter how bad things got. His results were nothing short of miraculous. He kept all his men alive through a year-long ordeal when they were stranded on Antarctica with no support. He knew that optimism was the highest quality a person could have when facing a survival situation, and he never allowed dark talk or bad attitudes.

Chapter **4**

Survival Style: Keeping Warm or Cool

I n any survival situation, you have to know how to warm up if you're cold and how to cool down if you're hot. At home, you control temperature with air conditioning, central heating, sweaters, flip-flops, or what-have-you. But if you find yourself in desolate snow-covered mountains wearing just jeans and a t-shirt, things are going to go bad, fast. Even if you have plenty of food and water, they're no use if you succumb to hypothermia.

In this chapter, we cover the basics of temperature regulation in wilderness survival situations. We tell you how to stay warm or cool with certain kinds of clothes (and how to improvise them) and discuss strategies for staying cool in hot environments. (We detail shelters for hot and cold environments in Chapter 6.)

Regulating Body Temperature

The human body, tough as it is, is really comfortable in only a pretty narrow temperature margin. Above 75°F (24°C), most people begin to feel too hot, and below about 50°F (10°C), most people start to feel chilly. Figure 4-1 shows specific effects of air temperature on the body.

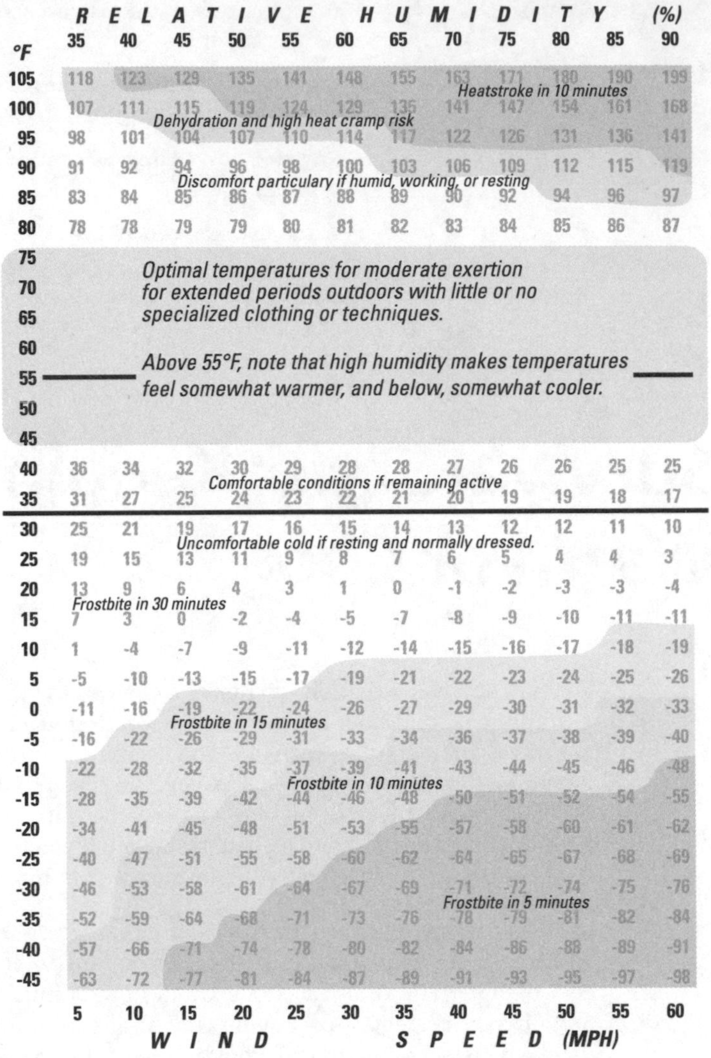

°F	35	40	45	50	55	60	65	70	75	80	85	90
105	118	123	129	135	141	148	155	163	171	180	190	199
100	107	111	115	119	124	129	135	141	147	154	161	168
95	98	101	104	107	110	114	117	122	126	131	136	141
90	91	92	94	96	98	100	103	106	109	112	115	119
85	83	84	85	86	87	88	89	90	92	94	96	97
80	78	78	79	79	80	81	82	83	84	85	86	87

Heatstroke in 10 minutes

Dehydration and high heat cramp risk

Discomfort particulary if humid, working, or resting

75
70   Optimal temperatures for moderate exertion
65   for extended periods outdoors with little or no
      specialized clothing or techniques.
60
55   Above 55°F, note that high humidity makes temperatures
50   feel somewhat warmer, and below, somewhat cooler.
45

°F	5	10	15	20	25	30	35	40	45	50	55	60
40	36	34	32	30	29	28	28	27	26	26	25	25
35	31	27	25	24	23	22	21	20	19	19	18	17
30	25	21	19	17	16	15	14	13	12	12	11	10
25	19	15	13	11	9	8	7	6	5	4	4	3
20	13	9	6	4	3	1	0	-1	-2	-3	-3	-4
15	7	3	0	-2	-4	-5	-7	-8	-9	-10	-11	-11
10	1	-4	-7	-9	-11	-12	-14	-15	-16	-17	-18	-19
5	-5	-10	-13	-15	-17	-19	-21	-22	-23	-24	-25	-26
0	-11	-16	-19	-22	-24	-26	-27	-29	-30	-31	-32	-33
-5	-16	-22	-26	-29	-31	-33	-34	-36	-37	-38	-39	-40
-10	-22	-28	-32	-35	-37	-39	-41	-43	-44	-45	-46	-48
-15	-28	-35	-39	-42	-44	-46	-48	-50	-51	-52	-54	-55
-20	-34	-41	-45	-48	-51	-53	-55	-57	-58	-60	-61	-62
-25	-40	-47	-51	-55	-58	-60	-62	-64	-65	-67	-68	-69
-30	-46	-53	-58	-61	-64	-67	-69	-71	-72	-74	-75	-76
-35	-52	-59	-64	-68	-71	-73	-76	-78	-79	-81	-82	-84
-40	-57	-66	-71	-74	-78	-80	-82	-84	-86	-88	-89	-91
-45	-63	-72	-77	-81	-84	-87	-89	-91	-93	-95	-97	-98

Comfortable conditions if remaining active

Uncomfortable cold if resting and normally dressed.

Frostbite in 30 minutes

Frostbite in 15 minutes

Frostbite in 10 minutes

Frostbite in 5 minutes

W I N D   S P E E D   (MPH)

FIGURE 4-1: General effects of heat and cold on the human body

Humidity (the amount of moisture in the air) can intensify the effects of heat, and wind speed can intensify the effects of cold. Note that in the top half of Figure 4-1, relative humidity increases to the right, showing your perceived temperature at different temperature and humidity combinations. For example, at 85°F, with a relative humidity of 85 percent, you actually feel a temperature of about 96°F. In the lower half of the figure, wind speed increases to the right. At −5°F with a wind of just 20 mph, for example, your skin feels a temperature of −29°F.

ZIPLESS AT 40 BELOW

In March 2007, I (Cameron) was trekking alone on Alaska's North Slope to learn about the beautiful world of the tundra in winter. One day, while testing a new clothing system, I felt myself getting colder by the minute. My experimental system wasn't working, and I knew that if I felt cold, my body was screaming at me to do something to warm up.

I should have listened, but I pressed on, thinking, "Oh just do another hour. You've been plenty cold before." This was an almost fatal mistake. Soon my body was conserving heat in emergency mode, calling warm blood in from my extremities to keep my core organs warm (fingers, toes, and nose freeze first). Before I knew it, my hands and feet were profoundly numb.

To warm up, I stopped dragging my sled and instantly tried to put on a heavy parka, one that I'd used to bring me back from the brink many times. I knew that if I just got the zipper up, my core temperature would rise enough that my body would let blood back into my fingers and toes.

When I had the zipper halfway up, though, the little metal pull-tab snapped off in my glove. It was a cheap zipper tab I'd sewn onto my customized parka. I stopped breathing. With my whole chest uninsulated, I was in real trouble, and my hands were so cold and useless that making some kind of repair was unthinkable. Without my hands, I might not be able to set up my tent and get inside, out of the wind, to get warm. This was no spectacular Hollywood moment, but the situation was potentially lethal.

With near-frozen hands, setting up my tent took an hour — it normally took about ten minutes. Using my teeth and the heels of my mittens as crude clamps, somehow I managed to get the tent up and crawled into my sleeping bag, and somehow I opened my thermos flask to get some hot liquid into my guts. An hour later, the crisis was over as hot blood flooded back into my fingers and toes. Rewarming was painful; it felt exactly like when you hit your thumb with a hammer, but it went on for half an hour or so, on every fingertip and toe.

My parka is in my closet now, and on my list of things to do before I go back to Alaska is "replace parka zipper with sturdier."

The body's *internal temperature* is different from the air temperature. Internal temperature is normally about 97–98.6°F (36.1–37°C); if it rises above 104°F (40°C), you suffer the effects of *heat stroke* (a form of hyperthermia), and if it dips below 95°F (35°C), you begin to suffer from hypothermia. We introduce these conditions later in this section, and we discuss how to recognize and deal with them in detail in Chapters 17 and 13, respectively.

The sensations of uncomfortable heat or cold are your body's signal that something's wrong! Don't try to just headbang your way through uncomfortable temperatures. If you feel uncomfortably cold or hot, use the techniques we describe in this chapter to regulate your temperature so that you don't end up in a dire situation like we describe in the sidebar "Zipless at 40 below."

The cold continuum: What happens as your body cools

When the body cools below the optimal temperature of 97–98.6°F (36.1–37°C), you begin to feel the effects of hypothermia. *Hypothermia* is a debilitating reduction of body temperature (you can identify hypothermia by the symptoms we outline in Chapter 13). Unless you do something to stop cooling, you can easily slip into a lethal hypothermic coma. It's that serious. Table 4-1 shows you what can happen when your body cools.

TABLE 4-1 **What Happens as Your Body Cools**

Stage	Body Temperature Range	Symptoms
Mild hypothermia	95–90°F (35–32°C)	Shivering, clumsiness
Moderate hypothermia	90–86°F (32–30°C)	Loss of shivering; loss of muscular coordination, increased clumsiness
Severe hypothermia	Below 86°F (below–30°C)	Confusion, loss of vision, apathy, coma, death

Luckily, you can do plenty of things to stay warm, and we cover them in most of the rest of this chapter.

People have survived many situations that tables and charts, or doctors themselves, would call "clearly unsurvivable." Never give up; however cold you or your companions are, don't write anyone off. Keep at it. Keep trying.

The heat continuum: What happens as your body heats

When the body overheats, the effects can be as lethal as when it cools beyond a certain point. *Hyperthermia* occurs when your body suffers from overheating. You can identify hyperthermia by the symptoms we detail in Chapter 17.

Table 4-2 shows you what can happen when your body heats. Body temperature begins to be dangerous around 104°F (40°C), and by 106°F (41.1°C), brain damage can occur. Around 120°F (48.9°C), your body goes rigid, and soon thereafter you die. But you can do plenty to prevent this scenario as we outline in this chapter.

TABLE 4-2 **What Happens as Your Body Heats**

Stage	Body Temperature Range	Symptoms
Moderate hyperthermia	104–106°F (40–41.1°C)	Nausea, vomiting, dizziness
Severe hyperthermia	106–113°F (41.1–45°C)	Brain damage
Profound hyperthermia	Above 120°F (48.9°C)	Muscle rigidity, coma, death

Relying on Layering for Warmth

All clothing that keeps you warm works on the same principle; it traps a layer of warm air, normally warmed by your own body, between you and the elements. Layering involves using several garments to trap layers of air (such as wearing three thin sweaters instead of just one thick one), and it's an important basic principle of cold-weather clothing. This section explains the importance of layering to keep you warm and suggests how to layer your own clothing.

Avoiding a cold sweat

You should wear several layers of clothing that you can add to or take off, depending on your activity level, adding layers when chilled and removing layers when starting to sweat.

Sweating is an effective bodily cooling mechanism, and for this reason it's your number-one enemy in cold-weather situations:

>> Sweat deprives you of bodily fluids, leading to dehydration, which worsens hypothermia.

>> As sweat evaporates, it cools your body and brings on hypothermia faster than if you were dry.

>> Sweat can soak your insulating layers, making them stick together so that they no longer effectively trap a layer of warm air, ruining their insulation properties.

Although a single, heavy layer — such as a parka — helps keeps you warm, it also makes you sweat, even if you're just moving around camp or chopping wood. But with thinner layers, you can add to them or strip them off according to your circumstances.

If you're breaking up firewood, plowing your way through knee-deep snow, or doing other similar heavy work, strip off a layer or two to prevent sweat from soaking your insulating layers. On the other hand, when you're doing less strenuous work — such as butchering an animal, setting traps, fishing, or washing plant foods — you're best off wearing more or heavier layers to keep warm.

Because wet clothes are poor insulators in wet conditions, use whatever you can (such as the space blanket or a plastic bag from your survival kit detailed in Chapter 2) to keep your clothes dry.

Choosing your layers

A simple layering system for temperatures around freezing includes the following:

>> **Base layer:** Thin long-john type garments are fine. Avoid cotton because it's poor at insulating you when wet. Wool and synthetic base layers are ideal.

>> **Thermal layer:** For sweaters, trousers, socks, gloves, and hats, use wool or pile (also called *fleece*), which is a kind of synthetic wool, as these retain their insulation properties when wet.

>> **Shell layer:** Wear a shell layer to protect you and your insulation layers from wind and moisture. Ideally, the layer is *breathable*, allowing sweat vapor out, but *waterproof*, meaning it doesn't let water droplets in — that's the main characteristic of waterproof/breathable shell layers, such as those made of Gore-Tex or its many equivalents.

TIP

Ideally your shell layer will have zippers under the arms and down the legs; zipping these up or down allowing you to remain properly ventilated so you sweat less.

When you begin to feel too warm, start by taking off the shell layer, and then, if needed, remove the second (thermal) layer, still leaving you with the base layer.

Improvising Cold-Weather Clothing

If you don't have access to nice, dry, cold-weather clothing, you have to improvise. You just need to know a few basic skills and apply them with some creativity to improvise with cold-weather clothing.

For improvising cold-weather clothing, the best guides are the native people of the polar regions, who've adapted to cold conditions for thousands of years. In this section, we describe how to stay warm outdoors, using a lot of advice based on native methods. Figure 4-2 shows the native dress of Arctic Canada and a hypothetical cold-weather wilderness survivor.

Note the following items of clothing:

>> A hide jacket trapping a layer of air against the skin (Figure 4-2a)

>> Fur used to block wind from the face (Figure 4-2b)

>> Heavy mittens (Figure 4-2c)

>> High boots for deep snow (Figure 4-2d)

See how the hypothetical cold-weather survivor fashions similar clothing items (Chapter 16 provides how-to info for making improvised goggles, mittens, gaiters, and snowshoes):

>> Cloth used to insulate the head and neck and to block wind (Figure 4-2e)

>> Improvised snow goggles (Figure 4-2f)

>> A heavy jacket trapping a layer of warm air next to the body (Figure 4-2g)

>> Mittens improvised from heavy socks (Figure 4-2h)

>> Improvised gaiters/boot covers (Figure 4-2i)

>> Fabric sewn to a coat to provide an insulated sitting surface (Figure 4-2j)

>> Improvised snowshoes (Figure 4-2k)

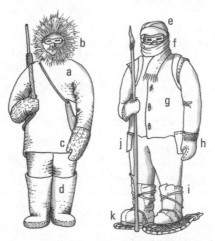

FIGURE 4-2: Native Arctic clothing (left) and a cold-weather survivor in improvised clothing (right)

The techniques we describe in this section do require a few basic tools. You can't do much without a knife and some kind of needle and thread (you should have these supplies in your survival kit, which we describe in detail in Chapter 2). You can improvise cutting tools and even needle and thread, but everything is easier if you just always have your survival kit on hand.

Extreme sewing: Using needle and thread to save your life

Improvising clothing requires you to join together pieces of textiles or other flexible material. The best way to do so is with needle and thread. Knowing how to use both is a great outdoor skill that can keep you alive. If you don't have a needle in your survival kit, you can improvise one from a piece of plastic, a splinter of bone or antler, or any one of many other materials (to see how, head to Chapter 14).

After you have a needle, you can improvise *cordage* (thread) from any number of materials. Natural cordage for sewing includes *sinew* (the tough, stringy tissues stripped from animal joints) and tough plant fibers. Thankfully shoelaces or laces pulled from a hood, wiring ripped from the wreckage of a machine, and dental floss work as well and may be easier to come by, though they make different sizes of holes in the fabric you're sewing and will need a larger needle.

TIP

To thread your needle, slip the cordage you're using through the eye and pull through a good measure; put a knot in the thread at the other end of the cordage to prevent the thread from pulling through the fabric (refer to Figure 4-3a). Join the two materials (Figure 4-3b) and begin sewing. Pull the needle out and end by tying a final knot to prevent the seam from coming apart.

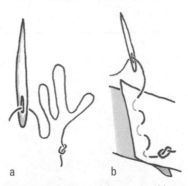

a   b

FIGURE 4-3: Using an improvised bone needle to sew a flat seam

Fighting hypothermia with improvised layers

If you find yourself in a situation in which your clothing is inadequate for the cold and you are in imminent risk of hypothermia, you must surround yourself with insulating layers of air quickly. For a detailed explanation of the principle of layers, see "Relying on Layering for Warmth," earlier in this chapter.

In cases where there are no man-made resources available of any kind, you should stuff dry grass, leaves, and moss into your clothes, or better, between the layers of clothing you are already wearing. This will create that all-important space of dead air that insulates you from the cold. Even more, if you are facing a long wait, such as when the sun is setting and you will have to survive a cold night, you should add an extra layer of insulation by constructing a shelter (see Chapter 6 for options). These two methods can help you fight off hypothermia when no other resources are available.

Vehicle wreckage can supply many materials for improvising cold-weather clothing. Creativity and persistence, as always in survival situations, are key. Here are some ways to improvise cold-weather protection from wreckage:

>> **Car seat covers:** They're often made of a flexible plastic, and you can easily cut them away and (if you have needle and thread) sew them into an improvised shell layer to protect you from wind, rain, and snow. Or cut off the covers and sew them into a parka, cape, or mittens. Use the padding inside these seats as insulation (the thermal layer) by stuffing it inside your outer layer.

>> **Plastic sheet, tarp, or garbage bag:** You can easily convert one of these plastic items into a poncho simply by cutting a foot-wide slit along a fold, near the center, for your head to pass through.

>> **Cardboard:** You can sew cardboard together to make large sheets for use as a poncho, though it breaks down in rain after a while.

>> **Duct tape:** Duct tape is one of the wonders of modern civilization, and it's useful in a hundred wilderness survival scenarios. You can use it to patch holes in your clothing, tape

over a cloth hat to make it waterproof, and even tape over sneakers to help keep out rain. Keep some in your survival kit. Instead of carrying a bulky roll of duct tape into the wilderness, you can wrap a few yards around a cigarette lighter for easy access later. Note duct tape becomes brittle in really cold conditions; medical (cloth) tape is better then.

>> **Newspapers or magazines:** Crumpled newspaper and book or magazine pages can be stuffed inside your clothes to trap insulating air inside.

Putting together animal skins

In survival situations where you are hunting or trapping, animal hides may be used to help you keep warm (Chapter 8 explains trapping).

Animal hides must be processed before use as clothing; the basic steps are:

1. **Scrape off the loose, fatty tissues from the inside (the non-fur side) of the skin.**

   These tissues will rot and degrade the hide if not removed; de-fat the hide with a knife or improvised scraping tool, using a shaving motion.

2. **Dry the hide(s) draped over vegetation or next to a fire; this can take a few hours to overnight.**

   The resulting hide will be stiff, but it can be made more pliable by pounding the hide with a heavy stone.

When ready, let one hide overlap the other a bit and start sewing to join the overlapping margins. Soon you'll have a towel-sized skin that you can use as a hat or a light cloak. Be creative and make whatever garment you need.

TIP

If you wear the fur on the inside of a garment (next to your skin), you get a warmer garment because the fur traps insulating air. Also, processed animal hides stiffen over time. Keep them pliable by bending and wringing them with your hands every day.

WARNING

Process and store your animal skins away from camp when you're not wearing them, because their odors may attract bears or mountain lions.

Having the right headwear, handwear, and footwear

It's particularly important to keep your head, hands, and feet warm in the wild because

>> So much heat is lost from the head.

>> If your feet freeze, you can't travel.

>> If your hands freeze, you can't even make a fire or set up a camp.

Also take care to keep your wrists and neck insulated; in both places, the skin is particularly thin, and you can lose heat from these regions very quickly. You can use duct tape (or any kind of tape) to tighten your cuffs *a little* if they don't already have Velcro tabs for adjustment. This prevents losing warm air from your shirt or jacket cuffs.

Keep the following in mind about these important body parts:

>> **Your head:** The first thing to do when you feel cold is get a hat on. The scalp contains so little fat that you lose a great deal of heat though the head. Slowing or stopping that heat loss can help keep your whole body warm.

>> **Your hands:** Mittens are usually warmer than gloves, and they're easy to improvise from a pair of socks.

>> **Your feet:** To keep your feet warm, you can take several steps:

- **Loosen the laces on your boots or shoes.** Don't loosen so much that they fall off, but make them loose enough that your blood (which warms your skin) can circulate easily.

- **Add layers to the inside of your footwear.** This can be as easy as slipping on another layer of socks, being sure to keep your laces somewhat loose. If you don't have extra socks, improvise them by making a simple tube of cloth sewn down one side and across the toe-end. This doesn't have to be particularly comfortable; it just has to help trap warm air inside your shoe or boot.

- **Insulate the outside of your footwear.** The padding from seat cushions can be useful as insulation that you layer on the outside of your footwear. Cut the padding into slabs and sew or tie them on, paying particular attention to the toe area.

Using Other Ways to Keep Warm

In addition to wearing layers of dry, air-trapping clothing, you can keep warm by staying active, covering yourself with blankets or other insulation, and using fire. We cover fire later in this chapter and discuss shelters in Chapter 6. For now, here are some additional good ways to keep warm.

Staying active

Bodily movement generates body heat. On really cold mornings, you may want to do some jumping jacks, run in place, or windmill your arms (which drives blood back into your fingertips).

Be careful to not over-exert, as this can cause you to sweat, which can soak your clothes — and then they can freeze solid. (Check out the earlier section "Avoiding a cold sweat" for more on the dangers of sweating.) Also, exercise burns calories that you may not want to expend, depending on your food situation.

TIP

During a hard day in the Arctic winter, we constantly adjust our clothing systems to prevent them from being sweated up and freezing solid. If you're going to do some vigorous exercise, remember to strip off a layer before you start, but put it back on moments after you stop moving.

Staying warm when you're staying still

A cold night can turn into an eternal agony; it seems that the sun will never come up. But remember, it will! You just have to get a few hours through the night; use the following methods:

>> **Insulation from cold surfaces:** Always use some kind of padding to insulate you from cold surfaces; for example, sit or sleep on dense piles of vegetation.

>> **Hot rocks:** Pull warm rocks from your campfire to slip inside your clothes. Be careful that they're not hot enough to burn you, though.

>> **Huddling with your companions:** If you have companions, huddling with them allows you to conserve the group's body heat by having it all under one cover. Use any type of cover you have as a blanket to stay warm (you should definitely have at least one space blanket in your survival kit; see Chapter 2).

>> **Candles:** If you have a candle, hunch over it to keep your hands warm and to allow you to inhale warm, dry air. Eight-hour candles are specifically made to get you through a long winter night.

Cool Threads: Clothing for Staying Cool

One of the principles of dry hot-weather clothing is shielding from the sun. Although on vacation you may want to get a tan by wearing a t-shirt and shorts outdoors, doing this day after day, all day, can be fatal in a wilderness situation. Instead, you need to wear loose, flowing robe-like clothing as well as a substantial head covering to protect yourself from the sun.

TIP

Regardless of what you're wearing, if it's really hot and you're trying to walk your way out of the survival situation, you would do best to travel at night, when it's cooler (deserts may be very cold indeed, but it's easier to keep warm by moving than to keep cool when it's very hot). We tell you how to work and travel at night in Chapter 17.

We think the best guides to surviving in a hot wilderness are the native people of such areas, and in this case, we look to the nomadic Bedouin folk originally of the Arabian Peninsula. Figure 4-4 shows a Bedouin in native dress, and shows a desert wilderness survivor in improvised clothing. Note the following items of clothing:

>> A long cloth used to completely protect the head and neck from the sun (Figure 4-4a)

>> Long, flowing, robe-like clothes that let air circulate next to the skin but shield the skin from direct sun (Figure 4-4b)

>> Lack of shoes (Figure 4-4c)

Going barefoot is an aboriginal custom you shouldn't emulate. Bedouin folk go shoeless from childhood, and their feet are very tough. Your feet aren't accustomed to going barefoot, so make sure you wear improvised shoes at least.

Now check out the wilderness survivor in improvised clothing:

>> Survivor's t-shirt head-garment that completely protects the neck and head (also note use of sunglasses and face mask) (Figure 4-4d)

>> An untucked shirt to let air circulate (Figure 4-4e)

>> Flaps of cloth sewn to cuffs protect the back of the hands from sunburn (Figure 4-4f)

>> Improvised sandals (Figure 4-4g)

FIGURE 4-4: A Bedouin in native dress (left) and a desert wilderness survivor in improvised clothing (right)

This section introduces specific types of clothing and principles to remember about clothing for hot conditions.

Wearing a hat and eye protection

Long exposure of the bare head to sunlight can lead to hyperthermia (heat exhaustion). Simply wearing a hat can greatly improve your chances of survival. A loose-fitting hat with a wide brim that shields the entire head is ideal.

A hat also cuts down glare. You can also reduce glare by putting soot under your eyes, or, obviously, with sunglasses. If you don't have sunglasses, you can improvise them from a strip of stiff cloth, a piece of bark, or plastic. You can protect your face from the sun simply by hanging a handkerchief below the eyes: Pin or sew it to your headgear. Check out Chapter 17 for ways you can improvise these types of eye protection and headgear to keep cool.

Close-fitting headwear, like a baseball cap, can be too hot if not ventilated; you can cut some slits or poke some holes in the fabric to let it breathe a little.

Considering other clothing concepts to keep cool

As you adjust your clothing for hot conditions, keep the following pointers in mind:

» **Select light colors.** White or other light colors reflect the sun instead of absorbing its rays as darker colors do.

» **Wear loose-fitting clothing.** Hot-weather clothing should be loose and flowing rather than tight, allowing a little ventilation to keep your skin cool. Note the Bedouin's loose, flowing robes in Figure 4-4.

» **Be prepared to add or subtract layers.** Adjust your clothing according to the conditions. At night, be prepared to bundle up, because hot areas can get very cold, particularly on cloudless nights when there's no cloud layer to trap the Earth's warmth.

» **Use ventilation.** Keep ventilated by unbuttoning your cuffs and shirt neck. Wear your trousers loose, or better yet, roll them up to your knees and wear your improvised robe over them.

» **Drape yourself with a damp cloth.** Wet skin cools much faster than dry skin, and if you have the luxury of excess water, you can keep cool by draping damp fabric over your body while resting in shade. As the water evaporates, it carries excess heat away from the skin.

Chapter **5**

Making Fire in the Wilderness

B eing able to start a fire to stay warm may be a matter of life or death in the wilderness.

But you don't just start a fire — you build one! With that in mind, remember that most people have trouble getting their fires started in the wilderness because they hurry the building process and use a haphazard selection of starter materials. Think of your fire as a well-designed structure — a good design can keep you alive.

In this chapter, we show you how you go about constructing a fire. We also show you some interesting alternatives to matches and lighters, as we give advice for the toughest task of all: starting a fire in the rain.

Fire Building 101

Every fire needs three things: fuel to burn, heat to ignite the fuel, and oxygen to breathe.

This section explains what you need to do to get a fire going, including different fire-building options, depending on your situation.

Get ready, get set: Upping your odds for a sustainable flame

Before you start your fire, you must be completely prepared for that important moment when the fire goes from being a small flame to a self-sustaining survival tool.

Here are important things to consider as you think about making a survival fire:

>> **Watch out for Mother Nature.** Make sure your fire-building site is protected from heavy winds and rain that can extinguish it or make starting it difficult.

>> **Take time to build your fire.** Be patient and build with care.

>> **Gather the driest wood you can find.** Wood is dry when it snaps cleanly in your hands. This wood ignites quickly and burns well. *Green wood* still has a little moisture in it, which makes it hard to ignite. If you have to work a stick or twig in your hands to get it to break — or if it holds together by fibers when you bend it — then it isn't dry enough.

>> **Use the thinnest possible kindling.** Twigs less than ⅛ inch (3 mm) in thickness (thinner than your shoelaces) make the best kindling. You can find out more about kindling in the section "Gathering fuels for your fire" later in this chapter.

>> **Be ready to feed your fire.** As soon as your fire ignites, you need to feed the flame quickly and steadily without overdoing it; you can smother a burgeoning fire very easily. Keep in mind that fires ignite and burn unevenly. Flames may crop up in places you don't expect. A few twigs, placed well over a burgeoning flame, can be all you need to get it going. Have an extra pile of dry kindling next to you to feed the flame as it arises, because a fire is very precarious when it first starts. This is critical!

Gathering fuels for your fire

To get a fire going, you need the right materials. The three types of fire fuel are:

>> **Tinder:** Tinder is the first material to be ignited, so it must be the most flammable. Make sure you have plenty of it before you strike your first match. Good tinder includes straw, grass, scraped fibers or husks from trees or dried fruit, lint from your clothing, dry shavings from a stick, dry pine needles or leaves, a ball of dry toilet paper or newspaper (although when paper is damp, it's worse than useless), and even sap from pine trees, which burns hot and bright. Be sure to collect tinder if you see it when traveling, and keep it dry.

>> **Kindling:** Kindling is the first real fuel to burn, and it's composed of thin twigs (pencil-thick at most) and/or splinters of wood split with an ax or knife.

>> **Main fuel:** This fuel is usually composed of wrist-thick or larger branches and even logs. You can also burn dried animal dung, as well as natural tar or oil that seeps from the ground; these areas may be marked on maps.

Once you've gathered your fuels, arrange them into one of the tried-and-true fire structures described in the following section.

Arranging your campfire structure

The tinder and kindling must be prearranged in a carefully built *campfire structure*. Different fire structures are useful for different purposes. Knowing the following types of fires and how to build them can help you conserve your fuel, dry out wet fuel, signal for help, keep you warm at night, and ensure that you have embers ready in the morning to easily restart the fire.

TIP

Whatever fire you make, pile up some dirt, rocks, or vegetation around it, like a screen, just before going to sleep to help reflect the heat into your shelter area on a cold night. Also, you should have a signal fire structure on standby at all times as a beacon to rescuers — for more on signal fires, see Chapter 12.

Getting lit: Building a general-purpose teepee fire

Generally speaking, the easiest type of fire to ignite is the teepee fire. It's good for a crisis because it starts almost every time.

Take your time making a teepee with carefully constructed sections of tinder and kindling to take full advantage of the fact that fire generally burns upward:

1. **Put the lightest, driest tinder at the very bottom — wispy-fine fibers are the best.**

2. **Use thin kindling (twigs) to build a teepee-like structure above and around the tinder, so this larger fuel is poised to catch fire.**

3. **Have fuel ready to add carefully to the fire once the tinder is really flaming.**

   Only experience can teach you how to grow the fire without smothering it.

Figure 5-1 provides helpful visuals for building a teepee fire.

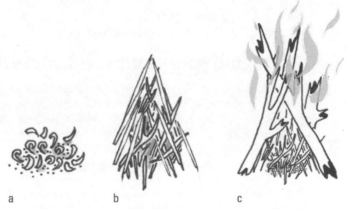

a   b   c

FIGURE 5-1: Making a teepee fire — tinder (a), a teepee of kindling (b), and fuel added to the teepee (c)

Using other fire structures

The teepee fire structure discussed in the previous section is easy to build, so it's a great go-to fire structure; check out Figure 5-2a for a visual. A couple other handy structures that also work well for fire starting and fire maintenance include:

>> **Star fire:** When the fuel is really large and hard to break up (as with large logs), push it into a star or cross fire (see Figure 5-2b) so that just the tip is burning at any given moment.

You can rejuvenate a star fire by pushing more of the log into the fire as it burns, or easily extinguish this fire by pulling the star apart by the cold ends of the logs.

>> **Pyramid fire:** A pyramid fire (see Figure 5-2c) built with plenty of fuel collapses in on itself overnight, providing a good pile of embers to use to relight the fire in the morning.

a   b   c

FIGURE 5-2: Teepee, star, and pyramid fire structures in action

The first spark: Igniting and oxygenating your fire

With your fuel assembled and your preparations made, you need a method to ignite your fire and to keep it "breathing" with oxygen. In the section "Got a Light? Exploring Methods for Starting a Fire" later in this chapter, we describe using matches, lighters, and other sources of ignition. But consider these tips before you apply the first spark to your fire so you can keep it breathing:

>> **Ignite your fire at the lowest spot you can.** Fire generally burns upward, so the lower you ignite it, the better.

>> **Blow gently on your fire or fan it.** The best way to convert a tiny flame into a large one is to give it some air (oxygen). Properly oxygenating a fire is something you have to learn

by experience. Here are some methods you can try to keep your fire "breathing" with oxygen:

Lean in close and blow gently on the burning fuel.

Fan the flames — sometimes gently, sometimes more vigorously.

Direct your breath to a specific point at the base of the growing fire with a tube, a piece of hose, a straw, or some kind of pipe.

TIP

Practice building fires with different kinds of tinder and kindling in different conditions. If you blow too hard, you might knock over the delicate assembly of burning tinder or over-oxygenate the tinder so that it burns out in a brief flash. A long, gentle stream of air is normally best, but depending on many variables, including different types of fuel, you may need to blow harder, or fan the flames. This practice is the best way to learn how much is too much.

Got a Light? Exploring Methods for Starting a Fire

In this section we discuss the different methods you can use to start your fire. We begin with the most obvious ways to get some flames going and then work our way down to techniques you can use when you have no apparent resources whatsoever. Even though a task like striking a match may seem like a simple act, each method listed here requires a little forethought, especially when your life depends on staying warm.

Best-case scenario: Using matches or a lighter

Knowing you have quality fire-starting tools is important and will give you confidence in the wilderness. We list the best options below, and then work our way down into less-optimal scenarios.

Matches

Matches are cheap, simple, and can be carried in waterproof containers in any survival kit (see Chapter 2). Be sure to pack wooden matches because paper matches often fall apart with just a little humidity or jostling.

Lighting a match seems straightforward — until your life depends on it. Then you must take your time to think through just what you're going to do, particularly if you have a limited number of matches. In most wilderness survival situations, you'll have a limited number of matches, and you won't have much room for error. When this happens, you must strike each match correctly to conserve your precious supply. Always use a stabbing motion with wooden matches — never drag the match! If you drag the match, you will break the match or tear the head off it before it lights.

See Figure 5-3 to become a pro at outdoor match-striking, so that you're always conserving your supply.

1. Turn your back to the wind, crouch near the tinder pile, and cradle the box securely in one hand, cupping it against any breeze.

2. Hold the match in the other hand and stab down deliberately across the striker patch.

3. After the match is lit, give it a second (or three) to fully ignite the first quarter of the wood.

4. Carefully move the lit match toward the tinder (unless you've struck the match right next to the tinder, which is preferable if there's a breeze or it's drizzling rain).

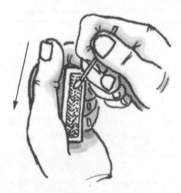

FIGURE 5-3: How to successfully strike a match so it doesn't go out and is useful for fire-building

Lighters

The main kinds of fire-lighters are cigarette lighters of either the disposable Bic type or the more durable Zippo type. Each type uses a steel wheel to create a spark against a flint. Disposable types give a couple thousand lights compared to the Zippo's 200 lights. However, the Zippo can be refilled (with liquid fuel) whereas most disposable types are not refillable. These pros and cons are something to consider when you are building your survival kit (see Chapter 2). Piezoelectric lighters make a spark without the wheel-and-flint combination, but they are not as versatile, especially when out of fuel, so we don't recommend them as survival kit fire-starters.

As a backup, it can never hurt to have a full disposable lighter in a small plastic baggie somewhere in your backpack, but even if your lighter and backup lighter are out of fuel, you can still light a fire if your tinder and kindling are prepped; see the "Starting a fire with a dead lighter" sidebar.

When you use a lighter, conserve fuel by facing away from wind and using it right at the base of the constructed fire structure.

STARTING A FIRE WITH A DEAD LIGHTER

Even after your lighter has run out of fuel, you can still get fire from it. The trick is to force the lighter's spark into the very best tinder you can get: dry lint pulled from cotton socks or some other cotton garment is ideal. Here's how to do it:

1. **Pull off enough lint to make a wad about half the size of a golf ball.**

   Make sure the lint is pulled apart as much as possible. Don't compress the lint or roll it into a ball. When you're finished, you should be able to see through the lint. This process is time consuming — it may take you as long as an hour — but it really works (see the nearby figure). Note that a lint cone is almost a sure-thing, but it will blaze up quickly and may last less than 5 seconds, so use it wisely. Light it right next to your fire structure so you can apply the flames immediately.

2. **Roll a tissue or a small length of toilet paper into a cone.**

   You can use any type of paper for this, but tissue is the best. When you have a cone, mount the lint ball just inside the very end of it — think of the shape of a snow cone. This paper apparatus is your fire-starter.

3. **Take a lighter and flick it into the wad of lint at the end of your paper cone.**

   The sparks should fly into the wad and ignite it.

4. **If the lint hasn't ignited after a dozen or so attempts, take the metal housing off the lighter and try again.**

   If you have a pocketknife or some other straight edge, you can pry the housing off pretty easily. You may have to use your fingernail. Make sure you don't accidentally dislocate the steel wheel or the flint. The wheel and flint shouldn't be attached to the housing in any way, so they shouldn't move when you're taking the housing off. If they move during the process, stop what you're doing and reexamine. After the housing comes off, the lint should ignite on the first few tries.

The lint ignites very quickly, so you need to have everything prepared beforehand, including expertly prepared kindling so it catches properly.

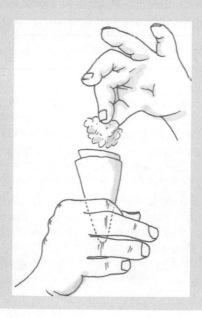

When the going gets tough: Fire starting alternatives

You can start a fire with many alternative methods. In this section, we show you some of the best techniques you can use if you don't have matches or a lighter.

Starting a fire with common, everyday items

You may be surprised at the wide array of everyday items that you can use to start a fire. Be sure to practice these at home before you go outdoors:

>> **Magnesium bar:** A magnesium bar (also known as a *metal match*) is a block of magnesium inlaid with a strip of flint. This handy item should be in every survival kit, and can help you start a fire even when damp because they produce a shower of white-hot sparks! Your local outdoor store may not carry them but they are easy to find online. For more on these, see Chapter 2.

>> **Magnifying glass or similar lens:** You can use a magnifying glass to focus the sun's rays onto tinder and ignite it. Doing so is easy, and it takes only seconds to figure out. If you don't have a magnifying glass, you may be able to carefully remove lenses from binoculars or a rifle scope. Eyeglass lenses may work for starting a fire, but many don't; try at home some sunny day to see if you can manage it with your prescription. Check out Figure 5-4.

>> **Stone and steel:** Steel produces a spark if struck against some kinds of stone (including flint and chert). Check the local creek bed for a variety of stones, and then try striking a heavy knife against them. The sparks from this method are relatively small so try to use the lightest tinder you can find. Lint pulled from clothing is ideal (see the sidebar "Starting a fire with a dead lighter" earlier in this chapter).

>> **Batteries and steel wool:** Many alkaline batteries (including car batteries and the common 9-volt rectangular batteries used in transistor radios) have enough charge to start a bit of steel wool (good to carry in a survival kit) on fire. Make sure the steel wool is fine — more hairy than wooly. If you're using common soap pads, you have to pull them apart until they're wispy-thin.

FIGURE 5-4: Starting a fire with a magnifying lens

Anytime you can connect the two poles of a live battery with the steel wool, you have a chance of getting ignition. Here's how:

- **9-volt:** Wrap your steel wool in tinder or toilet paper and rub the 9-volt battery's poles in the wool.

- **Other batteries:** When using any other type of battery, you must pull the steel wool apart and form a cord that can reach both poles.

WARNING

Be careful not to shock yourself if you're using a car battery. Insulate yourself from the steel wool or wire by holding it with thick, dry cloth.

The steel wool ignites almost immediately, so have your tinder ready.

» **Machinery batteries and wire:** If you're lucky enough to have machinery nearby, such as a car or tractor, you can make a spark by attaching a wire to each terminal of a battery and then touching the tips of the wires together. Doing so produces a serious spark that you can use to ignite tinder.

» **Weaker batteries in series and wire:** If your batteries are weak, try connecting them in a series. Eight 1.5v AA batteries can deliver the same 12v as a car battery. You must connect these negative-to-positive in some way and then connect a separate wire to each end of the stack. Once this is set up, you must touch the free ends of the two wires together to get a spark. A fiddly project, but it can be done.

»» Smart phone battery or backup battery: Many people carry smart phones and smart phone battery banks as a backup in the wilderness. In an emergency, each may be used to ignite tinder. As you will see, though, these methods may be destructive to the phone or battery and the accessories, so think carefully before using them.

> **For battery banks:** Plug in a USB charging cable, cut off the phone-charging plug, and pull apart the wiring. The black (or white) wire should be – (negative) and the red (or orange) should be + (positive). Touching these wires should produce a spark. Alternately, the wires can be used to ignite steel wool (see above).

> **For smart phones:** You have to break open the phone case. Most cases open without tools, but you should look up instructions for your make and model online to be familiar with how to do this. Next, remove the battery. It should have several metallic plates or "contacts" somewhere on the surface. At least one should be marked with a + (positive) and one with a – (negative). Hair-thin wires or lengths of foil paper (like that from chewing gum packaging) can be held to these contacts to ignite foil paper or make a spark.

Experiments show that an ignition drains about 3% of your battery power, so even a low battery may give you several chances.

When all else fails: Using the bow fire method

Humans have made fire for hundreds of thousands of years, if not a million or more. Still, many aboriginal people prefer to keep a fire going after it's lit rather than building a new one every night. You can learn a lot from them that can help you survive outdoors. One lesson is that fire may be started by friction, using simple tools. This section explains the "bow fire," the friction method that is most likely to work in a wilderness survival situation.

When making any type of friction fire, you're not trying to get a flame; you're trying to get an ember. The ember should be placed in the lightest, driest tinder you can find and then tended, sometimes by blowing gently, until the tinder catches. It may take multiple tries to get a live ember into your tinder.

A *bow fire* uses a curved piece of wood (the bow), strung with a cord of some kind, to spin a spindle that creates friction. This makes an ember that you can use to light tinder.

The most important parts of making a bow fire are

>> Selecting good pieces of wood and cordage

>> Manufacturing good components

>> Being patient and persistent in using these tools to start a fire

Craftsmanship and patience count!

If you don't have a knife or blade of any kind, you can use stone tools to build the bow fire. It will take much longer to do it that way, of course, but it can be done. The sharp edges you will need to carve the wood can be made by simply smashing rocks on top of other rocks until you get the edge you're looking for. For a more detailed explanation on how to make stone tools, see Chapter 14.

The bow fire method is probably the most practical way to make an improvised friction fire. Practice making this type of fire at home before trying it in the wilderness.

To make a bow fire, follow these steps (see Figure 5-5):

1. **Choose a straight, symmetrical length of wood for your spindle.**

   The spindle needs to spin very quickly, so you want to spend time making this stick as perfect as you can. Even small imperfections can render the spindle useless. Select dry spindle wood to work with, and you must whittle it as straight and symmetrical as you can (see Figure 5-5a).

   An ideal spindle is around 6 to 8 inches (17 to 20 centimeters) long and about an inch (3 centimeters) in diameter. One end of the spindle should be whittled to a sharp point (see Figure 5-5b) and the other end should be whittled to a shallow taper (picture a used crayon — not blunt, but close; see Figure 5-5c). The sharp point allows for maximum spinning speed and the tapered end allows for maximum friction.

2. **Make a baseboard with a notch in it.**

   The baseboard is a slab of wood where the lower end of the spindle will rotate, creating friction. This friction will create the ember. The baseboard should be made of dry wood and should be carved or cut to be as flat as possible. Cut a divot into the baseboard that fits the blunt end of the spindle (see Figure 5-5d). After shaping the divot, and ensuring it fits the lower end of the spindle, cut a V-shaped notch from the edge of the divot out to the edge of the baseboard (see Figure 5-5e). When an ember ignites, you want it to exit the spindle divot by this notch and fall onto a leaf or some other holder that can be used to move it to your tinder.

3. **Make the handhold.**

   The handhold is a piece of wood, sized to your hand, that you will use to apply downward force on the spindle. Carve a small divot in the center of the handhold. Make sure the handhold divot is shallow, but just deep enough to hold the top end of the spindle (see Figure 5-5f).

4. **Make the bow.**

   Ideally, you want to use a slightly curved branch about two feet (60 centimeters) long, and about an inch or more (3 centimeters) in diameter, cut from a living tree (see Figure 5-5g). Strip bark from the branch and run the shaft through dirt or sand to dry it. Then notch the ends of the bow to better grip the bowstring cordage; simple grooves should work (see Figure 5-5h). Don't cut too deep!

5. **Place the baseboard on the ground with a leaf or other dry catching surface under the notch (see Figure 5-5i).**

6. **String the bow and insert the spindle.**

   Use string or some other durable cordage to make the bowstring (see Figure 5-5j). Shoe or boot laces make good bowstrings. (If you do not have string or shoelaces, check out Chapter 14 for making improvised cordage.) Tie the cordage to one end of the bow and stretch it tightly so that when you tie it to the other end it is taut, just as it would be if you were to use this set up for archery (a bow and arrow). Lay the spindle across the line. Force one end down and around the line, and then take both hands and force the spindle upright, so that the line snaps taut around the spindle (see Figure 5-5k). You're now ready to start spinning the spindle.

7. **Spin the spindle until you get an ember.**

   Place your foot on the baseboard to hold it in place. Exert downward pressure on the spindle with the handhold. Start spinning your spindle slowly. At this stage, you're learning to coordinate holding the bow, holding the handhold, keeping the spindle upright, and keeping your baseboard steady with your foot. It sounds more complicated than it is and is easier to do if you just practice a little, using Figure 5-5l for reference. Concentrate on keeping a good connection with all the components. Try to keep the spindle perpendicular to the bow string because that cuts down on the problem of having the spindle slip out of the string, which is the most frustrating part.

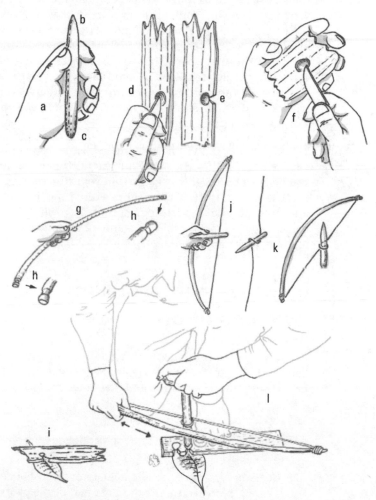

FIGURE 5-5: Building a primitive fire using a bow

TIP

You can use waxy leaves, pine needles, or some other slippery substance in the handhold divot to make the spindle spin easier. Don't use water or oil because liquids swell the wood.

Embers build in the notch of the baseboard; they're the beginnings of your fire. After starting slowly to learn the motion, you can move a little faster. Only when you see white smoke rising from the divot should you really go fast to generate an ember. Once you see the light from an ember, try to tap or knock it out of the groove and onto your catching surface. You will then transfer your ember to your tinder. You will most likely have to blow on the ember to get the tinder to ignite. For more on the fine art of blowing on a fire, see our instructions for starting a fire in the section, "The first spark: Igniting and oxygenating your fire," earlier in this chapter. Keep in mind that once you get an ember, you must act very quickly to get a fire going. Otherwise, the ember will die before you can take advantage of it, and you will have to start all over again.

TIP

The best tinder is the lint cone, which is described in the sidebar "Starting a fire with a dead lighter." If you use this tinder, you must be thoroughly organized in your fire-making operation because though the lint ball ignites every time, it only burns for a few seconds. Consequently, you must have slightly larger tinder, like dead grass or leaves, standing by to keep the chain of ignition-to-campfire going.

Battling the Elements: Making Fire in Wet Conditions

When things get wet, making fire is more difficult, but if you're persistent, you may be able to get a fire going. First and foremost, look for dry tinder, kindling, and fuel in the following places:

>> Under rock shelters and in caves

>> Under or inside downed trees or logs (found lying on the ground)

>> Under heavy snow pack (if temperatures are just under freezing, everything above the snow may be dripping with melt water, but deep under the cold snowpack may be colder, dry wood)

>> In animal burrows, such as squirrel or marmot dens

>> In the center of anything made of paper or fibers, like the inner layers of a roll of tape, or the very bottom layer of a large pile of grass

>> In trees, either dead standing trees or dead branches on live trees

Sometimes you can take sticks that are slightly wet and whittle away the soaked parts to produce somewhat dry kindling.

Also search your clothes and possessions, especially the inside of your wallet, for dry tinder. Sometimes papers or even paper money deep inside a wallet or pocketbook remain dry even though everything else around you is soaked. If you aren't completely soaked through, you can try making a tinder pile using lint from your underclothes. Lint ignites almost every time. The problem is having enough. Making a lint ball large enough to start kindling can take as much as an hour.

In wet conditions, try to build your fire on a somewhat dry base and under some kind of shelter. Look for a base of board or a piece of metal is good, and cloth or plastic cloth can work in a pinch. Use anything you can for shelter, as long as it keeps the drops off your fire for a moment.

TIP

Consider trying to start your fire without the use of tinder. Many times, when it's wet, tinder is harder to ignite than kindling — especially leaves or paper. If that's the case, make a small tee-pee of twigs and try lighting the thin stems directly. The kindling must be exceedingly thin, though — the thinnest twigs you can find. In wet conditions, a dense teepee made of wire-thin twigs is frequently the only way to get a fire started. The section, "Building a teepee fire," earlier in this chapter, can tell you more about building a teepee fire.

You'll note that in describing dry conditions, we haven't mentioned using gasoline or stove fuel to start fires; that is because you want to conserve such accelerants. But in wet conditions, if you have liquid fuels, this is the time to use them (sparingly, a few drops may be all you need) to start damp tinder or kindling.

Safely Extinguishing a Fire

Before you leave camp, you must extinguish all fires. No exceptions. A forest fire can start in less than a minute.

TIP

You know when a fire is extinguished because you can place naked hands on the dead coals.

Extinguish fires with water or, if you are conserving water, bury the fire with dirt built up to at least 1 foot in thickness. Don't use grass or moss; these might reignite. Place heavy stones on top of the dirt to discourage animals from digging up the fire and reigniting it (animals can smell anything aromatic that has fallen into the fire, such as fat, oil, or food, from a great distance).

Chapter **6**

Home, Sweet Hut: Simple Survival Shelters

When you're in a wilderness setting, getting in from the elements can be a lifesaver. A shelter can keep you warm in cold environments, cool in hot conditions, and dry when it's raining. Being sheltered is also a morale boost; you have eked out a little bit of control of your situation. Sometimes you can take shelter in natural formations, such as caves, but many times you need to build your own haven. That's okay, though, because most survival shelters are easy to make.

In this chapter, we show you the simplest and most effective shelters you can find and make. In Part III, we cover shelters for specific conditions (snowdrift shelters, for example, or desert sunshades and jungle hammocks). For the moment, we look at the simplest ways to take shelter outdoors.

Grasping the Importance of Shelter

Shelter is important in survival situations for physical and psychological reasons. Physically, the human body is pretty frail. A few hours in the sun can burn you severely, and a cold night can incapacitate you. A good shelter:

>> Gets you out of the direct sun, which can prevent sunburn and stave off hyperthermia (heat stroke)

>> Can be warmed, preventing hypothermia and frostbite

>> Protects you from wind and rain and sometimes insects and predators

>> Includes an insulating bed that keeps your body heat from being sucked into the cold earth

To make a shelter in the wilderness, you can try to make do with natural shelters or build your own. Whenever you're in a survival situation, keep a constant lookout for good natural shelters. If you're pretty sure you're going to be stranded outdoors overnight, finding or making shelter is a top priority. The upcoming sections describe the main natural-shelter alternatives.

REMEMBER

Keep your camp orderly and clean; this is good for morale and also for finding equipment the moment you need it.

Before Making Camp: What to Do

Having a shelter is good, but it should be considered part of the overall campsite. Here are the most important things to think about camp-wise.

Understanding priorities

When it becomes clear that you're going to spend the night out, you should prioritize your actions in getting shelter:

1. **Decide where you want to locate your shelter.**

    See the section later in this chapter, "Selecting a good campsite," for why the location is important.

2. **Gather some tinder, kindling, and firewood and put them near where you intend to build your shelter.**

   You don't want to search for these supplies at night. If you can, cover them to keep them dry (even if it isn't raining now, it could be in ten minutes!). See Chapter 5 for more on fire-making.

3. **Build (or find) your shelter.**

4. **Clearly mark your location so you can be seen from the air.**

   Use the methods we describe in Chapter 12.

5. **Now that camp is made, settle in for the night.**

   Quality sleep is important to keep up your strength and morale, but psychological factors may make it hard to sleep in a survival situation. See Chapter 3 for ways to proactively cope with stress.

REMEMBER

As a rule of thumb, never rest or sleep directly on the ground — it sucks heat from your body. Insulate yourself from the ground with a layer of vegetation, such as pine boughs, or use extra clothing.

Selecting a good campsite

If you're going to build or find shelter, you need to choose an appropriate campsite. Take some time to select a campsite; a good location can protect you from wind, rain, and other elements. Before you start building or searching, consider the following:

>> **When you're near water, look for higher ground to make your camp.** Cold air flows downhill, so riverbeds and lakesides are colder than slopes that lead down to them, particularly in the early morning.

WARNING

Beware of *flash floods,* sudden bursts of water that can turn a dry riverbed into a raging torrent. Look for high-water marks, such as water stains on rock faces or vegetation trapped by running water in trees or bushes. Be sure your camp is considerably higher than the usual high-water mark. For more on the dangers of flash floods and how to spot high-water marks, see Chapter 17.

>> **When on the spines of exposed ridges, beware of lightning hazards.** Although you may want to build your rescue signals on a ridge, actually camping on such exposed ground is a lightning risk.

>> **When you're in the mountains, watch out for the telltale signs of avalanche or rockfall.** Either of these can wipe out your camp in an instant. See Chapter 16 for more on avalanche hazards.

>> **Keep aware of high-wind hazards.** Check trees to see whether they're all leaning the same way or are missing limbs on the same side; these signs can indicate the prevailing wind direction. Set up your shelter in a protected area if you can, because incessant wind really can wear you down psychologically.

Using Natural Shelters

Natural shelters come in all shapes, sizes, and kinds, but they really boil down to two types: trees and caves/rock overhangs. This section looks at these two shelters and discusses which critters to watch out for before you move in.

Trees

In many survival situations you can turn to trees for shelter. Any tree that has been hollowed out by fire or downed for some other reason, and rotted from the inside-out, makes a decent shelter. Put down some vegetation, such as leaves or pine boughs, as insulation from the cold ground. Figure 6-1 shows two examples of tree shelters.

Hollowed logs are often as populated as apartment buildings, crawling with ants, termites, spiders, millipedes, and a multitude of other wonderful bugs. If you're desperate for shelter and have the ability to make fire, you can try to evict these inhabitants by building a fire next to the tree and fanning dense smoke (produced by throwing live vegetation on the fire) onto the log, but this is a lot of work that may or may not pay off.

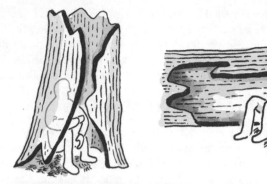

FIGURE 6-1: Taking shelter in a hollow tree (left) or log (right)

Caves and rock overhangs

A cave or rock overhang is an ideal shelter for a person lost in a wilderness. With *caves* — actual cavities in rock faces — smaller is normally better because small caves are easy to heat up with a good campfire. It is virtually impossible to warm the space under *rock overhangs* — simple rock overhangs, but at least they can keep you dry if you can get back behind the dripline. Figure 6-2 shows an example of using a cave entrance for shelter.

FIGURE 6-2: A cave can be a great shelter

If the cave is very deep and you can't find the back, resist the urge to explore by making a torch or using a flashlight. Stay in the first few feet of the shelter, just deep enough to keep out of the elements. Your objective is simply to survive. You can easily get lost, take fatal falls, or even get trapped by flash floods in a dark cave.

Checking for current residents

WARNING

Although natural shelters can be ideal, you need to make sure no one else calls yours home. Bears den in caves throughout North America from fall to spring. You can spot some clues near the cave entrance to find out whether the place is vacant. Caves occupied by larger mammals often display the following telltales: pawprints, food debris such as bones, animal feces (or *scat*), animal fur or hair, and strong wet-dog-like odors.

TIP

If you suspect a bear lives in the shelter, back away slowly and then get the heck out of there. It's tough to say how far you should go to stay safe in this situation, but you may want to travel several hours to get out of the bear's territory — even that may not be enough. If it's a mama bear inside with her cubs, you sure don't want to challenge her for the shelter.

If you're satisfied no larger animals are home, you can continue to explore a natural shelter:

>> **Use a long and sturdy stick to knock on the shelter.** Be ready for a raccoon, bird, or some other animal to explode out of the entrance.

>> **Creep closer and look closely.** Don't assume there's nobody home, because some animals freeze rather than run when frightened.

>> **Carefully explore the inside with the end of the stick.** Use the stick like a poker.

TIP

A good fire may deter animals from coming back to the shelter at night. Build the fire near the hollow tree or right at the entrance to the cave or rock overhang. Take care to shield the fire from strong winds near the entrance and be sure to place your fire so it can't be extinguished by rain.

Putting a Roof over Your Head: Building Simple Shelters

If you're going to be out even just one night, building a shelter is well worth it. Doing so is easier than it sounds. You can build a simple and effective shelter within an hour with just a few materials — either found in the wild or carried in your survival kit. In your kit, you should have the following three shelter-building tools:

>> **Knife (or other cutting and chopping implement):** See Chapter 14 for how to improvise knives and chopping tools from stone.

>> **Tarp:** A tarp can help waterproof the shelter. A large plastic bag or three may work in a pinch.

>> **Cordage:** Use cordage (rope, shoelaces, wire, strips of cloth, whatever you have) to lash wooden parts of a shelter together; parachute cord is ideal. If you're running low, you can cut open parachute cord to get at multiple strands inside it, tripling your cordage length. In the same way, you can unbraid twisted rope, which is made of several strands.

Making a tarp shelter

A simple plastic tarp is invaluable outdoors, sheltering you from rain, sun, and wind. If you can make a fire near the entrance and block the rear entrance with brush or a backpack, you have a shelter that can keep you alive indefinitely.

WARNING

If you build a fire in your shelter, always be careful not to light your shelter on fire. Keeping a pile of sand or dirt (or, if you can afford it, a jug of water) next to the fire can help you put out a fire before it spreads.

The basic tarp shelter uses a line tied between two trees as the peak of the tarp. All you need are a couple trees about 10 to 20 feet (3 to 6 meters) apart, a length of cordage, your tarp, and a few stakes that you can use to anchor down the corners, as in Figure 6-3a.

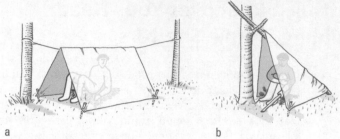

a   b

FIGURE 6-3: Two types of tarp shelters

To create a basic tarp shelter, follow these steps:

1. **Tie the length of cordage between two trees.**

   The tighter you tie it, the better. You want the roof to be straight, not bowing down.

2. **Drape the tarp over the cordage, making the peak of the roof.**

3. **Use stakes to secure the corners of the tarp by hammering them into the ground.**

   Stakes should be green wood cut from living trees, not the more brittle wood you find lying on the forest floor. If your tarp has *grommets* (metal-reinforced holes) on the corners, put the stakes through them to prevent the tarp from tearing under pressure.

If you're in a hurry or are weak and need to rest, you can make an alternative tarp shelter, as in Figure 6-3b. This shelter uses a ridge pole and is simpler to set up, but it's a little cramped, so after the storm passes or you're more fully rested, you may later decide to use cordage to make a roomier, more permanent shelter.

TIP

Whichever type of tarp shelter you fashion, use some foliage (such as pine boughs) to insulate the ground so you don't rest directly on the earth.

Building a downed-tree or other A-frame shelter

Downed-tree or A-frame shelters can provide a little more protection from the elements than a simple tarp shelter if the downed tree (or A-frame materials) has a lot of vegetation still on it. You can always supplement these shelters with a tarp for waterproofing. They should always be equipped with an insulated sleeping/sitting area and a fire with a *fire reflector* (a screen of sticks, placed vertically in the ground, to reflect the fire's heat back into the shelter area). Figure 6-4 shows examples of these types of shelters.

FIGURE 6-4: A downed-tree shelter and an A-frame shelter

Both shelters use a *ridgepole* (a pole at the peak of the shelter) flanked by walls. In the case of the downed-tree shelter (see Figure 6-4a), the ridgepole is simply a tree trunk that's fallen (you can tell it yourself if you have an ax). Crawl under the tree and cut out tree limbs that hang down to the ground, making a hollow under the ridgepole; you may also want to cut off branches that stick up above the ridgepole to prevent them from catching wind and shaking the shelter.

Here's how to build the A-frame shelter:

1. **Gather wood to make the frame.**

    In the A-frame (see Figure 6-4b), the ridgepole is a sturdy sapling supported by about six *uprights;* green wood won't crumble like dead wood from the forest floor, but use what you can get.

2. **Build the frame as in Figure 6-4b.**

   Lash the uprights to the ridgepole at an angle of 45 degrees or more. Lower angles don't shed rain or snow as well.

3. **Pile branches with vegetation against the ridgepole, at the angle of the uprights, to make the walls.**

In either case, a tarp draped over the ridgepole (and tied down or staked down, as seen earlier in Figure 6–3) can help water-proof the shelter. Build an insulation bed under the shelter and a fire with a fire reflector and with luck you should have a decent night out.

Constructing an insulated shelter

The shelter described here is extremely basic and is meant to be used in situations when you have no resources at all. This shelter works by creating a thick layer of dead air between your body and the outside. On a cold night, this shelter will not be toasty warm, but it can prevent hypothermia, especially when combined with layers of dead air in your clothing. For instruction on how to layer clothing with dry leaves, grass, or debris, see Chapter 4. You can make this very simple shelter by doing the following:

1. **Next to a log or long rock, make a 2-foot-thick (0.6-meter) bed of leaves, grass, moss, pine needles, any other dry vegetation, clothing, or other items that can insulate you from the ground (see Figure 6-5a).**

   Lay on it in a sleeping posture occasionally while you're building it to be sure it is the right size for you (see Figure 6-5b).

2. **Lean four or five 5-foot-long (1.5-meter) branches against the log or rock, forming a sloping roof over the bedding (see Figure 6-5c).**

   This is the frame for your shelter. Don't make it too big. You want this shelter to be tight-fitting so it insulates you almost like a sleeping bag.

3. **Pile a 3-foot-thick (0.9-meter) insulating layer of leaves, grass, moss, pine needles, any other dry vegetation, clothing, or other items on top of the roof (see Figure 6-5d).**

If you have a waterproof tarp, you can tie it to the roof to help you stay dry.

4. **Mark the outside of the shelter so it can be clearly seen and then squirm inside, sealing the opening with a backpack or more vegetation; then try to sleep.**

You can improve your morale with just a few hours of good sleep. Figure 6-5e shows you snug inside the shelter!

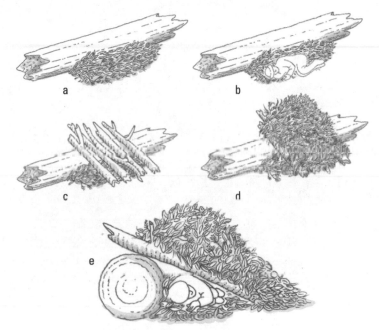

FIGURE 6-5: A simple insulated overnight shelter

IN THIS CHAPTER

» Knowing how much water you need

» Knowing where to look for water

» Collecting rain and condensation

» Extracting drinkable water from plants

» Filtering and purifying liquids

Chapter 7

Liquid Capital: Finding Drinking Water

Regardless of the wilderness setting you find yourself in, finding and storing water is your third priority after you do all you can to protect your body temperature (see Chapter 4) and make sure you're prepared to signal for help (see Chapter 12).

In this chapter we familiarize you with the threat of dehydration and show you how to find water, how to extract it from various sources, and finally how to filter and purify it for consumption.

Taking Steps to Conserve Water

In a survival situation it's imperative to conserve your bodily water reserves. This can stretch your survival time significantly.

Determining your water needs

Under average, moderate conditions, you lose from 2 to 3 quarts (2 to 3 liters) of body water per day. If you don't replenish this water, you begin to feel the effects of *dehydration*, which is when your body doesn't have enough water to perform its normal functions.

Dehydration usually starts with a drop in your energy level, followed by headache, confusion, dry mouth, quivering muscles, and extreme fatigue. If the average person doesn't replace the water lost on average every day, they will likely lose consciousness after three days and perish after five.

After you know the averages, you need to know the extremes:

>> In temperate conditions, at rest, you may only lose about 1 quart (1 liter) of water per day.

>> In a hot climate, you lose about 1 gallon (4 liters) just doing day-to-day activity.

>> Strenuous all-day activity in a hot climate like a desert may cost you over 5 gallons (more than 20 liters), which, if not replaced, is fatal.

For more on the special problems of hot climates, see Chapter 17.

TIP

Urine color is a good indicatory of hydration level; anything darker than a wheat color indicates dehydration.

Stretching your water supply

Your body uses water all the time, even when you're at rest. This occurs by urination, perspiration, and respiration (breathing). Though you can't stop this water loss, you can slow it down, and in a survival situation, that's your goal. Here's how to do it:

>> **Stop water intake in the short term.** Stop consuming your water supply for a short while. Any water you consume before bodily reserves are used will be lost through urination. You have to make a judgment call here: Adrift in a life raft in moderate conditions, you can go the first 24 hours without any water at all. In hot desert conditions (or in extreme cold) you may not be able to last that long.

>> **Don't consume diuretics.** *Diuretics* are liquids that cause excess urination, such as coffee, soda, alcohol, and salt water.

>> **Limit strenuous movement.** Limit your physical exertion to the minimum.

>> **Keep cool.** Find shade or erect a covering to make shade. Splash any liquid that you can — even salt water — on your body. Don't lie on hot surfaces like the ground. In cold conditions, strip off layers of clothing if you begin to perspire.

>> **Avoid eating.** You need water to digest food in general, but especially fats and proteins. If you have to eat, try to eat carbohydrates.

>> **Keep your mouth closed, breathe through your nose, and limit talking.** These reduce the loss of water vapor.

>> **If you're at high altitude, descend.** The higher you are, the harder you breathe, and the more water vapor you lose.

Rationing water in more severe situations

Base any water-rationing program on your environment. You have to find a balance between extending your life and impairing your physical capacities so much that you can no longer function. For instance, consider the following:

>> At sea in a raft, the minimum you need is around 1 cup (237 milliliters) of water per day. This is the smallest amount you can consume and still survive for more than a week or so, and this pertains only to ideal conditions.

>> If you're on land, especially in hot conditions, cutting down to 1 cup of water per day when you have 2 or 3 gallons (7.5 or 11.5 liters) lying around is counterproductive, because you end up physically incapacitated long before you consume your water.

Identify how much water you have, how many people you must supply, and how long you expect to be stranded. This is hard to estimate, but you have to start somewhere. Discuss any type of water rationing with your companions thoroughly. Make sure everyone in your party feels they're included and that they're being treated fairly. You should also discuss plans for finding water, which we cover later in this chapter.

Avoiding Certain Liquids

WARNING

You may be tempted to drink whatever fluids you can find in a survival situation. However, some liquids cause more trouble than they're worth. Here's why you should stay away from them:

>> **Salt water:** Salt water increases urination leading to dehydration. Although some survival texts claim you can consume salt water, they're almost invariably based on faulty sources, or they don't take into account the practical problems (namely, that as soon as you start drinking salt water, it's very hard to stop), or they ignore volumes of research. Our thorough research makes it clear: never drink salt water. For more on the problems of drinking salt water, see Chapter 20.

>> **Animal blood:** Digesting animal blood consumes your bodily water supplies; and blood often carries pathogens that you don't normally contract because you cook the meat. Consuming blood also puts you at risk for vomiting, which further dehydrates you. (*Note:* We endorse only one exception to this rule: drinking turtle blood at sea. For details, see Chapter 20.)

>> **Urine:** Drinking unpurified urine is highly inadvisable; it can be a diuretic and a poison. And as soon as you begin to dehydrate, your urine only becomes denser and saltier. Under no circumstances should you ever drink dark or thick urine. For more on the bitter controversy surrounding drinking urine, see the nearby sidebar.

THE CONTROVERSY OVER DRINKING URINE

Of all the issues we address in this book, none is more controversial than the question of whether drinking urine extends your life or hastens your demise. The truth is that some castaways and wilderness survivors have endured extended dehydration times while drinking urine, and some have probably hastened their deaths from drinking it.

You can read stories from the past and present in which people drink urine and then stay alive well beyond the average survival time. The problem is that knowing what the people could've endured had they *not* drunk urine is practically impossible. In some cases, survivors have gone seven full days — an unusually long survival time — without any liquid at all. Some didn't even lose consciousness during these extended times, even though they drank nothing at all. So just because a survivor drank urine *and* had an unusual survival time while dehydrated, doesn't necessarily mean that urine-drinking and extended times are related.

The argument is divided into three camps: Those who absolutely oppose drinking urine, those who favor it, and those who oppose it but who've read enough case studies to know that the question probably doesn't have an easy answer. This last camp, which consists of some famous survival experts, usually addresses the issue in a highly diplomatic fashion or simply tries to ignore it altogether.

That leaves us with some facts:

- Urine is sterile when it comes out of the body.
- Urine will keep for about two to three days, depending on how it's stored.
- If you're properly hydrated at the start of the survival situation, your first urination would be the purest.
- Drinking urine before you've exhausted all other possibilities is a bad idea. You don't know whether you're drinking something that's harmless or something that's a diuretic.
- The more you dehydrate in a survival situation, the more salty, toxic, and diuretic your urine becomes. If you're cycling your urine through your system, you need to know that this can hasten a shutdown of your renal system.
- In the last stages of dehydration, the uric acid in unpurified urine strips the membranes from the inside of your mouth and severely aggravates the cracks in your lips. Both are exceedingly painful traumas.

Based on this information, we suggest that you avoid drinking urine and look for other water sources. If you have no other water source and you're desperate, consider running urine through a *solar still* (discussed later in this chapter).

If you're in dire straits, you can get drinkable water from salt water or urine through distillation. See "Distilling salt water and urine," later in this chapter, for details.

Knowing the signs of a low-grade or even possibly poisonous water supply is essential. Here's what to watch out for:

>> An acrid, foul, or sewage smell

>> Skeletons of dead animals nearby

>> No plant life whatsoever near the water source

>> Bubbles, foam, or thick green slime on the surface

>> Milky colored water (especially from glaciers)

>> A profusion of cattails or rushes in a stagnant area

You want the highest quality water you can find — before you filter and purify. For more on purifying water, see "Filtering and Purifying Water," later in this chapter.

Finding Bodies of Water

You can find drinkable liquid in almost any environment; you just have to know where to look. After you find that liquid, you may then have to transform it into something you can safely consume. (For a look at cleaning water, check out the later section titled "Filtering and Purifying Water"; for tips on recognizing contaminated water, see the preceding section.) This section identifies water sources and helps you locate water.

Locating water in drainages

One of the first places to look for water is in a *drainage*, which is any place where rain trickles down and collects. Most drainages are at the bottoms of slopes. Valleys and canyons are drainages, as are creek beds, culverts, gullies, ditches, runoffs, and depressions in the land, such as ponds or lakes.

Sometimes the nearest drainage is obvious: It's the raging river right next to the trail. Many times, however, you have to examine your surroundings to determine the pathway rainwater takes after it falls on the ground. Drainages may hold water for months after the last rain.

If you find a drainage that seems dry, work your way downstream until you find a puddle; in temperate or near-temperate climates, you can almost always find one. If you're in bone-dry conditions, dig for water underneath the drainage.

Looking for other signs of water

You should keep a sharp lookout for signs of water at all times — even before the survival situation occurs. Places to look for water include the following:

>> **Where you see a profusion of green vegetation:** This is especially true if the vegetation is bunched in a low spot of the terrain

>> **Beneath a damp surface, such as damp sand or mud:** This may indicate ground water. You may have to dig down and allow the water to seep into the hole.

>> **At the foot of concave banks of dry rivers:** For more on dry riverbeds, see Chapter 17.

>> **In holes and fissures in rock faces:** Rock formations often contain cracks and hollows that hold water for months at a time between rains. You may have to use a tube or straw made from a reed to suck up the water.

>> **Under patches of shade:** Even in Spring or summer, patches of shade (from vegetation or rocks) sometimes preserve clumps of snow.

>> **Along game trails:** Game trails are narrow pathways that animals of the area beat through the grass. Many times these trails lead to water — especially the trails that go downslope or converge at watering spots visited by animals at dawn or dusk.

>> **Areas with birds, especially smaller birds:** If they fly low and straight, they're usually headed for water; after they drink, they usually have to fly from tree to tree to rest. Large birds of prey, however, like eagles, hawks, owls, or buzzards, aren't indicators.

>> **Areas with bees, flies, and ants:** Bees fly to water, as do green flies. Trails of ants crawling up trees frequently lead to pockets of water trapped in hollows.

Catching Rain

All too often, survivors miss their golden opportunity to collect rainwater because they didn't realize that you have to be highly prepared to really take advantage of rainfall. Make sure you get organized before the first drop falls.

Catching rain is about funneling water down a *catchment plane* into a container. The plane can be a plastic poncho or tarp (see Figure 7-1a), but you can also use metal sheeting, broad leaves (Figure 7-1b), fabric such as canvas, or even wood to channel drops into your containers.

As in any survival situation, containers are king. If you believe rain is coming, collect or build as many water-collection containers as you can. You can use old bottles (those with a wider mouth are best), shape paper or heavy cloth into a container, make bowls from large pieces of bark or leaves, and/or channel water into natural hollows such as a tree crotch or a divot in a boulder. If you have a large tarp you can make the catching plane the container simply by using it to line a large, shallow pit and let it fill like a small pond (see Figure 7-1c).

FIGURE 7-1: Ways to catch rain

If your collection materials are clean, you can drink the collected rainwater straight, without purifying it. If your catchment plane is dirty or fouled with saltwater, pour off the first water you collect, keeping it for other purposes such as washing.

Collecting Condensation

Even if water isn't falling from the sky or running on the ground, you may be able to collect water vapor in a variety of ways. In this section, we tell you how to gather dew and collect the water that evaporates out of plants.

Gathering dew

You can frequently collect enough condensation or dew to stay hydrated. This water must be purified only if you think the surface it comes from is somehow contaminated. Here's how to collect dew:

>> Take your shirt off, tie it to your ankle, and walk through wet vegetation; then wring out the water into your mouth.

>> Look for puddles of condensation that form in the pits of rock faces and inside bowl or pitcher shaped leaves.

>> Soak up the drops on metal or glass surfaces with your shirt or a sponge. You can also use a credit card or something like it to coax the drops into a container.

Dew usually forms sometime during the cold of night, not at dawn.

Making a transpiration bag

You can get water from plants by using a *transpiration bag*, which simply is a plastic bag that you wrap around a tree or bush that captures the water that naturally evaporates from vegetation. Droplets form inside the tightly sealed bag and then trickle down to collect in the bottom.

You can use any plastic sheeting to make a transpiration bag — just make sure you have a tight seal around the vegetation, and try to make sure that it's exposed to direct sunlight. Check out Figure 7-2 to see how a transpiration bag works and how to use a tube to suck out the water.

If a plant is poisonous, the water you collect from it is poisonous. For more on poisonous plants, see Chapter 8.

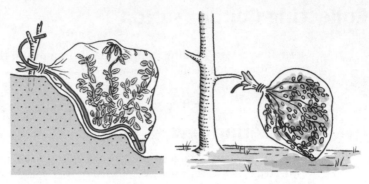

FIGURE 7-2: Transpiration bags on the ground and on a tree

Setting up a solar still

A *solar still* is a tightly sealed evaporation unit that allows droplets to form and then trickle down to a collection cup. You can use this method to get water from vegetation, to desalinate salt water or purify urine or other contaminated water. Sometimes just the wet earth below the topsoil can be enough to produce drops if you build a solar still over a freshly dug pit.

You can follow these steps to make a basic vegetation still, but this setup (shown in Figure 7-3) also works for all the applications previously listed in this chapter. Solar stills like this produce only a tiny trickle of water, so build as many as you can.

1. **Dig a pit and fill it with freshly cut plants, the wetter and fleshier the better.**

    REMEMBER

    Poisonous plants produce poisonous liquid in solar stills. Don't put plants that ooze milky fluid or sticky sap in a solar still (with the exception of the barrel cactus — see Chapter 17).

    TIP

    To purify contaminated liquid, place a container of it in your pit in place of the vegetation. If you don't have vegetation or liquid but the ground is wet, you can simply put plastic over the empty pit, and the groundwater will evaporate into the still.

2. **Put a collection container in the center of the pit, on top of the vegetation.**

3. **If possible, extend a tube from the container at the bottom to the rim of the pit.**

Using a tube vastly improves efficiency. With the tube in the cup, you can suck up the condensation without disturbing the evaporation process inside the still.

4. **Drape plastic sheeting over the pit; then take a slightly pointed stone and push the plastic down gently to form a slope.**

This allows the condensation to roll down and drip into the container. You want to end up with a miniature stalactite shape just over the container. You can try canvas if no plastic is available.

5. **Heap sand or stones around the edge of the plastic sheeting to anchor it in place.**

Make sure you get a good seal around the plastic.

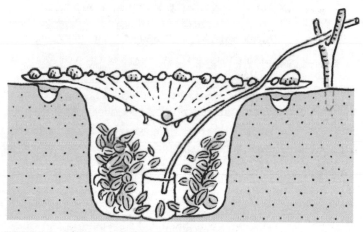

FIGURE 7-3: A basic solar still with vegetation

Extracting Water from Plants

You can get the water you need from nearby vegetation, but you have to be on guard for signs of poisonous liquids. This section identifies trees and plants that provide safe drinking water.

WARNING

Consider any plant liquids that are sticky or milky to be poisonous and unfit to drink!

You can frequently find water in tree hollows and in pitcher- or cup-shaped leaves. Or you can extract water from trees if you know the right methods. Here's how:

>> **Palms:** Coconut, buri, nipa, rattan, and sugar palms all contain drinkable liquid. Bend over a flowering stalk of palm and cut the tip off to allow the liquid to drip into a cup. Make a new cut every 12 hours to renew the flow.

>> **Banana and plantain:** Cut down the tree and then convert the stump into a reservoir by hollowing it out. The tree's liquid rises and fills this reservoir quickly. Check out Figure 7-4. At first, the liquid is too bitter to drink, so you have to sit through two to three fillings before the liquid is palatable. One tree can provide you with three to four days' worth of liquid.

>> **The flowers of cactus:** Eating the bulbous flower of a cactus can provide much needed liquid. For more on consuming cactus flowers, see Chapter 17.

>> **Umbrella tree:** Found in western tropical Africa, this tree has leaf bases and roots that can yield water.

>> **Traveler's tree:** Water collects at the bases of the leaves of this fanlike tree, which grows in Madagascar.

>> **Baobab tree:** Water collects and is stored in the bottlelike trunk of this tree, which grows in Australia and Africa.

Other plants that yield water include the following:

>> **Bamboo:** Green bamboo may contain water. You can either cut the sections open and drain them or bend the entire cane over, cut the top off, and let the water drip into a cup. If the water is clear and doesn't smell bad, you can drink it straight; if it's brown or smells fermented, you have to purify it (see the next section). Brown canes sometimes contain water as well.

REMEMBER

>> **Coconuts:** Drink only from mature, brown coconuts. Young, green coconuts contain an oil that acts as a laxative, and too much of it can cause diarrhea.

FIGURE 7-4: Cut down a banana or plantain tree to get water in the trunk reservoir

>> **Fleshy plants:** Cut down plants with fleshy centers and then squeeze or mash them to extract the liquid. ***Warning:*** Some varieties of fleshy cactus are poisonous. For information on cactus, poisonous and not, see Chapter 17.

>> **Vines:** To extract water from a vine, first cut it at the highest point you can; then cut it at a lower point to allow the liquid to drain down. If you cut low first, the water is drawn back up the vine. Don't drink any vine liquid that appears sticky, milky, or anything other than clear.

Filtering and Purifying Water

Any natural body of water can contain bacteria, parasites, and toxins, any one of which can make you ill. Nearly all water-borne diseases involve a violent bout of diarrhea, which accelerates dehydration. To avoid sickness, consider all water dangerous, regardless of how clear it appears. Filter and purify all your water to the best of your ability. This section explains methods you can use to purify or treat water, starting with the most effective one — boiling.

In most rainy environments it's vastly better to get an organized rain-catching operation going than to mess around with continually having to filter and purify water.

Boiling water

Boiling water for three minutes is the best course of action in a wilderness situation; this should kill all harmful microorganisms. If you have a tin cup or some other metal container and you can get a fire going, always boil your water.

Boiling water in a plastic container is possible, but you risk destroying the container. Put some thought into this procedure before you risk it. The key is to suspend the plastic container from a tripod and never allow it to touch hot flames or coals. (For instructions on building a tripod, see Chapter 14.) The plastic should turn black, but you obviously want to watch for the deformities that indicate the plastic is melting.

TIP

Before boiling any water, consider filtering it first to remove larger particles. See the later section "Improvising filters" for details.

Purifying water with chemicals

If you can't boil your water, you should purify it with chemicals (preferably after filtering — see the later section "Improvising filters").

Water purification tablets (often iodine-based) come with instructions for use; follow these carefully to be sure your water is purified. *Household bleach* may be carried in a small bottle in liquid form; two or three drops per quart (or liter) is standard for disinfection of suspect water.

For small amounts of water, you should wait at least 30 minutes for the chemical to kill enough germs to make the water safe. For gallon jugs and larger, wait two hours or more.

Distilling salt water and urine

If you have the necessary tools and time, you can convert salt water or urine into drinkable water by heating it in a metal container, collecting the steam in fabric, and then wringing out the water from the fabric into a container. Or you can distill salt water and urine in a solar still. For more on this, see the section, "Setting up a solar still," earlier in this chapter.

Distillation is the only method that makes salt water or urine drinkable. Using water purification tablets doesn't do anything to make salt water or urine safe. Some filters can desalinate salt water, but you must read the label on the package of the filter to make sure it's built to do this highly specialized task.

Using commercial water filters

Commercially made water filters use a hand pump to force water through filters and/or purifying chemicals. Many aren't guaranteed to filter out all harmful microorganisms (or to desalinate salt water), so research before buying. These devices can be too heavy and bulky for a survival kit, so you should learn the other methods we present in this chapter.

TIP

Some filters are essentially large plastic straws that you suck water through, the water being filtered in the straw. These are handy, but they are easily broken or clogged, so it's important to know other methods.

Improvising filters

An *improvised water filter* can remove excrement, leeches, body parts of dead animals, and many other unpalatable things from suspect water. They will not purify water but are important to use before chemical treatments or boiling. As seen in Figure 7-5, fabric (a t-shirt or sock for example) can be used as a crude filter, grasses or other stalky vegetation catch larger debris, gravel and sand catch smaller debris, and charcoal from a campfire may improve the taste of filtered water.

Digging a seepage basin

A *seepage basin* is a meter-deep pit dug next to a body of water that allows water to seep in, being filtered by the intervening sand or gravel. Figure 7-6 displays a generic seepage basin. You can place the basin next to nearly any body of water; at the seaside, make the basin beyond the first or second line of dunes.

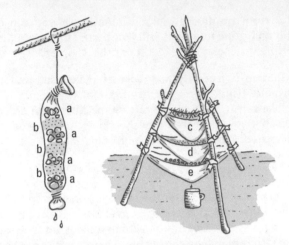

FIGURE 7-5: Sock and tripod filters using fabric, vegetation, sand, and charcoal

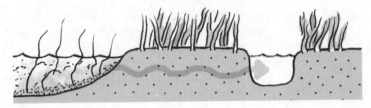

FIGURE 7-6: A seepage basin

IN THIS CHAPTER

» Understanding calories

» Finding safe plant foods in the wilderness

» Hunting with improvised tools

» Trapping and fishing

» Cleaning, cooking, and preserving wilderness foods

Chapter **8**

Gathering and Hunting to Stay Alive in the Wilderness

After you solve your most immediate survival problems — maintaining good health, keeping a tolerable body temperature, and securing a water supply — you need to start thinking about food. Although people can and have gone for weeks or even months without significant amounts of food, having the strength to forage for food and firewood, maintain your camp, signal for help, or start traveling toward civilization (or whatever else you need to do) all require food.

Humans have lived off the land for a lot longer than they've been going to the grocery store, but most civilization-dwellers need to learn about ancient methods of finding natural food in the wilderness. In this chapter, you can discover what it takes to find and prepare safe wilderness foods.

Managing Food and Energy in the Wild

In survival situations, eating comes to mind quickly because most of us are accustomed to eating every few hours. The first step in managing your food supply is accepting that you will probably be eating less often. Next, you must begin thinking in terms of calories in and calories burned.

Calories = energy

Calories are units of energy; average adults need about 1,500 a day just to keep the body running. A little study can familiarize you with how many calories are in various foods; for example, a spoonful of sugar has about 20 calories, a big spoonful of peanut butter is about 100 calories. You bring *calories in* by consuming foods like these, which fuels your body's activities.

The average adult burns about 3,000 calories in a good day of hiking (double that for a cold day) and about 500 calories per hour of moderate kayaking – examples of *calories burned.* You can get these calories either from what you eat, or by burning your own body's energy reserves (fat and muscle). The average adult has enough body fat to fuel the body for many days without eating, even though you would feel very hungry.

If you burn more calories than you bring in by consuming food, your body begins to burn its caloric reserves for fuel, eventually, leading to starvation. Although we tend to avoid high-calorie foods in daily life, in survival situations you want as many calories as you can get. You not only need *calories in* to replace *calories burned* but also some extra calories for a safety net.

Plan ahead: Estimating how many calories you need

Although this chapter is about finding wilderness foods in a survival situation — one in which you've lost or eaten all of your food — it's good to start out by packing enough calories for what you plan to do. Begin by estimating roughly how many calories you'll need per day by figuring your anticipated calories burned.

Just for some examples, here are the average caloric costs for an average adult of some common wilderness activities:

>> **A day of moderate hiking with a moderately-heavy pack:**
3,000 calories

>> **Several hours of canoeing and swimming in calm, not-too-cold water:** 3,000 calories

>> **Resting for a day (these are calories burned just to keep the body going):** 1,500 calories

>> **Hiking in deep snowy terrain without snowshoes:**
5,000 calories in a day

TIP

The University of Kentucky lists the average calories burned per hour for a wide variety of activities at https://www.uky.edu/hr/wellness/exercise-calories-burned-hour. Use these as a very broad reference for calorie counts, and don't get hung up on details. We suggest rounding up to the nearest hundred.

To understand what your calorie needs will be, you have to consider the other side of the equation, too: calories in. Anticipate what you could encounter in your travels that can satisfy your need for calories. This list gives you a few examples of calories available in some common wilderness foods:

>> **A raw trout of about 6 pounds and about 14 inches long:**
3,500 calories

>> **A single wild coconut:** 1,400 calories

>> **A single large snail:** 70 calories

>> **A large handful of wild blueberries:** 100 calories

By anticipating how many calories you expect to be burning daily and what sources of calories you may encounter in the outdoors, you can increase your survivability.

Unfortunately, as of this writing no quality non-commercial websites list calories contained in wilderness foods. You'll have to do some research to find out about the caloric value of the kinds of foods you would encounter in the areas you plan to travel.

As you research this topic, be aware that many people in the fields of nutrition and wilderness foods have highly personal opinions on what you should eat in the wild, and it's unlikely that anyone is entirely right about everything.

Rationing and preserving

TIP

If you have packed food for your trip but are suddenly lost or stranded, you must think about rationing. The following ideas are worth remembering:

>> **Don't eat for the first 24 hours.** Your body can handle this time just fine on its own, and you may as well get used to a little hunger. At most, nibble at your survival kit foods.

>> **Don't eat if you don't have a good supply of water.** Digestion requires water.

>> **Eat what will spoil earliest first.** Consume foods that will spoil, such as meat, before foods that keep well, like dry rice or any canned or packaged food.

>> **Arrange your food by dividing it into portions per person per day.** Start by assuming you'll be out for a week (most lost hikers are found well within this time frame). If you're dealing with relatively small quantities of food, say, back-packing meals, lay the food out so you can inspect it visually. Doing so allows you to be sure the food isn't spoiling, and it shows you how serious the situation really is.

>> **Immediately consider using any existing food as an emergency supply and plan to subsist on what you can hunt and gather.** If you can find food in the wilderness, this leaves your nonperishable civilization foods — such as granola bars or a can of chili — as a reserve that you can count on.

>> **Consider ways of preserving your incoming food supply.** Keep a supply of food coming into camp and being stored, while eating only a portion. You can rely on that supply if you have to travel or you're injured and unable to check your snares and fishing traps for a while. Find out how to preserve food in the section later in this chapter, "Drying and smoking food for later."

TRYING NEW FOODS

You want to survive, don't you? Then get over food taboos. If you can stomach it without throwing up or setting off your food allergies, you're getting calories to your body, and that's the point. Of course, if you're vegetarian or vegan, you may have some serious philosophical soul-searching to do if you get into a wilderness survival situation.

Diversifying your diet

REMEMBER

Calories represent energy, but the body has other requirements for food beyond calories. The body needs and can digest protein (like meat), fats (like animal or plant oils), and carbohydrates (like plant roots and tubers). Eating a lean-meat-only diet is unwise and may lead to *protein starvation* in which you are getting enough calories but are malnourished nonetheless, which can lead to sickness and death. So it's always best to diversify your diet with some protein, some carbs, and some fats if that's possible in your wilderness survival situation.

Now that you're thinking in terms of calories, it's time to apply this idea to survival situations. Where are you going to get those calories? Unless you have a tremendous amount of nonperishable food on hand (for example, you are trapped in a cabin stocked with food or are adrift at sea on a disabled vessel), you should begin to think about living off the land.

Prioritizing Plants in Your Wilderness Diet

Plants are an excellent survival food source. Humans can safely eat thousands of kinds of plant species, they are easy to gather, and most are easy to prepare. But you do have to know which plants are safe to eat, which you can learn about in this chapter. We also introduce you to a variety of common edible wilderness plants.

Perusing the salad bar: Where to find a variety of plants

One of your first tasks in finding plant food is to find a decent vantage point, sit down, and take a careful look at the terrain. No matter how uniform the area you're stranded in appears, you can probably find some variations in the landscape (ecological *niches*) where different kinds of plants thrive. Even in a desert, you can find vegetation niches — including open ground (in direct sun) and shaded terrain (under the edges of large boulders) — if you look carefully.

TIP

Instead of wandering aimlessly in search of plant foods, systematically search each vegetation niche to increase your odds of finding different kinds of plant food.

Understanding a plant's edible parts

You can divide each plant into segments that you can consider eating. If the flower doesn't look at all appetizing, maybe the leaves are more palatable, or maybe the roots can supply food. This section presents some common guidelines for consuming different types of plant parts. Also check out the related section, "Cooking food you can eat now," later in this chapter.

Fruits

Fruits are the ripened reproductive elements of plants that have flowers. They often contain large numbers of seeds. Fruits are normally safe to eat unless they're fermenting (the sickly-sweet smell is unmistakable) or moldy.

WARNING

Be aware of the poisonous berry varieties in the areas you're most likely to visit — do some research before you go hiking or camping, and recall this fun little saying when deciding whether to try wild berries:

> *Red, white, or yellow might kill a fellow!*
>
> *Black or blue, that's for you!*

Of course, no single rule is entirely accurate — so to be sure berries are safe, always use the Universal Plant Edibility Test that we describe later in this chapter.

Leaves

You can eat many leaves safely. Although you want to avoid leaves with hairs or spines, even these can sometimes be softened by boiling, as in the case of stinging nettle leaves.

Flowers

Soft flower petals are often edible. Boiling reduces their sometimes-bitter taste.

WARNING

Flowers may cause allergic reactions because they're often coated with pollen.

Mosses and lichens

In the Arctic, reindeer (caribou) and people alike eat tundra mosses and lichens. These grow in small tufts or clumps, often clinging to rocks. Learn which are poisonous before you travel!

Nuts and seeds

Nuts and seeds are high in calories because they contain oils, which are essentially fat. Except in the case of fruit seeds, nuts are often encased in hard shells that can take time to process. Some people have nut allergies. Although many seeds are poisonous or can make you very sick, cooking them can be an effective way to make many of them safe. Find out what kind of nuts exist in the wilderness you plan to visit.

Roots and tubers

Roots and *tubers,* which are swollen underground stems, are the plant's nutritional feelers. They can contain quite a bit of water when you dig them up. You can dig out and pry up roots with a stout wooden staff. Try not to take so many that you kill the plant. Some roots and tubers are poisonous, so use the Universal Plant Edibility Test later in this chapter if you have any doubt.

Identifying some common edible plants

Thousands of edible plants are available to you in the wild. Here we just identify some of the most common varieties in various climates. We can only scratch the surface here, but this list can guide you to further research what's available in your area. (*Tip:* Identifying plants can be tricky business, so perform the Universal Plant Edibility Test later in this chapter if you're not certain of a plant's identity.)

Edible Temperate Climate Plants

Amaranth	Persimmon
Arrowroot	Plantain
Beechnut	Pokeweed
Blackberries	Purslane/little hogweed
Blueberries	Sassafras
Burdock	Sheep sorrel
Cattail	Strawberries
Chestnut	Thistle
Chicory	Water lily and lotus
Chufa	Wild onion and garlic
Daylily	Wild rose
Nettle	Wood sorrel
Oaks	

Figure 8-1 shows some examples of temperate climate plants.

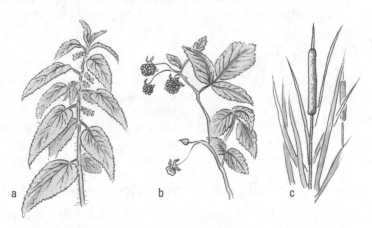

FIGURE 8-1: A nettle (a), blackberry (b), and cattail (c)

Edible Tropical Climate Plants

Bamboo	Mango
Bananas	Palms
Breadfruit	Papaya
Cashew nut	Sugarcane
Coconut	Taro

Figure 8-2 shows three examples of tropical climate plants.

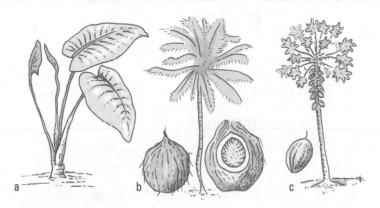

FIGURE 8-2: Taro (a), coconut (b), and breadfruit (c)

Edible Desert Climate Plants

Acacia	Date palm
Agave	Desert amaranth
Cactus	Prickly pear cactus

Figure 8-3 shows three examples of desert climate plants.

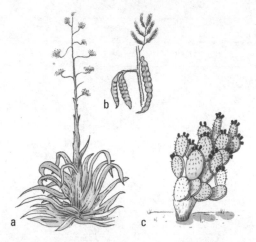

FIGURE 8-3: Agave (a), acacia pods (b), and prickly pear cactus (c)

Edible Arctic Climate Plants

Crowberry	Rock tripe
Dandelion	Salmonberry
Mountain sorrel	Willow shrub
Reindeer moss	

Figure 8-4 shows three examples of arctic climate plants.

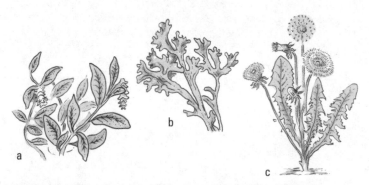

FIGURE 8-4: Willow shrub (a), reindeer moss (b), and dandelion (c)

Dulse	Laver
Green seaweed	Mojaban
Irish moss	Sugar wrack
Kelp	

Figure 8-5 shows three examples of edible plants at sea.

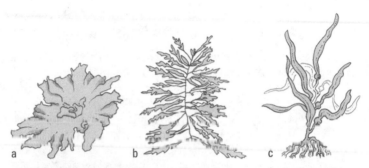

FIGURE 8-5: Green seaweed (a), mojaban (also known as sargassum) (b), and kelp (c)

Is it safe? Deciding whether to eat an unknown plant food

The preceding section lists some safe plants to eat. How do you know, though, if you're in the wild and come across a plant you're unfamiliar with? In this section, we list some signs that you should avoid a plant altogether, and we tell you how to test plants that are still in the running to be your next meal.

Knowing which plants to avoid

WARNING

To help you figure out which plants not to eat, keep these rules in mind. Don't eat the following:

>> Any plant with a milky sap

>> White, yellow, or red berries

>> Red plants

>> Plants with hairs or spines

>> Plant bulbs (except onions or garlic); beware that the death camas *(Zigadenus venenosus)* bulb, which looks very inviting, can kill

>> Any plant food with an almond scent (this may indicate a powerful toxin)

After these rules, what's left? A lot! In fact, you can eat many thousands of kinds of plants. If a plant doesn't automatically score a spot on the forbidden list, you can check your next potential meal by using the Universal Plant Edibility Test, which we cover next.

Taking the Universal Plant Edibility Test

When you're considering eating any unfamiliar plant food, you must carry out the Universal Plant Edibility Test (but don't use the test for fungi, because some are lethal even in small doses — see the nearby "Hold the mushrooms, please!" sidebar). This test determines whether a given plant is safe to eat. The test takes a whole day, and you can only drink water during that day, so it's quite an investment. The return, though — knowing that you can safely eat a certain plant — may well be worth it.

You can find the test in Table 8-1. If you get through a step without having a bad reaction, proceed to the next one. And if you go all the way through without any problems, congratulations! You can consider the part of the plant that you've eaten to be safe to eat.

HOLD THE MUSHROOMS, PLEASE!

However enticing mushrooms look, the species you're hungrily eyeing may be a deadly mimic of the kind you grew up finding in forests back at home. That's why in survival situations we suggest that you treat all mushrooms just like you treat all snakes: as though they are lethal. Now, having said that, if you're in the most desperate straits, have only fungi to eat, and can't hold out any longer, three rules can help you stay alive. Don't eat any fungi with:

• White gills (the papery 'fins' on the underside of the cap)

• A cup-like basin at the base

• Rings around the stem

TABLE 8-1 **The Universal Plant Edibility Test**

Step	Test	Duration	Possible Bad Reactions
1	Hold a piece of the plant on the sensitive skin inside your elbow joint or on the forearm.	15 minutes	Rash
2	Touch a small piece of the plant to your lips.	5 minutes	Burning sensation
3	Hold a piece of the plant on your tongue.	3 minutes	Stinging sensation
4	Chew a small piece of the plant and hold the chewed vegetation in your mouth — without swallowing.	15 minutes	Burning or stinging sensation
5	Swallow the vegetation you've been holding in your mouth.	Wait 8 hours	Vomiting or diarrhea
6	Eat another small portion (about ¼ cup).	Wait 8 hours	Vomiting or diarrhea

Hunting and Trapping Food

Foraging for plant foods is a great way to bring in calories, but there is a catch: most vegetation only gives you about half the calories you would get from the same amount of animal tissue. Animal tissue technically includes any body parts, but in many cases, we're talking about meat (muscle tissue) and animal fat. If you can get these to supplement your wilderness survival diet, all the better.

Even though getting meat may be more difficult than gathering plants, it's not impossible. Indigenous people worldwide are experts at acquiring animals as food, often with relatively simple technologies. We can learn a lot from them; for example, instead of trying to run down an animal or lunging for it from a bush, you can emulate native people by using a hunting tool that extends your reach, for example, a throwing stick or net. You can also improve your survival chances by focusing on what animal foods you can gather with even less effort, like grasshoppers, mealworms, clams, and other little critters that are yours for the taking (see the nearly sidebar, "Finders keepers: Foraging for food," for details).

This section helps you find animals you may want to hunt and includes info on how to make and use snares and weapons, such as a bow and arrow, spear, and bola. Finally, we tell you how to get to the meat.

Looking for tracks and critter highways

To hunt or trap successfully, keep an eye open for places where animals often travel, feed, drink, and/or sleep. Animals often travel repeatedly on *game trails,* or faint clearings through vegetation, which you can spot in many environments (see Figure 8-6). You may also notice trails marked with animal tracks and/or scat (droppings).

FIGURE 8-6: Look for faint (or distinctive) paths through vegetation

Snaring small animals

Snares capture animals that you can later collect and eat. A *snare* is essentially a loop of wire or very strong cordage that traps an animal by entanglement. If the snare closes around the throat, the animal may die before you reach it. If the snare only snags the animal's leg, you may have to kill the animal when you check your snares. Snares are best for capturing smallish mammals, such as squirrels and rabbits.

Setting up your snares

Making snares is fairly easy; most just require a good piece of wire or very thin cordage. You can strip suitable snare-making wire from mechanical vehicles and devices. You need lengths well over 1 foot (0.3 meters) long. If the wire is sheathed in plastic insulation, strip it off before making the snare. Snaring is highly regulated, though in a survival situation it is acceptable.

To create a basic snare, follow these easy steps:

1. **Make a snare loop about 4 inches (10 centimeters) in diameter (for the neck of a squirrel) or larger if you're trying to snare a larger animal.**

2. **Tie the snare off with a snare knot.**

   To tie a snare knot, loop the end of the line around twice and then thread the end through the first loop. Make sure you pull the knot tight. Check out Figure 8-7 for an example.

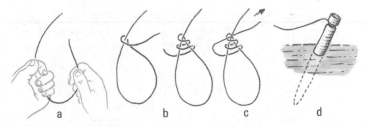

FIGURE 8-7: A snare knot

3. **Arrange the snare loop so that it lies right in the animal's path.**

   For optimal placement, first study the game trail or branch on which you're deploying the snare.

4. **Tie one end of the snare wire to a sturdy tree or firmly-buried stake, and regularly check on it to see what you've caught.**

TIP

When you make a snare, wear gloves (if you have them) to prevent your scent from getting on the wire, which alerts the animal of danger. Or you can camouflage your scent by burying the snare wire in dirt for 24 hours before deploying it, using pieces of cloth or socks on your hands like gloves.

There are three main kinds of snare:

>> **Branch snare:** Place snares in a series on branches where you've seen animals like squirrels travel frequently (see Figure 8-8a).

>> **Burrow-hole snare:** You can spot animal burrows in many places, such as near the banks of rivers or under heavy brush. Place a burrow-hole snare (see Figure 8-8b) just outside the entrance to a burrow. It traps the animal as it exits or enters.

When setting up a burrow-hold snare, firmly anchor a strong stake near the burrow. Better yet, anchor the snare to an existing branch, sapling, or trunk so the animal doesn't spot some new element in its environment.

>> **Game-trail snare:** A game trail snare has lightweight brush walls that corral the animal into the snare (see Figure 8-8c). Most animals are unwilling to travel backward, so they run into the snare instead of backing away from it if they spot it.

You make a game-trail snare by suspending a slipknot loop over a trail. Place the wire on two small, forked twigs just above ground level so the animal's neck goes into the snare.

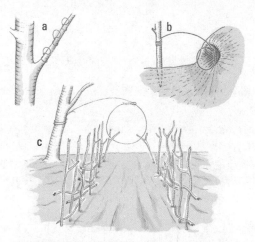

FIGURE 8-8: Different types of snare setups

You can use bait to lure animals into snares, but we suggest focusing on laying out many baitless snares and checking them often. Baiting is complicated, and some baits alert the animal that something is amiss. If you do use bait, you need bait that the animal is familiar with or bait that's unfamiliar but attractive to the animal.

Checking snares and collecting your catch

Check and maintain your snares regularly. Sometimes the snare kills the animal, but a predator gets to it before you do. Other times, you may come back to a snare and find it holding a wounded, desperate, and potentially dangerous animal. Kill a snared animal quickly and humanely. A sturdy club works fine. (For advice, check out the later section "Going in for the kill with a club.")

TIP

Be equipped with a spear (or bola, or other weapon that extends your reach) anytime you venture away from camp, so that you're ready to kill animals you come across while making or checking your snares. We discuss these other weapons in the upcoming sections.

Using a throwing stick

You may wonder why we don't cover how to make and use an improvised bow and arrow for wilderness survival. We both agree that this is more something that people expect in a survival manual, than something that is actually realistic. The task is time-consuming, needs just the right materials, and also takes time to master. Instead, we focus on a simpler and more practical hunting tool, the throwing stick.

A throwing stick, although not as sexy as a spear or bow and arrow, can be effective for maiming small animals such as rabbits, squirrels, and birds. A throwing stick is larger than a stone and more likely to hit the target. It's especially useful when you throw it into groups of smaller animals, such as a flock of birds.

To make the simplest throwing stick that is 1- to 2-foot long (0.3- to 0.6-meter long):

1. **Find a green branch or sapling that's from 1 to 2 inches (2.5 to 5 centimeters) in diameter (see Figure 8-9a).**

Try to find a branch that's a little heavier on one end.

2. Strip the main branch of all bark and whittle away any smaller connected branches.

3. Whittle one end down to be slightly smaller in diameter than the other (see Figure 8-9b) unless it's already a little heavier on one end.

Throw the stick so that it hurtles through the air horizontally, something like a Frisbee, using the thinner end as the handle (see Figure 8-9c). Throw low to the ground to hit small animals. It will take a few hours of practice to learn to hit a target the size of a bowling ball from about 20 feet (7 meters) away.

More elaborate hunting sticks are whittled into shape from curved sticks, with a wing-shaped cross-section that develops lift and can fly long distances, like the traditional Australian *boomerang*. Look this up if you're interested, but we find it too involved for most practical purposes.

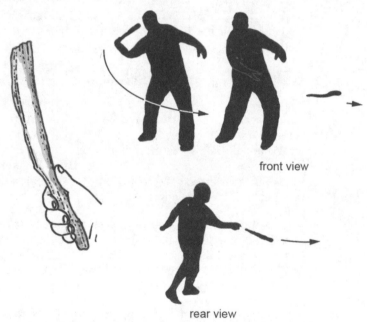

front view

rear view

FIGURE 8-9: Using a throwing stick

Making and using a spear

A spear is a good implement for nearly any wilderness survival situation. You can use a sturdy spear for self-defense from animals, as a probe for checking out murky water or thick brush, as a support when crossing a strong stream, for tending your campfire, as a lever to raise logs or rocks, and many other things. For hunting, spears can wound larger animals enough that, although the animal flees the attack, you may be able to follow its blood trail (the *spoor*) until the animal dies or is so weak that it's easier to kill.

Constructing a spear isn't difficult. Just follow these steps (see Figure 8-10):

1. Select a green sapling, thicker than a broomstick, and cut it down (see Figure 8-10a).

2. Strip the bark from the sapling and cut the length to about 6 feet (1.8 meters); see Figure 8-10b.

3. Sharpen one end of the sapling with any knife you have available, be it metal or stone, as in Figure 8-10c.

4. Harden the sharp end of the spear by holding it over a fire for a while, being sure to rotate it (see Figure 8-10d).

   Rotating the spear over a fire drives some of the water out of the wood, blackening the tip and making it very hard; now it will puncture rather than just bend. *Note:* If you're going to add an armature (keep reading for instructions), you don't have to sharpen or harden the tip with fire.

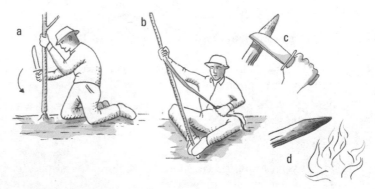

FIGURE 8-10: Building your own spear

If you prefer, you can mount an armature on the end of a spear. An *armature* is any hard, sharp item that can serve your needs. You need to bind an armature carefully and very tightly onto the working end of the spear so it doesn't work loose. Begin by splitting the end of the spear by hammering a knife into the end (see Figure 8-11a). Then slip in the armature (see Figure 8-11b) and wrap the whole assembly tightly with strong cordage (as in Figure 8-11c); be sure to wrap below the armature to prevent the spear from splitting. You can use any type of cordage, although wire tends to slip.

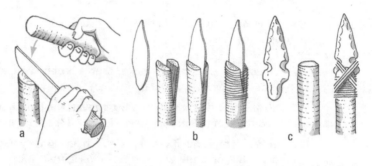

FIGURE 8-11: Lashing an armature onto a spear

Good items for making an armature include the following:

>> **A large nail:** This is good for spearing fish and other shallow-water animals. However, since it is not barbed, larger fish can squirm away.

>> **A sharpened sliver of hard plastic:** For example, pulled from vehicle wreckage. Grind the sliver to shape on an abrasive stone.

>> **A sharpened splinter of bone or antler:** See Chapter 14 for how to process bone and antler into sharp slivers. These materials are ideal for whittling in barbs to better hold the speared animal.

>> **A sharpened sliver of stone or glass:** These take more time and effort to shape than bone or antler splinters, but they can be very effective.

If you can put notches into the sides of the armature, your cordage has something more to grab, which holds the armature more firmly.

Despite what you see on TV or at the movies, few indigenous people worldwide actually throw spears at animals to kill them. Throwing your spear will probably just result in a fleeing animal and a broken spear tip. For attacks at range (or a significant distance from you), a throwing stick, net, or bola are much more likely to land you some food than a spear.

Making and using a bola

People have used bolas for thousands of years to hunt all kinds of animals, including birds and rabbits. *Bolas* are simply strings weighted at one end. When they find their target, they wrap around the legs or body, immobilizing the prey and allowing you to move in for the killing blow with a club.

Bolas are easy to make; just stick to these steps:

1. **Find several smooth, round stones, each an inch or so in diameter.**

2. **For each stone, cut a piece of cloth or other textile about 4 inches (10 centimeters) square (see Figure 8-12a).**

3. **Wrap each stone in its own cloth (see Figure 8-12b) and tie off this cloth tightly with cord (see Figure 8-12c).**

4. **Connect all the cords and make a loop for swinging the bola (see Figure 8-12d).**

TIP

You need to practice using bolas accurately. Whirl a bola well above your head (see Figure 8-12e) and then release to send the weapon at the target. Whirling a bola without knocking yourself out takes practice. In the heat of the hunt, whirl the bola only one or two times before releasing so you don't alert the prey.

Using a throwing net

If you happen to have some netting, you can improvise a throwing net. The point of a net is to entangle things that otherwise are too fast and maneuverable to catch; fish, yes, but also birds on the ground and insects if the mesh is fine enough.

TIP

Net-making is a long and complex task we don't cover in this book, but you can try to improvise a hunting net from an old hammock, the mosquito netting from a tent, or even cargo netting from airplane wreckage.

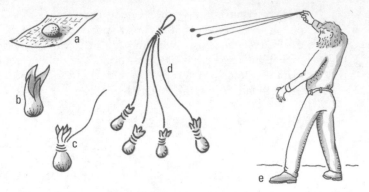

FIGURE 8-12: Crafting and utilizing a bola

Whatever the mesh size, a throwing net should have weights fastened to the perimeter. Try tying in stones or pebbles or sewing them on the perimeter in small scraps of cloth.

You throw a hunting net like a giant frisbee, not at the target but somewhat ahead of the target, in its direction of travel.

Going in for the kill with a club

Many animals won't be killed by a snare, spear or bola. Many times, you have to follow a blood trail to the injured, exhausted animal and then kill it with your club.

TIP

To make a killing club, select a 1- or 2-inch (2.5- or 5-centimeter) diameter sapling and cut a 3-foot (0.9-meter) length from it. Strip the bark (which would otherwise decay and skip around like a sheath) and lash a wrist-loop of some kind of cordage around the base so it doesn't fly out of your hand.

Be prepared to attack with a purposeful explosion of energy; just like you, an injured animal will fight hard to stay alive. Use a ruthless, lightning-fast attack, aiming at the neck to kill the animal humanely and quickly.

WARNING

Don't underestimate any animal's ferocity or the damage it can do even with small claws and teeth! The danger from infection is real.

Butchering your next meal

After you make your kill, you need to take quick action and butcher the animal before it starts to decay. Butcher animals at least 50 yards (45 meters) from your camp, near water if possible, so you don't attract predators and scavengers to your campsite.

Skinning a larger animal

To butcher a larger animal, follow these steps:

1. **Hang a large mammal by the hind limbs, cut deeply across the neck, and let the blood drain away (see Figure 8-13a).**

   WARNING

   You can capture and consume the blood instead of draining it away, but consuming it can carry a heavy risk of infection. So we don't recommend it except in the direst of circumstances.

2. **Cut along the dotted lines shown in Figure 8-13b to facilitate removing the hide.**

   You're not butchering the animal (taking it apart) yet, just removing the hide.

3. **Cut with just the tip of a sharp knife slipped under the skin (see Figure 8-13c) and cut the genitals as shown to prevent infection.**

4. **Remove the hide, cut away the intestines, and generally empty the body cavity (see Figure 8-13d.)**

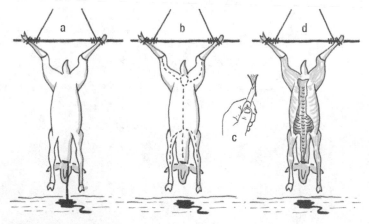

FIGURE 8-13: Butchering a large mammal, such as a deer

You're now ready to cut the muscle from the bones and cook it. In survival situations, you want to eat as many parts of the animal as you can stomach: lungs, knuckles — everything but hooves, bones, and hide are pretty much edible (though carnivore livers can be toxic).

TIP

Keep the bones (and, if available, antlers) of any mammal larger than a small dog. Bone and antler are excellent raw materials for making survival tools (as you see in Chapter 14), as are the hide and *sinews* (stringy tissues that hold the limbs together), which you can use as cordage.

Skinning a smaller animal

To skin a small animal, follow these steps:

1. **Make an incision though the skin (but not deeper than the skin) across the back, as in Figure 8-14a.**

2. **Grab the two sides of the hide by slipping your fingers under it and pulling outward (see Figure 8-14b).**

   When the skin snags at the paws, you can easily slice it off with a knife. Small mammals don't need to be bled if you're going to roast them whole next to a fire, which is a good way to cook them.

3. **After you skin the animal, remove the meat.**

   For information on getting that meat into edible form, see the section, "The Wilderness Café: Preparing Food Outdoors," later in this chapter.

FIGURE 8-14: Skinning a small mammal

Getting Your Hands on Freshwater Fish

In addition to gathering plant foods and hunting, fishing is a good way to live off the land. You can often find fish in large numbers, and with some ingenuity (and patience), they can be relatively easy to get your teeth into! This section focuses specifically on freshwater fish, including info on catching them in different ways and how to clean and cook them. (Check out Chapter 20 for more specific information on fishing at sea.)

Finding fish

Before you can enjoy the delicious taste of a bluegill, perch, trout, or some other freshwater fish, you need to know where to catch them. Fish like to take cover in certain places in rivers and streams, for example:

>> In *eddies* (mini whirlpools), where they can rest (see Figure 8-15a)

>> Just downstream of rocks or gravel bars, where they can rest (see Figure 8-15b)

>> In the shade under overhanging vegetation or logs, where they can hide (see Figure 8-15c)

FIGURE 8-15: Where to fish a stream

Fishing with a hook and line

Fishing with a hook and line (also known as *angling*) is relatively straightforward. If you have a wilderness survival kit (see Chapter 2), you may have a line and hooks ready to go; you only have to bait them, weight them, and set them in the water. If you don't have hooks, you can improvise them from many materials, including wire, safety pins, or splinters of bone, antler, or plastic. You can set out as many fishing lines as you have hooks.

Here's how to fish without a reel:

1. **Tie a hook, weight, and float to the line; tie the other end to a 5- or 6-foot (1.5- or 1.8-meter) pole, cut from a living tree.**

   You may want to put the hook at the end of the line, with a weight — any piece of stone or metal — above the hook, or vice versa. The weight keeps the line from pulling out horizontally in a current.

   A *float* — which you can make from any piece of floating material, such as cork — can show you that a fish is taking the bait. Figure 8-16a shows a hook baited with a worm, using a float but no weight. In a waterway with a little current, use a weight, as in Figure 8-16b.

2. **Bait your hook and drop the line in the water.**

   Bait is a topic for a whole encyclopedia, but here we can say that winged insects, worms, and grubs are all good bait.

3. **Check your lines every few hours and bring in your catch by taking in the line, hand over hand.**

Have a club ready to kill hooked fish, which may flop right back into the water if you're not careful.

Put out multiple fishing lines and check them often, just like snares. The beauty of this system is that it works 24/7.

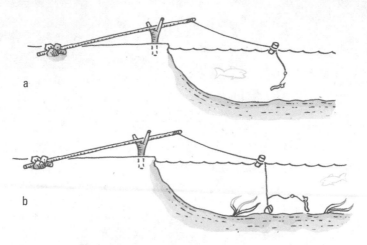

a

b

FIGURE 8-16: Fishing with a hook and line but no reel

Making and using fishing spears

Catching fish with a spear is common worldwide even today. You can master this technique with some practice. To make your spear, stick to these easy steps (and check out Chapter 14 for more on tying knots):

1. **Cut down a long sapling (up to 8 feet, or 2.4 meters) and strip it of bark.**

2. **Cut a notch into the base of the spear to attach a lanyard (see Figure 8-17a).**

   A *lanyard* is a simple leash made of any durable cordage that prevents you from losing your spear in the water.

3. **Use a clove hitch to tie your lanyard into the notch at the base of the spear (Figure 8-17b).**

4. **Finish the leash with a bowline knot, leaving a loop large enough to slip your hand in and out easily (refer to Figure 8-17c).**

5. **Fashion some barbed armatures from bone, antler, or even hard plastic or wood; attach the armature to the spear.**

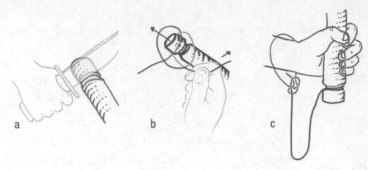

FIGURE 8-17: Crafting a fishing spear and fastening it to your wrist

We show you how to attach armatures in the earlier section "Making and using a spear." You should catch fish with barbed spear armatures; these prevent the fish from wriggling off the spear. Figure 8-18 shows a range of possible designs. Lashing several armatures to the spear increases your odds of spearing a fish. Make your lashings tight. You can help secure lashing with sticky tree sap.

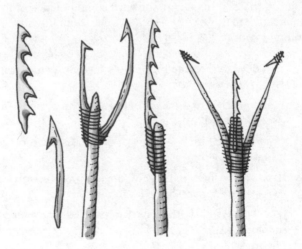

FIGURE 8-18: Barbed armatures can make spearing fish easier.

TIP

Here are some spear-fishing tips:

>> When spear-fishing from a bank, try to keep your shadow under you or behind you to keep from alerting fish of your presence.

>> If you wade into the shallows, don't go deeper than knee-deep and move slowly to prevent splashes that drive fish away.

>> Aim a little lower than the fish appears in the water. This corrects for the water's distortion of perspective, the fish's apparent position (in gray in Figure 8-19) is somewhat above its real position.

FIGURE 8-19: Fishing with a spear

Fishing with a net

Making a net is so laborious (and requires so much cordage) that we don't cover it in this book. However, if you come across an old fishing net (you may find one on the shore) or other mesh, you can try to catch fish by stretching it across a water course (a stream, for example) and weighting the bottom with rocks (you can suspend these in textile bags, as though making a bola). Secure the ends of the net or mesh, on shore, with stakes or by tying it to vegetation. Check the net every few hours.

Preparing fish to eat

You can boil small fish whole, without bothering with butchery, but any fish larger than the palm of your hand should be butchered to get rid of some harmful internal organs. Here's how to clean and cook a fish:

1. **Cut the fish down the belly and remove the guts, either by pulling them out (see Figure 8-20a) or by cutting them out with a knife (see Figure 8-20b).**

   You can use the guts as bait. Just be sure to store them away from camp to prevent attracting other animals.

2. **Decapitate larger fish.**

   You can boil the head for soup and cook the resulting fillet.

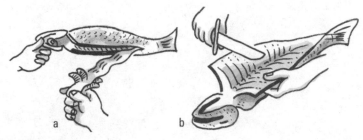

FIGURE 8-20: Cleaning fish

The Wilderness Café: Preparing Food Outdoors

You may not have a fancy cutlery set or a stove or a clean kitchen sink, but you can still prepare your food in the wilderness to make it safe and reasonably appetizing. In this section, we tell you how to prepare food before you eat it and how to preserve food for later. (For information on building a fire, see Chapter 5; for directions on lashing together a tripod that you can use to cook over a fire, flip to Chapter 14.)

REMEMBER

Whatever animal parts you don't eat should be burned (thoroughly, down to just ashes) or buried away from camp (at least 50 yards, or 45 meters) to prevent attracting other animals.

Cooking food you can eat now

With few exceptions, you should cook wilderness survival food to kill bacteria and parasites. Cooking can also improve flavor, soften food, and make some foods (like snails) more palatable. This section gives you an overview of how to cook and otherwise prepare foods in the wild.

Plant foods

Although not all plant foods require cooking, you should cook most of them. Microorganisms thrive on plant surfaces and in water that plants may be growing in. Boiling, steaming, and otherwise cooking plant foods can decrease their nutritional value, but it's worth knowing that you're not eating the colonies of bacteria that live in a single drop of swamp water.

You can boil plant foods, bake them in coals, or roast them over a flame. Here's how to prepare various plant foods:

>> **Fruits:** Wash fruits before eating them. Most fruits don't need to be cooked, though you can make some (like the *plantain,* a banana-like fruit) more palatable by cooking.

>> **Nuts and seeds:** Wash and shell the nuts and seeds on a large, clean working area, such as the surface of a clean tarp.

>> **Leaves and flowers:** Thoroughly wash leaves before eating them. Flowers should be washed and boiled.

>> **Moss and lichens:** Boil these before eating them.

>> **Roots:** You have to cook most roots to soften them up before eating. Bake them in coals or boil them. When they're softened, you can mash them if you like.

Mammal foods

WARNING

Although some wilderness TV shows have featured people devouring uncooked (or even living) animals on camera, don't do it. This is just a trick for dramatic TV, and it's a spectacularly bad idea. Cooking kills many potentially lethal microscopic life-forms; it's the main reason that humans cook food in the first place!

You can roast mammal meat on a rack or spit above fire, boil it in water, or bake it in clay or wrapped in thick layers of leaves. Mammal meat should be well-done, not raw or bloody, when you consume it.

You can split open mammal bones with a heavy rock (crush the bone on an anvil stone) to get at the *marrow,* a nutritious, calorie-rich buttery substance inside. You can also boil bones to extract every possible calorie and nutrient in a tasty broth.

The organs of mammals are normally good to eat, but be aware that the liver of many carnivores contains high concentrations of vitamin A, which can cause death. Don't eat carnivore livers.

Insects and invertebrates

Grasshoppers, snails, mussels, and other critters can be roasted on a rack over a fire or boiled. Some insects are so hard to process, though, that it's best to just crush them into a paste that you boil in water as a soup.

Insects are related to shellfish, so if you have a seafood allergy, leave insects off the menu.

Fish

Although you may get away with eating some fish uncooked (and you may have to if you're stranded in a dinghy!), fish should normally be cooked like any other animal tissues.

Fish are excellent survival food because they cook quickly and can be dried and preserved for a long time. Figure 8-21a shows how to rack a larger fish next to a fire for cooking (we explain smoking fish and other meat in the later section, "Drying and smoking food for later"); be sure to slice small flaps in the meat, allowing the filet to hang on the rack. You can simply skewer smaller fish on a clean stick next to a fire as in Figure 8-21b; when the fish is dry and flaky, it's ready to eat. Or use other methods, as long as you can prevent the body from falling apart when it heats up. Boiling prevents you from losing any of the fish in the fire.

Drying and smoking food for later

Preserve your survival foods if you're not eating them immediately; the wilderness is no place to waste anything! Dried food is less liable to attract insects and is slightly water-resistant.

FIGURE 8-21: Cooking large and small fish

You can mash fruit flat and spread it (not too thinly!) on a flat surface, like a rock, to dry in the sun. The resulting fruit leather makes a good trail food.

You can dry meat and fish on a rack — just be sure the wood for making the drying rack is clean. Also try to use *nonresinous* wood for smoking foods — smoke from resin sours the meat. To smoke fish and meat, follow these steps using a teepee-style rack (see Figure 8-22):

1. **Build your fire and let it die down.**

   You don't need a hot fire with flames to dry meat; in fact, it's better to dry food slowly, over coals.

2. **Build a tripod over the fire.**

   Make sure the branches are sturdy. We explain how to build a tripod in Chapter 14.

3. **After laying strips of meat (either mammal or fish) on the various rungs of the tripod, you can cover the structure with a tarp or even brush to concentrate the smoke.**

FIGURE 8-22: Smoking meat on a tripod

2

Exploring Advanced Survival Techniques

IN THIS CHAPTER

» **Understanding the basics of land navigation**

» **Using maps**

» **Relying on a compass**

» **Using GPS-enabled electronic devices**

Chapter 9

Finding Your Way with Basic Navigation Tools

n this chapter, we show you the basics of *navigation*, or other-wise staying oriented in the wild. We provide a map reading refresher and then show you how to use a compass and a GPS receiver. (For information on navigation using the stars and sun, see Chapter 10.)

TIP

Practice the skills of navigation at home, when you're not under pressure. Being able to orient yourself outdoors is a skill as fundamental to survival as making fire or properly using a knife.

Getting Your Bearings with Navigation Basics

Whether you're working your way back to civilization, moving toward a water source, or simply trying to figure out where you left your pack, being able to navigate is essential to your survival. You want to know not only where you are but also where you're heading. Even in the era of the GPS, you should keep in mind some basic navigational practices. These principles apply whenever you head into the wild:

>> **Try to know your position as closely as you can, as often as you can.** Many times, people get lost in the wilderness due to a momentary lapse in awareness. (If you have no idea where you are, see Chapter 11 for tips on what to do when you're lost or disoriented.)

>> **Trust your instruments.** When you're disoriented (and really frustrated!), you tend to ignore what your map and compass are telling you — especially when they don't seem to make sense. Maps and compasses can be wrong, but it's rare.

>> **Always orient your map.** Keep your map aligned with the terrain around you at all times. Check out the section "Orienting your map," later in this chapter, for more info.

TIP

To simplify the whole process of navigation, use your wits and instruments to find large landmarks; then use these large, easy-to-find landmarks to find smaller ones.

Setting a route with waypoints

Whenever you move through the wilderness, you should establish a route made up of a series of waypoints. *Waypoints* are prominent places along your route that give you the ability to know precisely where you are for a moment. You can use waypoints in two ways:

>> **Beforehand:** You can use waypoints as a way to break up your route into goals — places you want to reach, check off, and then move past. Plot your waypoints on a map or pick them out in the terrain in front of you.

>> **As you go:** You can use waypoints to record your course, which gives you a "trail of breadcrumbs" so you can make your way out of the wilderness. This is such an important part of navigation that practically all GPS units have a *waypoint function* that allows you to record your waypoints as you're passing them.

If you're operating in an area that doesn't have trails, you can always use handrails. A *handrail* is exactly what the name implies: a sturdy, reliable object or landmark — such as a large rock outcropping or a river or creek — that can guide you. Even if you seem to be going a long way out of your way, moving from large landmark to large landmark is almost invariably the fastest, easiest way to travel in the wilderness.

TIP

A handrail is almost always better than a beeline. A *beeline* is a straight line cut across the wilderness, and it often only *looks* like the shortest route. In reality, it's almost invariably the longest — especially when you're dealing with hilly terrain or dense underbrush in a jungle.

Using deliberate offset

TIP

Deliberate offset, sometimes called *aiming off,* is a navigation trick in which you intentionally miss a small landmark to hit a large one. Why would you want to do that? Because sometimes the waypoint you need to reach is so small that when you aim right for it, you miss it and go right past.

For example, you can use deliberate offset if you're trying to reach a house that sits near a road. Instead of trying to hit a bull's-eye and land on the front porch, aim a little off — say, a quarter mile down the road (see Figure 9-1). When you arrive at the road, you should know which direction to turn because you deliberately aimed a little off, and you can now turn and travel straight to the house.

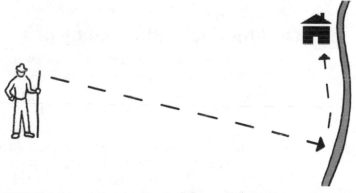

FIGURE 9-1: Using deliberate offset to find a small landmark

Maps Made Easy

When you head out into the wilderness, you need to bring along the appropriate kind of map and, of course, be able to read it. The following sections provide pointers for selecting a map and establishing a good foundation in map reading.

Picking an appropriate map

The best map is the one that gives you the most information. Select from the many maps available of the area you will be visiting. Most can be previewed online so you can make a good choice. Some of the most commonly-used wilderness maps are:

>> **State and national park maps:** These maps tend to focus on a specific park or wilderness area, indicating official campsites, trails, ranger stations, and so on.

>> **Travel maps:** These maps tend to show technological infrastructure e.g., roads, railways, cities, etc. Useful supplements but not to be relied on for wilderness travel.

>> **United States Geological Survey (USGS) maps:** The best maps for wilderness travel in the U.S., these maps often are referred to as *topographic* or *topo* maps. They display detailed contour lines indicating the shape of landforms, including mountains and valleys.

REMEMBER

The *key* or *legend* of a map introduces its symbols, colors, and scale. Start with any map by examining the key to understand what you're looking at.

Deciphering common map colors

The colors on your map can tell you a lot about the terrain. Table 9-1 lists standard colors used on many maps of the outdoors.

Measuring distance on a map

Often located at the bottom of the map, a map *scale* is expressed as a ratio, such as 1:75,000. What that means is that 1 inch on your map equals 75,000 inches in the real world. Now, 75,000 inches is not a useful figure, so the scale in miles and KM are normally shown on any map.

The best way to use the scale is to lay a flexible length of string or wire along the scale at the bottom, mark it at regular intervals (or miles), and then use this as a 'flexible ruler' to measure distance on the map. Since most wilderness travel is not done in straight lines, this string method is more useful than a rigid ruler.

TABLE 9-1 A Standard Map Color Key

Color	Feature	Comments
White	Open ground	Open ground may or may not be vegetated; if so the cover is not thick.
Green	Vegetation	Thicker ground cover in the form of some kind of vegetation.
Blue	Water	Blue typically indicates water; if you're in an area marked blue on the map, but the landscape is dry, beware that a flash flood or rising tide might flood your area.
Black	Manmade structures	Manmade structures are rarely drawn to scale. They're much smaller in real life.
Brown lines	Contour lines	These lines tell you what the land looks like in three dimensions. Check out "Using contour lines to identify the shape of the land" for details.
Blue lines	Navigation grids	These grids include latitude-longitude and UTM. For more on these, see "Understanding your coordinates," later in this chapter.

Using contour lines to identify the shape of the land

To read a topographic map, you need to know how to interpret *contour lines,* the mapmaker's way of expressing three dimensions on a two-dimensional map. Each contour line indicates a certain altitude above sea level, normally in feet or meters. The *contour interval* indicated on the map key tells you how many feet or meters are between each contour line. Figure 9-2a illustrates how tightly-packed contour lines indicate steeper terrain. More widely spaced lines, shown in Figure 9-2b, indicate gentle grades, easy slopes, and flatter terrain.

Many times, the contour lines form quickly-recognizable shapes on your map indicating common landforms (hills and valleys, for example). A little experience is all you need to quickly interpret topographic contour lines. The following list describes common contour line shapes, and Figure 9-2 shows how they communicate a terrain shape.

>> **V-shaped lines pointing toward higher elevation:** Drainages, like creeks, runoffs, washes, and sometimes canyons (as in Figure 9-2c)

>> **V-shaped lines pointing toward lower elevation:** *Ridge lines,* which are long crests, and *spurs,* which are small crests that protrude from the main crest (as in Figure 9-2d)

>> **U-shaped lines pointing toward higher elevation:** Valleys, usually gentler depressions than canyons (as in Figure 9-2e); densely packed lines near the base of the U usually mean a cliff or sometimes a waterfall

>> **Circles, especially circles decreasing in size:** Peaks and hilltops, as in Figure 9-2f

>> **Hourglass forms (two U-shapes butted against each other):** Passes in mountains and hills, as in Figure 9-2g

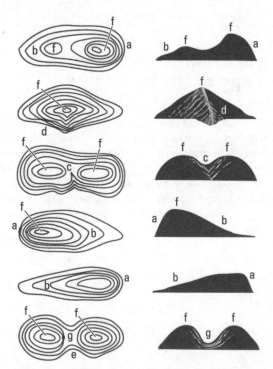

FIGURE 9-2: Landforms and how they appear on a topographic map

Establishing your coordinates

Globally, the most common location or coordinate grids for determining position are latitude and longitude and Universal Transverse Mercator (UTM).

Using latitude and longitude

Latitude and longitude are both measured in *degrees* from a certain point, and each degree is divided into 60 minutes. A minute is equal to about 1 nautical mile (about 6,076 feet), which is about 15 percent longer than a statute mile (5,280 feet; what most of us are used to). A minute — 1 nautical mile — is always identified by its unique symbol: '.

Latitude lines run horizontally, and they tell you how far north or south you are from the equator. There are 90 degrees of north latitude and 90 degrees of south latitude. You can't miss this type of helpful measurement on your map. It's always located along the side margin and is identified by the degree symbol, °.

When you stand on the equator, your latitude is 0°, and when you stand at the North Pole, your latitude is 90° North. If you stand on the South Pole, your latitude is 90° South. Easy, isn't it? A higher number means you're closer to the pole. You don't need a sailor's cap or a parrot for that. If you look at your map and figure out that your latitude is 26°11' North and the Coast Guard tells you over the radio that they're at 26°13' North, you know that they're 2 nautical miles north of you because they have a higher number value. The opposite is true when you're south of the equator — if a location has a higher number than yours, it must be south of you.

Longitude tells you how far east or west you are from the *prime meridian*, a vertical line passing through the Royal Observatory in Greenwich, England. There are 180 degrees of west longitude and 180 degrees of east longitude (making 360 degrees all the way around the Earth). If you're standing at 118°36' West and you need to go to 118°38' West, then you need to travel 2 nautical miles west, because your destination has a higher number.

Using the UTM grid

UTM stands for another kind of navigation grid, the Universal Transverse Mercator. This system is based on the meter, with grid lines drawn on maps at every kilometer (1,000 meters, or about 0.62 miles).

Using UTM is easy: the vertical lines drawn on your map are called *eastings*. Eastings are numbered, and their numbers increase as you move east. Moreover, the numbers count meters as they move across your map. For example, if you're near the easting 350000 m.E. and your map shows that the easting 351000 m.E. is near your camp, then you know that your tent is 1,000 meters to the east.

The light blue lines running horizontally across your map are called *northings*. Northing numbers increase northward. So if your GPS tells you you're located at 411536 m.N. and you look on your map and see that the river you want to reach runs along the northing 411000 m.N., then you know that the river is 536 meters to your south.

Navigating with a Map

Many times, you can navigate through the wilderness with just a map — especially if you're on well-marked trails. The problem is that your map can get you lost, too! The basic practices in this section can cut down on the unwanted angst.

Orienting your map

REMEMBER

Each time you use a map, begin by *orienting* your map, or physically aligning the map so that it matches the surrounding terrain. If the river is on your left and the hills are on your right, then you should rotate the map in your hands until the map reflects that real-world reality — even if it means turning the map upside down! Why? Because the very essence of map reading is about interpreting spatial relationships — how the real world really looks. You can orient your map in one of two ways:

>> **Eyeball it.** Look at the nearby features and then rotate the map until it's close.

>> **Use a compass.** If you have a compass nearby, use it; compass orientation is much more exact. For more on orienting you map with the use of a compass, see "Using your compass to orient the map," later in this chapter.

Keeping track of distance traveled

You can find your way in the wild with a map by *dead reckoning*, a method of estimating your position by keeping track of (a) your speed and (b) how long you've traveled. For example, if you walk at 3 miles (4.8 kilometers) an hour and you walk for about two hours, you can estimate that you've travelled 6 miles (9.6 kilometers).

When estimating how fast you're moving, you have to take into account difficulties in terrain, especially when you leave the trail. The accepted standard of rate of travel by foot is 3 miles per hour over flat terrain. Off of trails, though, your pace usually drops off to less than a mile an hour. One of the most common errors in dead reckoning is to overestimate your speed on foot.

When estimating your rate of travel and navigating through the wilderness, you frequently estimate distances to landmarks, even if it's just subconsciously. Here are a few situations in which just about anybody can assume landmarks are closer than they really are:

>> When looking uphill or downhill (watch out for this one especially)

>> Whenever a bright light is shining on your landmark, especially a large one, such as a mountain

>> Whenever looking across flatlands, such as a desert, or bodies of water

>> Whenever the air is unusually clear, such as after a good rain and when the air is cool and crisp

Getting Acquainted with Your Compass

A compass gives you the ability to stand anywhere in the world and determine which direction is north. If you know that, you can quickly determine all the other directions.

There are many kinds of compasses including GPS compasses, cellphone compasses, and *back-sighting compasses,* which have what look like gun sights mounted on them to tell you which direction you're currently pointing. But the best simple compass for wilderness travel is an *orienteering compass* molded into a clear plastic baseplate, like the one in Figure 9-3. Because this standard compass doesn't require batteries, you can rely on it to work whenever you need it.

An orienteering compass is *top-sighting,* which means it's made to be held low, so you can read it by looking down on it from above.

Learning the parts of an orienteering compass

The main parts of an orienteering compass are:

>> **Baseplate:** The flat plastic platform that the compass unit sits on (see Figure 9-3a)

>> **Direction-of-travel arrow:** The large arrow on the baseplate, where you read the bearing (see Figure 9-3b)

>> **Housing (bezel):** The transparent, rotating disc that protects the compass needle and it is marked with degrees (Figure 9-3c)

>> **Orienting arrow:** The red arrow painted on the inside of the housing (Figure 9-3d)

>> **Straight edge:** Simply the edge of the baseplate; it works like a ruler (Figure 9-3e)

>> **Needle:** The small, magnetized bar that swivels around inside the housing and always points to magnetic north (Figure 9-3f)

Being aware of potential errors

Although compasses are great navigational tools, they aren't accurate 100 percent of the time. As long as you're aware of the two types of slight error, you can adjust the compass readings to correct the errors and determine what the true readings should be.

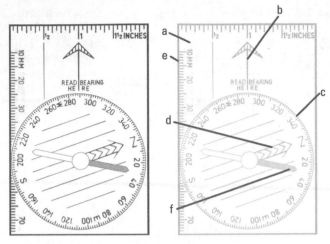

FIGURE 9-3: An orienteering compass

Understanding declination (or variation)

You probably know the exasperating truth by now: compasses normally don't point to the North Pole but rather toward *magnetic north*, which is normally hundreds of miles offset from the North Pole. On land maps, the difference between these two spots is called declination (on nautical charts, *magnetic variation*). *Declination* is the amount of error your compass has in any given area. You have to add or subtract this amount from your compass's reading to get true north.

At the bottom of your map, you should find the amount of declination you need to adjust for in your area. Look for a diagram with the annotations TN, which stands for *true north* (the direction to the North Pole), and MN, which stands for *magnetic north*, and then a number, like 13°. The declination may be east or west:

>> **East:** If magnetic north is located to the right of true north on the map, then the declination is east (see Figure 9-4a). Subtract the number of degrees from your compass bearing to point toward True North.

>> **West:** If magnetic north is to the left, the declination is west (see Figure 9-4b). Add the number of degrees from your compass bearing to point toward True North.

REMEMBER Some electronic compasses, such as those on GPS units and smart phones, automatically correct for declination/variation, and do point toward True North. Check the device or app settings to be sure!

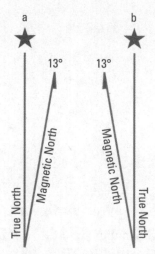

FIGURE 9-4: Typical east (a) and west (b) declination diagrams

Interference: Understanding local deviation

Sometimes nearby magnetic disturbances can influence your compass and cause it to have a second type of error: *deviation*. If you have stereo speakers nearby or if you have headphones on or if you're near a large block of iron — like an engine, for example — you can expect it to pull on your compass's magnetic needle.

The best way to find out whether you have this type of compass error is simply to move the compass around in one area. If you see the needle pulling to one side for no apparent reason, try to get as far away as possible from what you think is influencing the needle. Deviation can also be caused by metal belt buckles, necklaces, rings and so on, so check these as well.

Navigating with a Map and Compass

Using a map and a compass together can give you a lot of confidence in the wild (short of a GPS; see "Navigating with Electronics and Cellphones" later in this chapter for more on the GPS). But using them well usually requires a little practice before you get that wonderful ah-ha experience — so be patient and keep at it.

This section gives you directions for performing basic navigational functions with a common handheld, top-sighting orienteering compass.

Understanding common compass usage

Most of what you do with a compass requires only two or three actions:

>> **Taking a bearing:** A bearing is an imaginary line drawn from your compass to something you see, like a landmark. Simply point the direction-of-travel arrow at something in the terrain, and you're taking a bearing.

>> **Turning the bezel:** Turn the bezel (AKA housing) dial, usually while holding the compass stationary on the map.

>> **Using the compass like a ruler:** Line up the straight edge of the compass's baseplate on two points of the map, and then compare this distance to the scale marked on the map legend.

Establishing a field bearing

You can get started moving with your compass as your guide by taking a field bearing. A *field bearing* is a compass measurement that gives you the ability to establish an orderly course in the wilderness and navigate in a straight line. It doesn't require the use of a map. Check out Figure 9-5 while you're following these steps, and remember, you will find it a lot easier to do than it sounds, written out:

1. Point the direction-of-travel arrow in the direction you want to travel (see Figure 9-5a).

2. **Rotate the bezel (AKA housing) until the red end of the magnetic needle is centered above the orienting arrow (the magnetic arrow is pointing to north).**

   This is called *boxing the needle*. Figure 9-5b aligns north with the compass needle; the bearing to the landmark is 258°.

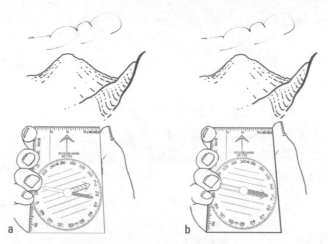

FIGURE 9-5: Taking a bearing in the field with an orienteering compass

3. **Read the bearing, in degrees, where the housing meets the direction-of-travel arrow.**

   This reading is your field bearing.

4. **Pick out a series of landmarks along this field bearing and make note of them.**

   You can begin walking toward the first landmark in the series — just don't touch that dial! Leave the housing of your compass alone. You're trying to navigate on a set course now. You want to reach your first landmark, make sure the next landmark lines up on your course, and then continue on.

Using your compass to orient the map

Using your compass to orient your map can go a long way toward helping you figure out where you are — especially if you're disoriented or lost. When you use this technique, you can rest assured that your map matches up with the physical terrain around you. That helps a lot if you're trying to figure out whether the trail is on your right or left — or behind you!

1. **Lay your map on a flat surface and place your compass on it, with the straight edge of the compass's baseplate lined up with any straight edge on the map.**

2. **Rotate your compass's housing until the N, located above the 360° marker, is centered on the red direction-of-travel line.**

3. **Rotate the entire map and compass around smoothly until the red end of the compass's magnetic needle is centered over the orienting arrow inside the housing.**

   You're *boxing the needle*. Your map is now oriented to magnetic north (see Figure 9-6a) — which isn't exactly good enough, because you want true north.

4. **Correct for declination.**

   Now you want to eliminate the error between magnetic north and true north. For example, if you have a 13° east declination, you have to subtract 13 degrees from your magnetic heading, which gives you 347° (360° – 13°). Rotate the housing to 347° and then box the needle by rotating the entire map again. (See the earlier section "Being aware of potential errors" for more on declination.)

When you're finished, your map and compass should look like this:

>> The baseplate of the compass should be lined up on one of the straight edges of the map.

>> The red needle should be hovering over the orienting arrow inside the compass housing.

>> The housing should be set to read 347° on the direction-of-travel arrow (corrected for declination).

When this is done, your map is officially oriented to true north, and it matches your surroundings exactly. Check out Figure 9-6b and practice a little; you'll find it sounds more complicated than it really is.

The following sections show you additional ways to use your map and compass. All these methods use this map–orienting procedure as their foundation.

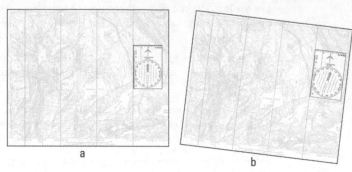

FIGURE 9-6: A map oriented with a compass both before (a) and after (b) correcting for declination

Setting your course from a map bearing

If you know where you are on the map and you know where you want to go, you can take a bearing from the map and then use it to make your way across the terrain. The upshot is that you can navigate toward a landmark that isn't yet in sight. Just follow these steps:

1. Orient the map (see the preceding section).

2. Lightly draw a straight line from your starting position to your destination.

3. Place the edge of your compass's baseplate on the line, with the direction-of-travel arrow pointing toward your destination.

4. While holding the compass and map firmly in place, rotate the housing until you've boxed the red part of the magnetic needle in the orienting arrow inside the housing.

5. Lift the compass from the map while keeping the red end of the magnetic needle boxed over the orienting arrow.

You're now pointing toward your destination.

After you set your course from a map bearing, you don't need to make any more adjustments to the compass or perform any adding or subtracting. You can begin moving from landmark to landmark.

MAKING IMPROVISED COMPASSES

You can make an accurate compass yourself if you can simply magnetize a small, thin piece of metal. The problem is that some metal won't magnetize! You need iron-based objects for this, which in this modern day means things made of iron or steel. Sewing needles work well, but some are now being made from non-magnetic nickel-plated brass. Paper clips also work, as do some double-edged razors and clips on the tops of writing pens.

To magnetize your needle, you can use

- The magnets inside stereo speakers — even the small ones like those found in headphones

- Stones containing iron, which usually means stones that are brown or rust-colored

- Materials that carry a static charge, such as pieces of fabric and human hair (the best fabrics are silk and nylon)

- Batteries and wire

Here's how to make your compass:

1. **Magnetize your "needle."**

   Whether using a magnet, stone, or your own head of hair, the trick is to stroke the piece of metal over your magnetizer slowly, repeatedly, and always in the same direction. For example, when using a piece of silk fabric, take your needle and stroke it 100 to 200 times across the silk — but always in the same direction. To use a battery to magnetize a needle, hook up a wire to the poles of the battery and then wrap the wire around your needle like a coil.

2. **Suspend your needle so it can rotate freely.**

   You can do this by hanging it from a string, a long hair, or by putting it on a floating object in a bowl of water. Floating objects include cork, wooden matchsticks, and the best of all, leaves. The container has to be nonferrous (not made of iron), like a plastic or porcelain cup or an aluminum mess tin. When free to rotate, the needle should align itself on a north-south axis.

Navigating with Electronics and Cellphones

The *global positioning system* (GPS) is a network of satellites that send precise navigation data to millions of receivers globally. In outdoor travel they are most often found in electronic devices such as *handheld GPS systems*, navigation systems (typically on larger watercraft), and smartphones.

This section familiarizes you with what GPS can and can't do and shows you some basic actions to make sure GPS works for you in wilderness situations.

What to expect from GPS

GPS-receiving electronic devices typically display your location in two ways:

>> They give you your position purely as a series of coordinates (latitude and longitude, or UTM), which you look up on a map to find exactly where you are. If you are reporting your position to Search and Rescue personnel, it's important to give them these numbers. In a survival situation, when you first feel that you're lost, get a position from your GPS and write it down. Any time you move more than half a mile or so, get a new position and write it down as well.

>> They directly show you your position as a point on an electronic map. Often this display also indicates the grid coordinates; if so, these should be noted so you can get them to Search and Rescue personnel if you are able to communicate with them. In a survival situation, when you first feel that you are lost, 'pin' or save your location on the electronic map, and keep track of future movements in this way.

Most GPS receivers also have a compass function or app to help you find North.

The GPS receivers used in phones, watercraft navigation systems, and hand-held systems are all accurate enough that they can be used for basic navigation and to identify your location close enough for Search and Rescue units to find you. Therefore, when using any of these systems, it's good to at least be familiar with the numerical grid information (latitude and longitude, or UTM) so that you can communicate your position to Search and Rescue services if you're in contact with them.

REMEMBER

Because GPS–receiving electronics rely on batteries, a good navigation package for the wilderness includes a GPS receiver (or a smartphone and/or handheld hiking aid), a paper map, and an orienteering compass.

Setting up your GPS system

For those carrying handheld GPS systems (such as the common Garmin, Bushnell, or Magellan units) it's important to check the GPS receiver's settings for the datum, position format, and unit format. The unit will come with instructions indicating how to set these. It may be important to know the settings when communicating with Search and Rescue, as different settings might give somewhat different position data.

If you are casually using a smartphone hiking app, you probably will not have to adjust these settings, but be ready to tell Search and Rescue personnel what kind of phone and app you are using; they can take it from there.

Datum

Datum is the survey information that was used to make a particular map, especially a topographic map. You must match the GPS unit's datum setting with that used to make the map.

To find out which datum was used to make the map you're currently using, look in the margins of the map for one of the following statements or abbreviations:

>> North American Datum 1927 (NAD27)

>> North American Datum 1983 (NAD83)

>> World Geodetic System 1984 (WGS84)

On the GPS unit select the datum that matches your map datum.

Position format

Regardless of whether your unit gives you a map or just coordinates, you must set the *position format*, typically latitude/longitude or UTM. Choose the one used by your paper map or the system you feel most comfortable using if the map has both. For more on how these coordinate systems work, see "Understanding your coordinates" earlier in this chapter.

Unit format

Finally, set the *unit format* to whatever you're most familiar with and is indicated on your map, typically miles, kilometers, or degrees.

TIP

If you're using the latitude/longitude coordinate system, you probably want to use nautical miles as your unit of measurement. If you're using UTM positions, using kilometers is best.

Using GPS in the wild

The most important action you can take with your GPS receiver (whether on a cellphone or handheld GPS system) is to record *waypoints,* or places of interest and importance that you pass along your travels. The single most important waypoint is your start point. Before entering any wilderness area, bring up the unit's menu, go into the *waypoint feature* (on a phone it may be a 'pinning' or 'save location' feature), and record your position at that moment. Regardless of where you go afterward or how lost you become, you can now go into the waypoint feature and ask the receiver where this starting point is — and how far from it you have ventured.

As you travel, continue to record waypoints. If you do become disoriented, you can go to the waypoint feature and find where the last waypoint was and backtrack. (Record these waypoint readings on a paper map, too, because GPS units can run down in the field.)

Depending on many variables, you may want to turn on a *tracking* feature on a phone or handheld GPS system. When this is on the unit automatically makes a record of your travels. The receiver has to remain turned on for this to work, so battery power is always a consideration. But if you have fresh batteries, this is a great feature because it gives you a "trail of breadcrumbs" that can help you find your way back or simply tell you how far you've gone.

GPS receivers may not get the signal transmitted from satellites if the sky is obscured by heavy vegetation or if you are deep in a canyon. Inclement weather, however, normally doesn't interfere with the signal. In any case, to catch a signal you can move to more open ground and/or wait out bad weather.

Using cellphones in the wild

A smartphone or cellphone with a mapping or tracking app can be a big help in the wild. But there are a couple of important differences between a typical handheld GPS navigation unit and a cellphone. First, the compass feature on your phone may not use GPS to indicate north; it probably uses a *magnetometer*, a device that detects the Earth's magnetic field. Consequently, it will usually point toward magnetic north, rather than true north; check the app settings to see whether or not this is automatically compensated.

Second, your cellphone's compass will likely be influenced by metal objects including jewelry or the magnets inside headphones. In our own experiments, we have seen some phone compasses come under the influence of nearby objects, while others haven't budged.

Third, most smartphones continually track movements of your phone regardless of any input by you, the user. There are also numerous tracking apps that can be downloaded from the net, which allow you to take a more proactive approach to navigation. These come in numerous varieties, including those that can detect when you have parked your car, which is especially useful for day hikers. Before setting off into the wild, you should experiment with these tracking apps to make absolutely certain that you can retrieve the information you need.

Finally, when relying on a phone for information in a survival situation, protect it from high- and low temperatures, impacts and fluids, and do all you can to preserve the battery — your life may depend on it.

Chapter **10**

Looking Up to the Sky: Celestial Navigation

People have been using the sun and the stars to find their way across land and sea for thousands of years. Sometimes this type of navigation can be complex, but more often than not, using the heavens to navigate is relatively easy.

In this chapter, we show you how to find direction using the sun, the stars, and a little ingenuity. Keep in mind that though these techniques are sometimes incredibly accurate, most are used to get your bearings or keep you going in a general direction. Still, if you don't have a compass or a GPS unit, you can rely on these useful methods.

Determining Direction with the Sun

The sun can be a great tool to help you find your way in the wilderness. You can use its position in the sky just like a compass by using a few easy techniques.

Whether you're using the sun or GPS, always keep your bearings while outdoors. Letting your attention lapse can get you lost quickly! When you get out of the car to start your hike, check to make sure you know where you are on the map or in relation to a distant landmark. Check again in fifteen minutes and again in another fifteen, and always try to maintain at least a general awareness of what direction you're facing.

None of the methods that follow are complicated; but keep in mind that the closer you are to the equator or to the poles, the less accurate these methods are. Luckily, the majority of the world's landmasses — including North America, Europe, and most of Asia — lie at latitudes that make these sun-navigation techniques useful.

TIP

Due and *True* North and South refer to geographical North and South, the direction to the Earth's North and South polar axes. *Magnetic* North and South are normally somewhat different; do some research to find out the magnetic *variation* (sometimes called *declination*) in your area. These are marked on flying and boating charts and most hiking maps.

TIP

You can improve the usefulness of all these techniques by carefully drawing a mock-up of a compass on the ground. After you find north and south, draw a north and south line, then draw a line 90 degrees to this line to indicate east and west. Likewise, if your technique gives you east and west, draw in north and south. Either way, you end up with a very helpful cross on the ground that you can use to make plans for traveling.

Locating east and west at sunrise and sunset

The sun rises in the east and sets in the west, regardless of where you find yourself on planet Earth. Just keep in mind that it doesn't always rise at *due east*, or precisely east, nor does it always set at *due west.* But you can take the dawn's early light to be generally east and sunset to be generally west anywhere in the world.

Finding north and south around midday

At midday, if you're anywhere in North America, Europe, or Northern Asia, the sun lies due south of you. For example, if it's lunch hour, say, between 11 a.m. and 1 p.m., you can rest assured that if you turn and face the shining sun, you're facing south. And behind you, over your shoulder, lies north. And of course, if you know where north or south is, you can instantly deduce the other directions. If you face the sun at midday in the Northern Hemisphere, east is on your left, and west is on your right.

Likewise, you can use this technique to find north in some of the southernmost parts of the Southern Hemisphere. At midday, if you're in New Zealand, Argentina, or South Africa, the sun lies due north of you. Basically, the farther South or North of the equator you are, the more this method is useful because at the equator the sun is more directly overhead.

Drawing a compass with the stick and shadow method

If you're in the wilderness without a compass or GPS, you can construct a reliable type of compass using the *stick and shadow method*. This direction–finding instrument can be highly accurate, and it works everywhere on Earth. Pick an area clear of vegetation and on relatively level ground and follow these directions:

1. **Plant a 3-foot-long stick and in the ground.**

   You can use practically any length of stick, but 3 feet (0.9 meters) is ideal.

2. **Place a rock right on the point where the stick's shadow ends (see Figure 10-1a); this point represents west.**

3. **Wait at least 15 minutes (you can estimate the time) and mark the new location of the shadow's point with another rock to represent east (see Figure 10-1b).**

4. **Draw a straight line from one rock to the next to indicate the west-east line (see Figure 10-1c).**

5. **Put your left foot on the first mark and your right foot on the second mark; you're now facing north. To complete the compass, make a cross by drawing a second line through the middle of the west-east line at a 90-degree angle (see Figure 10-1d); this is your north-south line.**

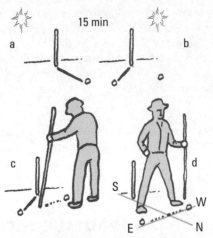

FIGURE 10-1: Creating a stick and shadow compass

Discerning direction with your wristwatch and the sun

You can determine direction easily if you have a wristwatch, either digital or analog. If it is analog, just use the hands as directed in this section. If your watch is digital, estimate the position of the hour and minute hands, and numbers around the watch face, perhaps by drawing the time on your hand with a pen.

The analog wristwatch method is simple:

1. **Point the hour hand of the watch at the sun.**

2. **Find due south by envisioning a line that runs between the position of the hour hand and the number 12 at the top of the watch face.**

   This line points due south. Using Figure 10-2a as a guide and a little practice, you can have this down in no time.

It can help to imagine that a line tracing from the hour hand to the 12 is the pointy end of a wedge (see Figure 10-2b); this point establishes north accurately enough for getting your bearings in survival situations.

The method shown in Figure 10-2 is for the Northern Hemisphere. For the Southern Hemisphere, use the same method, but point the watch's 12 at the sun (rather than the hour hand), and find the line running halfway between the 12 and the hour hand; this points north.

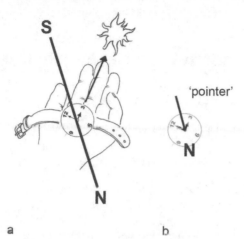

'pointer'

a   b

FIGURE 10-2: Using an analog wristwatch to find direction in the Northern Hemisphere

The wristwatch method is a little inaccurate if you are on Daylight Savings Time; if so, subtract one hour from the hour hand, and proceed as shown in Figure 10-2.

TIP

You can use the wristwatch method with the watch on your wrist, but it's much easier if you hold the watch in your hand. Ever better, lay your watch on the ground, rotate it to have the hour hand (Northern Hemisphere) or 12 (Southern Hemisphere) pointed at the sun, then draw the north–south line. Now draw a line perpendicular to these, forming a cross with N, S, W, and E as indicated.

Finding Direction with the Stars

At night, you can navigate your way through the wilderness using an ancient method, one that is as accurate as a digital compass. People have looked to the heavens to get their bearings for millennia. Knowing a few stars and constellations can quickly show you one of the cardinal directions, and from there you can quickly deduce the others.

This section provides the easiest methods for identifying direction with the stars. When the sky is good and dark, the main constellations will be visible, and with some practice you'll be able to find them (even without a smartphone app!). Don't be surprised if you find yourself checking every night for your newfound beacons in the sky.

Finding north with the North Star

You can count on the North Star, called *Polaris*, to be your most reliable signpost in the sky, because it's the only heavenly body that never moves or sets. (Actually, it does move, but only a tiny bit — so little, in fact, that you'd need instruments to detect its movement.) After you find the North Star, you can easily determine the other directions: south, east, and west.

You can find the North Star by first finding one of the two main constellations that lie on either side of it, the Big Dipper or Cassiopeia. These constellations point the way to the North Star and allow you to confirm that you have just the right pinpoint of light in the sky. The following methods work in any season for everyone in the Northern Hemisphere (see Figure 10-3):

>> **The Big Dipper (Ursa Major, or the 'Big Bear'):** The Big Dipper appears in the sky just as its name suggests: like an enormous ladle. You can find the North Star by following the pointer stars at the end of the bowl part of the ladle.

>> **Cassiopeia:** This constellation looks like a huge W, although it usually appears tipped over on its side. Find the North Star by following the stars that form the middle point of the W.

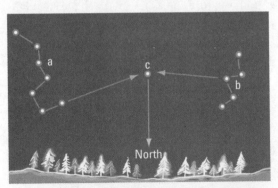

FIGURE 10-3: The Big Dipper (a), and Cassiopeia (b) can be used as pointers to find the North Star (c)

When you're facing the North Star, west is on your left and east is on your right. If you want to travel west, for example, you simply turn 90 degrees to the left and keep your right shoulder oriented on the North Star as you walk. The North Star lies almost directly over the North Pole, so when you're facing it, you're facing true north, not magnetic north, which is the direction your compass points.

The North Star is useful for confirming your direction and also for determining whether your compass is accurate. The North Star is true north, so if your compass says it's not, then the compass is not giving you an accurate reading. This can come from one of two problems:

>> **The area you're in has a wide magnetic *variation*** (sometimes called *declination* on land maps). This means that the compass, which works by reading Earth's magnetic field, is functioning just fine, but you will have to compensate a little for the small error, usually less than 30 degrees. Just make sure that when the sun rises and the North Star fades, you know the amount of error in your compass.

>> **The compass is not working.** If your compass needle points more than 35 degrees *away from the North Star* it is probably malfunctioning. It is true that some magnetic variations can be this high, but they are a rarity. If your compass is really off when you point it toward the North Star, it's possible that you're holding the compass too close to a large piece of metal and the metal is interfering with the magnetism of the compass (this is called compass *deviation*). Try moving away from metal (such as a car or boat) and remove metallic jewelry or watches to address this error.

Finding due south with the Southern Cross

If you're anywhere near the equator or below it, you can use the Southern Cross to orient yourself at night.

The Southern Cross appears in the sky just as advertised — like a cross — so locating it after nightfall is no problem. Just be sure you have the genuine article! Next to the Southern Cross lies a false cross (see Figure 10-4d). The only way to be sure you've found the right one is to locate the Pointer Stars, two bright stars near the Southern Cross's base. You should think of the Southern Cross and the Pointers as parts of the same body.

You can find south with the Southern Cross; just remember that the Southern Cross doesn't always sit directly over the South Pole. You find due south by using the Southern Cross and Pointers like a ruler. Just draw an imaginary line that cuts the space between the Pointers in half (see Figure 10-4a); draw another imaginary line straight down the center of the Southern Cross (see Figure 10-4b). Follow these two imaginary lines to a point in space where the lines cross (see Figure 10-4c); directly below this point lies due south.

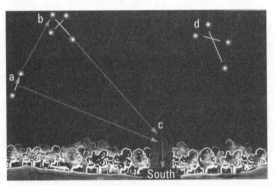

FIGURE 10-4: The Pointer Stars (a) and Southern Cross (b) can be used to find due south (c), but don't be fooled by the false cross (d)

Finding West and East by Moonlight

Because of the way the moon is illuminated by the sun, its position in the sky can help you find west and east.

TIP

If the moon has come up before sunset, its illuminated side indicates west. If it has come up after midnight, the illuminated side of the moon indicates east. Very helpful!

IN THIS CHAPTER

» **Traversing trails**

» **Knowing what to do when you're disoriented**

» **Sitting still or moving when you're lost**

» **Traveling over open wilderness**

» **Handling obstacles**

Chapter **11**
Trekking over Land

I t's not hard to picture the situation: you've been walking all day on a well-marked trail or in a seemingly familiar area, and now the sun is going down and suddenly nothing seems well-marked or familiar at all.

You can work your way out of this mess, but it'll take time, a clear head, and a lot of patience. This chapter explains how to traverse over trails and shows you the basics of traveling through the wilderness, including info on how to cross rivers and streams and what to do if you're lost.

Understanding Trail Travel

You may be wondering how difficult traveling on trails can actually be. You'd be surprised, brave traveler. Any wilderness area you go into is in reality a maze — a labyrinth of trails, false trails, animal trails, and washes. To avoid meandering or even getting lost in the wild, check out the following practical tips for successfully traveling trails. (And see Chapter 9 for the basics on finding direction.)

REMEMBER

Before you head out, let someone know where you're going and when you plan to be back. If you don't return as expected, that person can contact the authorities and help set the search-and-rescue teams in motion.

Knowing where you are

When traveling on a trail or doing some other activity in the wild, try to know your position as closely as you can, as often as you can. This deceptively simple principle can do more to keep you from getting lost than just about any other.

WARNING

Leaving the trail to take a shortcut gets more people lost in the wilderness than just about anything else. Many times, leaving the trail and heading directly for a large landmark seems like a shorter route, but doing so is frequently the start of trouble. Without the help of the trail, even experienced wilderness people sometimes become disoriented.

Another practice that gets people lost is leaving the trail to walk down a slope, such as down to a creek. When you walk down from a trail, you lose sight of it. You can still see signs of it, but many times they can be misleading. If you do walk down slope from a trail, always turn around and look behind you to make sure you know the way back.

TIP

People usually get lost in the wilderness due to a momentary lapse in awareness — *part-time navigation.* Many times, people who are bird-watching, berry-picking, or hunting end up lost because they're so concentrated on the task at hand that they only occasionally look up to see where they're going. They frequently find what they were looking for, but then they realize that they've strayed into an unknown area.

Knowing where you've been

Finding your way back is more important than forging ahead. You can stay out of trouble almost indefinitely if you can remember how to get back to where you came from, such as the car, the river, or the trail.

REMEMBER

Your greatest survival tool on the trail is the ability to stop, turn around, and look behind you. Always look behind you when you're walking on any trail — even if you don't expect to go back that way. People get lost in the wilderness every year because they get on the trail and think only about moving ahead. When they turn around to go back, the trail doesn't look the same — it has lots of turns they didn't see and lots of landmarks they aren't sure about.

The following is a list of problem areas to keep an eye on. When encountering these points, examine the area well enough that you'd know it in the dark or in a driving rain.

>> **Trail junctions and intersections:** Many times, a pathway joins the trail you're walking on and you don't realize it. When you come back down your trail, that seemingly harmless junction is going to be a fork — a fork you've never seen before. When you're hiking, turn around and look at each junction from the direction you'd see it from if you were returning. Stop and make sure your mind absorbs each junction.

>> **Old trails, false trails, animal trails, and washes:** Always watch for trail imitators and imposters. A single sudden rain can create a track that looks like a trail, but actually just takes you downhill somewhere.

>> **Tunnels through foliage:** These are especially bad because when you emerge from the tunnel your sense of spatial relationship — to where you once were — is often distorted.

>> **Rivers, streams, lakes, landforms, and manmade structures:** If you run into a landmark in the wilderness, keep in mind that it may have a *twin* — a nearby lookalike that can easily fool you in the rain or dark. Always look for distinguishing characteristics — unusually-shaped rocks and trees, and so on.

>> **An area outside your normal stomping grounds:** If you frequently hike in a particular area but then decide to push your boundaries a bit, look behind you as you leave familiar grounds.

>> **Your old stomping grounds:** Remember that when you go back to your uncle's old farm, or when you take the trail to your favorite old swimming hole, the lay of the land may have changed.

In the next section, we show you various techniques you can use to find your way back should you become disoriented.

Getting Back on Course When You're Disoriented

If you're disoriented, stop. Plant yourself. Take a deep breath and settle your mind. You can almost always find your way out of the wilderness if you can calm yourself and work the problem thoroughly.

More often than not, your instincts tell you to double your efforts, to try harder, to walk more — and to walk faster. But the instinct to double your efforts only makes things worse. If you find yourself off course and disoriented, this section can help you get back on track.

WARNING

Don't backtrack unless you're absolutely certain that you know where you came from. The most important thing to do when you're disoriented is to find out where you are *now*. Sometimes backtracking just gets you more disoriented. If you do backtrack, establish a range and mark your trail. For more on these basic travel practices, see the sections, "Traveling in a straight line" and "Marking your trail," later in this chapter.

Reviewing your calculations

If you're using instruments (like GPS) to find your way and you've become disoriented, make sure you haven't made a navigation error and are using the instruments correctly (for more on navigation, see Chapter 9):

>> **Make sure your map is oriented correctly.** Incorrectly oriented maps get more people in trouble than just about anything else.

>> **Make sure you're looking at the right map.** Keep in mind that you may have walked off the map or that you may have been navigating all this time with the wrong map!

>> **Check the date of your map.** Your map may be outdated and inaccurate — especially in the category of manmade features, which change often.

>> **Check your compass corrections.** Many times, you have to correct for compass error, which is the source of so many mistakes. Make sure your compass isn't being affected by some metallic or magnetic influence.

>> **Make sure you're navigating with the right units of measurement.** Not all maps use the same units of measurement, and many maps offer the ability to measure distances in two or three different units — miles, kilometers, and so on. When using a GPS receiver, make sure it's calibrated to the units of measurement on the map and to the *datum setting* (the frame of reference that matches the geographic features to map coordinates).

Using your senses to help you find your way

If you don't have maps or instruments, or if you've examined them and you still can't make heads or tails of where you are, you can try the following techniques to help orient yourself. This can help when combined with instructions provided in the upcoming section, "Taking action when you're disoriented."

Stop and observe

Stopping to observe your surroundings and thinking through your earlier movements can get you back on the trail. Try the following:

>> **In your mind, go back to the last point where you were certain you knew where you were.**
Make a list of what you've seen and everywhere you could've gone wrong. If you can figure out where you had your lapse in awareness, you can probably get out of trouble.

>> **In your mind, try to replay your entire hike, from when you left your base to where you are now.** What were the major features you passed? Did you cross a river or stream?

>> **Examine the features and landforms around you.** Any two landforms can look the same if you only glance at them, so don't assume that you've seen everything on the first glance. You usually can't distinguish one creek bed or hill from another unless you spend a minute contemplating it. Many features appear different in different shades of light.

>> **Watch for sunlight in thinning forests or scrub.** You may be next to a major trail or road that's only 50 feet away. A major shaft of sunlight can indicate a break in the forest from a road or a trail.

Listen

Sitting in the quiet can be brutal, but it works. To listen carefully, be still and hold your breath if needed. Here are useful sounds to listen for:

>> **River rapids, waterfalls, and surf:** Sometimes you can hear these sounds from miles away; rivers provide water and beaches are good open areas to be spotted by rescuers and where you can find lots of survival resources, such as rope and driftwood.

>> **Ground vehicles:** Wilderness vehicles include snowmobiles and ATVs; you may be near a road or highway if you hear a continuous low roar.

>> **Sounds associated with people:** Barking dogs, slamming doors, and laughter all carry quite a way and may be associated with people, especially at remote hunting or wilderness lodges.

Taking action when you're disoriented

If you've become disoriented, your priority should be to figure out where you are — not to travel more. If you can't establish your position on a map, or if you don't have a map to begin with, then you must do everything you can to understand your *relative position* — in other words, where you are in relation to some nearby landmark. Start by trying to orient yourself with the methods described in the earlier section, "Using your senses to help find your way." These may help expand your position awareness outward until you can either determine where you are on the map or how to get back to a place that you know, like a trailhead or parking lot.

To do this, you start by establishing a base, and plan on returning to your base as a part of the process of reorienting yourself:

>> **Make a map.** A homemade map can be of immense help. To make it, you may have to be resourceful. On paper or any other surface you can mark on, draw the nearest landmark — the trail, a creek, or a river — anything that can be used to establish your relative position. This allows you to start making sense of the world around you, and should prevent the meandering that can cause complete disorientation.

Take your time to make a good map. Your goal is to expand your map until, ultimately, it includes your last known landmark, or the place where you left the trail, which is the key to making it back to safety.

>> **Move to higher ground.** Higher ground allows you to see a lot of terrain and landmarks at once — this move alone might tell you where you are, and it helps you make a complete map of your relative position. Move to higher ground only if you know where higher ground is — and you're positive you'll be able to find your way back to your current position. Make sure that you add your current location to your map!

>> **Expand out in concentric circles.** Do this slowly. Venture out nearby and look at the lay of the land around your position. Do this in very small increments, and return to base frequently. You may be able to pick up the trail again this way. With each expansion, add to your map.

Before you move, make sure you'll be able to get back to where you are right now, your base. Continue adding to your map, marking your trail very prominently so you can always return to your mapmaking base. Check out the later section, "Marking your trail," for specific advice.

What to Do When You're Lost

It's psychologically important to admit it when you're lost so that you can start a plan of action to get found or get home. In this section, we discuss staying put and waiting for rescue, and we tell you what to do if you make the risky decision to move when you're lost.

Staying put so people can find you

If you're monumentally lost, or if you have good reason to believe that someone is going to come looking for you, in most cases the best idea is to stay put. For example:

>> You're separated from your hiking or tour group.

>> You've left word saying you'll be back.

>> You were involved in a crash or any other tragedy that should mobilize search-and-rescue services.

>> You know that search-and-rescue services are already looking for you. Many times, hikers or victims call in a rescue and then move, which is the worst thing they can do. Just moving a short distance might make you invisible to search-and-rescue services.

REMEMBER

If you have reason to believe someone may come looking for you, your responsibility is to stay alive and healthy so you can signal them. (Signaling for rescue is covered in Chapter 12.)

Even if your current situation is tough, try to do what you can to stay put. Here's how to ward off the cold and make yourself more comfortable as you sit tight:

>> **Make a fire and stay the night.** If you can get a fire going, you can turn the tables on the wilderness. For more on the fine art of starting a fire, see Chapter 5.

>> **Make a shelter.** A small, tight-fitting, hovel-like shelter can do much to insulate you. Building a shelter when you know there's a town nearby may seem crazy, but you must fight the ever-present threat of hypothermia. A simple but decent shelter can get you through the night — which is much better than wandering. For more on building your wilderness home, see Chapter 6.

REMEMBER

Always mark an improvised shelter, otherwise, you're building camouflage! Use brightly colored cloth, reflective metal, or any of the many methods we cover in Chapter 12.

Deciding to travel

Although staying put is normally best, there may come a time when you're convinced that the only way you're going to get home or be rescued is to move. In this section, we tell you how to move systematically when you're lost. In the next section, we explain how to travel over open wilderness.

WARNING

Making the decision to travel when lost must be your last resort; travel only if you must move because of safety reasons or you've logically concluded that no one is going to come looking for you.

Preparing to move

If you're dead set on moving, take the following precautions:

>> **Above all, make a plan (and a map).** Take a bearing on something — a tree, a rock, anything; don't just walk aimlessly. (For more on making a plan — and a map — see "Taking action when you're disoriented," earlier in this chapter. For traveling with bearings, see "Traveling in a straight line," later in this chapter.) If you're leaving people behind, make a timetable and a schedule of contacts (if possible) and thoroughly discuss what the plan of action is.

>> **Make the necessary preparations.** Carry water, make copies of maps, and carry as many tools as you can.

>> **Leave a message at your current location.** Write down the following information, all of which can be of immense help to rescuers if they find it:

- Who you are and how you became lost

- When you became lost

- A brief history of your situation

- What time you began to travel away from that location

- Where you intend to go

Display this note prominently, for example under a conspicuous pile of rocks, or hanging on a tree branch. If people come looking for you, this information may be the only hope they have of locating you. If possible, periodically leave small notes that searchers may discover as they try to track you.

>> **Leave highly visible markers behind you as you move.** These signs can significantly help rescuers track you through the wilderness.

Detecting signs of civilization

Always be alert for sounds and signs of civilization; see "Using your senses to help you find your way." Here are a few more things to watch out for:

>> **A glow on the horizon:** Even distant cities and towns might be visible as a glowing area brighter than the rest of the land you're looking over at night.

- **Reflections off of low clouds:** Especially when there is dense, white low overcast, you may see reflections from human-made light.

- **Power lines and railroads:** These are often arranged on straight lines cutting through dense forest. If you can make your way to these they might help direct you toward people and help.

- **Low-flying aircraft:** Aircraft ascend from, and descend toward, airports. If you see a series of aircraft moving in the same general direction, they may also indicate an airport.

- **Noise:** Keep your ears tuned for noises such as machinery, engines, and voices.

- **Squared land and fences:** If you have a view of the area around you, look closely for squares or rectangles in the distance. These shapes, often marking farmed land, are a dead giveaway for civilization.

- **Smells of food or industry:** Food smells and industry exhaust travel long distances. Many experienced navigators have followed their nose to safety.

Following water to civilization

You've probably heard the old adage that you can follow water to civilization, or perhaps you've heard that you should always work your way downstream. Nothing's wrong with this advice, except that it's not a guarantee. Sorry! You can follow a creek down to a river and then follow the river to a lake or the ocean . . . but you may be traveling for a very, very long time before you reach people.

WARNING

Don't travel in the bottoms of steep canyons or river drainages — especially if you have no way to get out in a hurry. The water level can rise swiftly, even if it hasn't been raining (or the rain is miles away). We've been on rivers when, unknown to us, the floodgates of a nearby dam were suddenly opened; the water rose 10 feet in 20 minutes.

Blazing Your Own Trail

Traveling through wilderness without a trail (often called *trail-blazing*) requires some special skills, which we cover in this section.

In a city, people might walk three miles an hour, but in wilderness terrain remember you will likely go about one mile per hour . . . and just a small amount of underbrush or other obstacles can slow you down to a literal crawl.

Managing meandering

Even when you have a clear plan in mind, when trailblazing through wilderness you will encounter obstacles such as rivers, hills, and canyons that force you to *meander*, or move in unplanned directions. Here are some tips to reduce the effect of these distractions:

>> **Without anything to orient you, you tend to walk in a series of arcs or in an aimless fashion.** Many theories suggest why humans tend to walk in curves or circles when outdoors; we don't know which is most accurate, but we do know that yes, people generally move in arcs or even circle back when trailblazing. Keep this in mind and try to avoid it by using a compass to help reach distinct landmarks in the direction you mean to go.

>> **You tend to make arbitrary turns when you reach obstacles you're unsure of.** People often take the path of least resistance, and many simply prefer to turn right or left at an obstacle, even though there's no real navigational rationale for this turn. Take your time and think through the reasons for turning away from the intended direction.

>> **People tend to turn away from irritants.** These include heavy winds on one side of your face, burning sun, briars and thorns, wet ground, and especially slopes. Whenever you walk on the side of a slope, you tend to want to walk either up it or down it (especially down).

Now that you know some ways you can get turned around, you're ready to try to walk in a (somewhat) straight line.

Traveling in a straight line

To travel straight while trailblazing, it's best to start by establishing a *bearing*. This is simply an imaginary line you draw from your position to a prominent landmark or feature that you want to reach. Even if you can see only 50 feet in front of you, establish a bearing to something you want to reach, a tree or rock, for example. This reduces wandering. One of the best types of bearings is the type you make with a compass. (For more on compass bearings, check out Chapter 9.)

Another good bearing is a *range*, an imaginary line that you draw through any three landmarks that line up in a column ahead of you. To make a range, you have two options (see Figure 11-1):

>> **Connect three landmarks.** Mentally draw a straight line through three landmarks ahead of you, such as a bush, a rock, and a hill. Try to follow this straight line even though you will meander here and there to avoid obstacles.

>> **Use a back bearing.** A *back bearing* is simply an imaginary line that runs from an object behind you, through your body, to an object in front of you. This also gives you a range because it gives you three things you can line up in a mental column for navigation.

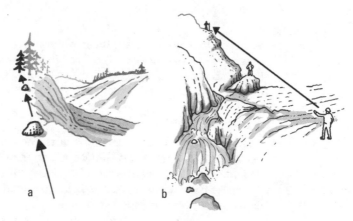

FIGURE 11-1: Making a range by visually lining up landmarks

Marking your trail

Marking your trail while trailblazing allows you to backtrack if you work your way into a situation where you cannot go ahead anymore.

Trails can be marked in many ways; with piles of rocks (*cairns*), by conspicuously breaking tree limbs at eye height, or tying brightly colored or reflective material to vegetation. Ensure your markers are visible from both sides of the tree or landmark, back and front, so you can see them when you look behind you and so search-and-rescue units can see them as they're following you.

In very dense vegetation you may need to shorten the distance between trail markers down to just 20 feet or less. Patience is the key in these situations. Trailblazing can be tedious but if you're thorough, this method can save your life in low-visibility terrain.

TIP

If you're lucky enough to be traveling with a group, you can blaze the trail by setting up a moving range, known as a *file*. Here's how (refer to Figure 11-1b):

1. **Send two people out in front of you.**

   One person is the *aimer,* and one is the *trailblazer.*

2. **If you're standing at the back of the line, use the aimer in the file to line up the trailblazer; then coach the two down the range using hand signals until they're almost out of sight.**

3. **After the trailblazer has gone as far as you want, the trailblazer sets a mark — *blazes the trail* — while the rest of the file moves forward.**

Crossing Rivers and Streams

Crossing water in a survival situation must be taken seriously; weak and demoralized, it's easy to be swept away. Essentially you must decide whether to wade across or build a flotation device such as a raft. This section covers these two choices. (Swimming in survival situations is a bad idea; everything will get wet, you may get cold, deep water may hide dangers, and many people are intimidated by swimming in natural waters). For info on crossing frozen water obstacles, see Chapter 16.

Wading

The first step in walking across a river or stream is to choose the best place to cross. From high ground or a safe tree, examine the river for possible crossings and look for a *ford*, a place where the river narrows or becomes shallow enough to cross easily. You may have to travel quite a way up or down stream to find a ford, but it's normally better than swimming.

If all you find is a dangerous raging river, far up and down stream, consider traveling along the river rather than crossing it. Or, consider waiting a few days; many natural rivers increase and decrease flow over days due to changing weather.

TIP

If the temperature allows, consider packing your clothes into a plastic bag or other container for the crossing to keep them dry. You may want to keep shoes on, though, to prevent injury by rocks or other objects in the riverbed.

When crossing water, you can use any one of the following techniques:

» **Crossing solo with a pole:** You can use a pole to help break the river's current. Find a strong tree branch or other pole, about 3 to 4 inches (7.5 to 10 centimeters) in diameter and about 7 to 8 feet (2 to 2.5 meters) long, and dig it into the riverbed *upstream* from your body, as in Figure 11-2a. This disrupts the flow so you can walk behind it, downstream. Drag the pole along the riverbed, moving it by small increments (if you pick it up it might be swept away and hard to push down again), and stay behind the break in the current.

» **Crossing with a group and a pole:** Use a strong pole that several people can hold onto. Have your group form a single column, lined up on the pole, as in Figure 11-2b. The lightest person should be the one farthest upstream.

» **Crossing with a group and a loop of rope:** Send the strongest person across first, on the inside of a loop of sturdy rope, with the other two people holding the remaining rope on shore. The second person holds onto the rope while crossing. The third person crosses on the inside of the loop, as the first person did. See Figure 11-2c.

FIGURE 11-2: Crossing a stream solo (a), in a group (b), and with a rope (c)

TIP

In a survival situation you should avoid *rapids*, fast-flowing and turbulent sections of water; but if you find yourself in swift water, try to float on your back with your feet pointing downstream. Survival may be possible if you can keep your feet in front of you and your buttocks high, avoiding underwater rocks and other obstacles. Focus on floating rather than swimming while in fast water; when the water slows, use your arms and legs to swim toward dry land.

Building a raft

You can improvise a flotation device (let's call them rafts to be practical) from one of at least three types of materials, or a combination of all three. We list these raft-building materials here in order of their practicality:

>> **Empty containers:** Anything that holds air can be tied together or put in a bag or tarp and tied up, as in Figure 11-3a.

>> **Logs and Styrofoam:** Styrofoam is the best. Always test the floatability of wood — many types don't float very well. Thick bamboo canes can quickly be lashed together to make effective rafts. You can tie logs or Styrofoam together with two pieces of rope for a basic raft shown in Figure 11-3c. It's not the most comfortable vessel, but you can steer and propel it with your hands and feet to get across moving water.

>> **Lots of logs or bamboo poles:** With these materials, you can build a conventional raft using crossbeams, as in Figure 11-3b. Use a simple levering process to tighten the ropes holding everything together. Simply wrap the line around a pole a few times and then pry upward.

TIP

As you plan on crossing a river with a raft, think about where you'll end up on the other side. The best choice for a landing site is a sandy bank. Know that your landing site will be downstream; how far depends on the speed of the water. The moment you start to move toward the opposite bank, the water will push you downstream. Don't try to fight this, just keep steadily headed to the other side.

a   b   c

FIGURE 11-3: Building rafts with empty containers (a), logs and poles (b), or logs and Styrofoam (c)

REMEMBER

Improvised rafts are vulnerable to capsize and disintegration. Small and narrow rafts are the most unstable. The best design is a large raft in the form of a square or circle. To avoid having your raft fall apart, overbuild it. Use as much cordage as you can and tie your knots tightly. (For more on ropes and knots, see Chapter 14.)

Because a trapped-air raft is the most practical (if you have just a few materials), we walk you through how to build one with a plastic sheet (check out Figure 11-4):

1. **Pile 1.5 feet (0.5 meters) of brush, foliage, or plastic containers on top of a plastic sheet or tarp.**

   Don't use foliage that has thick branches for this because they poke holes in the raft. If you're using a poncho, tie the hood closed and lay the poncho down, hood up.

2. **Tie together two sturdy poles or branches into an X and lay the X on top of your foliage; then pile another 1.5 feet of foliage on top of your X.**

3. Wrap the edges of your plastic around the foliage and tie them in place using any cordage or vines you can find.

4. Place your wrapped foliage package on top of a second tarp or poncho, open side down.

5. Wrap the second tarp or poncho around the first and tie the whole package together.

Place the entire raft in the water like it is, with the second poncho or tarp on the bottom. The tied part of the second poncho or tarp — the open side — should be face up.

With any kind of raft, remember, it doesn't have to be pretty or support a lot of people for a long time; just make it big and stable enough to get across the river so you can continue overland travel.

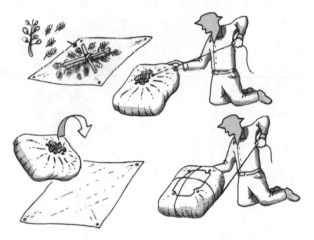

FIGURE 11-4: Making a trapped-air raft to cross rivers and streams

IN THIS CHAPTER

» **Understanding the ins and outs of signaling**

» **Learning about appropriate signaling tools**

» **Using radios and cellphones to signal**

» **Preparing for the arrival of a rescue helicopter**

Chapter **12**

Signaling for Rescue

You can kick up quite a bit of commotion in the wild and still not be noticed. What seems obvious to you can be completely invisible to a potential rescuer. Understanding what people can actually see and hear — what really gets you noticed — is part of the art and skill of signaling.

In this chapter, we show you ways to get the attention of anybody who's looking for you — and even those who aren't. We show you how you can get attention, how to use communication devices to signal for help, and how to prepare for the arrival of help from the skies.

Signaling Basics

When you're in the wild and need someone to find you, you send out a *signal* — basically anything that gets you noticed. You will want to be noticed by *search-and-rescue* (SAR) units and anyone else who may be able to help you. This section helps you establish a firm signaling foundation so you're easier to find.

Picking a good location

To make a visual signal, the first consideration is *maximum visibility*. Prime real estate for good signaling is usually

>> The highest elevation you can safely get to

>> A spot that can be seen from all sides

>> An expanse with few natural objects that would distract rescuers; for instance, an open field with no large boulders

TIP

If you can't stay at your signaling spot, make a signal pointing to where you are. Large, well-contrasted, and angled arrows make excellent signals. For more on these types of signals, see "Mastering the Language of Signaling" later in this chapter.

Making your signal stand out

The basic philosophy of visual survival signals is *bigger, brighter, different.* These three ideas encapsulate the entire spectrum of signaling. Anytime you can do something bigger, brighter, or different — especially in a conspicuous spot — you're improving your chances of being found.

Bigger

Bigger means anything that makes you, or your signal, larger. A human being is actually a very small thing on this Earth, so whenever you can be a part of something larger, you're making yourself more visible.

TIP

If you've been in an accident, stay with your downed aircraft or near the debris field of your damaged or capsized vessel. Debris fields represent a much larger position marker than your body — and search-and-rescue units look for them specifically.

If you're in a group, stay together and form a symbol such as straight line, or anything else that contrasts with the prevailing terrain. If you're in the water, link arms with others in your group.

Brighter

Brighter means a more intense signal. Brighter can mean more light at night, such as more fire or more flares, but it can also mean using the brightest colors you have available. Here are some ways to make your signal brighter:

>> Make more than one fire, or make a larger fire.

>> Put reflectors near anything that puts out light.

>> Use colored objects, such as clothing, for your signals. If your undershirt is brighter than your outerwear, consider putting the undershirt on over the outerwear.

>> If you have brightly colored objects that you can lie out on the ground around you, do so.

Different

Different refers to anything that contrasts with its surroundings or that appears wrong or out of place in the prevailing terrain. For example, stamping a straight line in desert sand or deep snow, where such straight lines are not normally found.

Most of Nature's lines are curved, so any straight line is a good signal; so are right angles.

TIP

Being persistent

Unfortunately, getting someone's attention may take a while. Don't expect to be seen easily or on the first try. Many survival tales recount being flown over several times before rescuers found the survivors. Be prepared to signal repeatedly.

It's common for search-and-rescue units or people going about their business to pass right by someone who's signaling frantically. Many times, airplanes or ships change course and only appear to be heading your way. This can be frustrating in the extreme and demoralizing. But you must continue to signal until you're certain they're coming for you.

Learning the Language of Signaling

Effective use of distress signals increases your odds of being rescued. These internationally recognized symbols mean only one thing: someone is in peril.

This section introduces the language of signaling.

Using three of anything to signal distress

Anytime you use three of any type of signal, you're sending out a strong, universally recognized message. Three loud noises, three bright flashes, three fires built in a triangle — all of these are recognized as distress signals, and they fall into our criteria of "bigger, brighter, and different." (See the earlier section "Making your signal stand out.")

SOS and Mayday: Calling for urgent help

You can use *SOS* (a 'help' signal from the days of early radio communications) or *Mayday* anytime, anywhere — you don't have to be on the water or in the air, and you don't have to be an official, like a ship's captain, to use them.

REMEMBER

Use SOS or Mayday only when you're in grave danger and need immediate assistance. SOS and Mayday are the most serious distress signals you can send.

Sending SOS

To send SOS, you use three short signals, three long signals and then three short signals again, like this: ... --- ...

You can bang on a piece of metal (perhaps from the wing of a downed plane) to get attention — bang three times in short succession, three times with a longer wait between them, and then three times again in short succession. Same thing if you are using a flashlight shining through darkness at a possible rescue vehicle or persons; three short flashes (all in the space of one second), three long ones (one second long each) and then three short flashes again. Most potential rescuers will recognize the international SOS signal.

TIP

If you have a walkie talkie or other radio (on a boat or airplane, for example) and batteries are running low, SOS is a good way to signal. Radio operators will be familiar with the signal. Just press the TRANSMIT key three times quickly, three times slowly, and three times quickly again. This transmits brief bursts of static that radio operators can hear, and they may then try to call you back.

Calling Mayday

The most common radio distress signal is *Mayday* (from the French *m'aidez* or "help me," the international term of serious distress.

You can spell Mayday on the ground or on the roof of downed aircraft or shelters, but its most common use is in radio communications. For more on how to use Mayday over a radio, go to "Sending a distress call over the radio," later in this chapter.

Sea stuff: Saying Pan-Pan when you're not in immediate danger

Pan is the international code word you use when your situation is serious but not life-threatening (e.g., your boat is sinking but very slowly). Pan is usually used only on the sea, but it is recognized internationally.

Pan is spoken twice, three times in a row. It's pronounced so that it rhymes with swan: "Pahn-Pahn, Pahn-Pahn, Pahn-Pahn."

Using ground-to-air emergency code

Large symbols that you make on the ground around you are referred to as *ground-to-air emergency code*, or simply *patterns*. These are formed by arranging debris, colored items, branches, rocks, earth, snow—anything that can form large patterns, say 20 feet long.

Here are the main patterns and what they mean:

>> **Require assistance:** V

>> **Require medical assistance:** X

>> **Proceed in this direction:** ↑

Using your body to signal

You can communicate with low-flying aircraft and ground units on nearby hills by standing still and intentionally forming signals with your arms and body position. There are four main widely-recognized postures:

>> **Need help, or pick us up:** Raise both arms into the air, similar to signaling a touchdown in football (see Figure 12-1a).

>> **Land here:** Crouch and hold your arms straight out, parallel to the ground (Figure 12-1b). Point toward the specific area where you want the aircraft to land.

>> **Don't attempt to land here:** This is vigorous waving motion you use to prevent an aircraft from landing in a hazardous area (Figure 12-1c).

>> **Urgently need medical assistance:** Lie on your back with your arms straight overhead and your legs extended (Figure 12-1d).

WARNING

Don't wave at aircraft with one hand if you're in trouble. Waving with one hand means that you don't need assistance. If you're in peril, you must put both hands in the air.

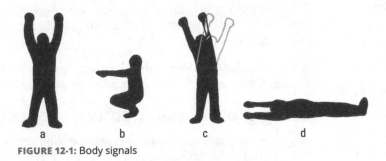

a   b   c   d

FIGURE 12-1: Body signals

Signaling with Signaling Tools

Creativity and persistence are key to effective signaling. In this section, we take a look at basic tools that have proven very effective in saving the lives of survivors. (For info on radios and other electronic devices, see "Signaling with Electronics," later in this chapter.)

Noisemakers and horns

Repeated patterns are the best type of audio signals, and distinct patterns of three sounds are usually recognized as distress signals. Here are some good noisemakers:

>> Whistles of all types

>> Aerosol noisemakers, like the type used at sporting events

- ⟫ Gunshots
- ⟫ A steel pot or a metal airplane wing or any other large or hollow piece of metal you can beat on

Almost any noisemaker we list here is better than the human voice. Yelling is exhausting and not as effective as other noisemakers.

Mirrors and other reflectors

A mirror or other reflector can sometimes be seen from 50 miles (80 kilometers) away. If you have access to a survival kit (find out how to build your own survival kit in Chapter 2), look inside for a signal mirror. If you don't have that luxury, practically anything shiny will work, for example:

- ⟫ Mirrors in cosmetic cases, cars, or planes
- ⟫ CDs, DVDs, or computer discs of any kind (these are very good)
- ⟫ Any piece of glass (a dark backing, like mud smeared on the back, can sometimes increase its reflecting ability)
- ⟫ Plastic space blankets, especially when stretched tightly over a pot or some other object to smooth out the reflective surface.
- ⟫ The glass screen of cellphones
- ⟫ Food or other packets that have foil interiors
- ⟫ Glossy book covers
- ⟫ Polished metal lids
- ⟫ A split log with water splashed on (the exposed white wood inside shines when it's soaked)
- ⟫ Flashes on cameras or cellphones
- ⟫ Belt buckles or any kind of metal on clothing or backpacks

Aim a reflected light signal by putting your hand out before you in line with the target, line up the mirror so it reflects light on your hand, and then quickly remove your hand. Check out the Cheat Sheet at www.dummies.com to see how to aim your signal mirror.

Even if you can't actually see someone to signal, continually sweeping the horizon with your mirror or other reflector is a good idea (ships or planes may be too far to see).

Fire

Fire can be used to signal day or night. Make yours different from a simple campfire in the following ways;

>> **Three fires in a triangle:** Pilots should recognize and report this signal. Space fires at least 75 feet apart. A straight line of three fires is sufficient if there isn't room for a triangle.

>> **A fire that flares up sharply:** Oil, gas, or any other petroleum products are good for making your fire flare up brightly when you see or hear SAR units; you can also use paper, leaves, or grass.

>> **Large bonfires:** Many pilots will report a bonfire in wilderness areas, and SAR will check them out. Keep in mind that big fires can quickly get out of control and put you in more peril.

For more on starting fires, check out Chapter 5. And for tips on escaping a forest fire, flip to Chapter 24.

Smoke

Smoke is also a good visual signal; it will be investigated by SAR in the air or on the ground.

Producing an abundance of smoke that contrasts with your environment is the key. You can create contrast and abundance in one of two ways:

>> **Black smoke:** This is your best bet in snowy conditions or when you have overcast skies. Only certain materials can produce large amounts of black smoke, so if these materials are in short supply, you may want to consider building a large fire of other materials and hold your black-smoke producers in reserve. You can then throw these items on the fire when searchers are in your vicinity. Dark smoke comes from

- Engine oil, vegetable oil, animal oils, and fats
- Rags soaked in oil
- Rubber or rubbery products, like tires
- Plastic

>> **White smoke:** White smoke is very effective in green forest environments. You can create a surge of white smoke by partially smothering a fire with:

- Green leaves or grass, or wet leaves or grass
- Moss
- Green branches
- A small amount of water or wet clothes

Pitch, sap, or resin — or wood that contains it — can make either white or black smoke, so you have to experiment.

Smoke isn't very effective in windy conditions. If it's windy, consider some other type of signal and save your materials for making colored smoke for when conditions are calmer.

Shadows

You can use shadows to make contrasting patterns that are visible from the air in sunny conditions. Sharp, hard angles and straight lines get you noticed, especially when using shadow. Make patterns at least 20 feet long. For more on the size of signal patterns and how to aim your signal mirror, see the Cheat Sheet at www. dummies.com.

You can make shadow patterns with:

>> **Built up mounds of earth.** This is useful in desert conditions, but the mounds must be substantial. To make this signal stand out, pile up sand or dirt at least 1 foot. Alternately, drag your heel in loose sand or soil to make long, straight pattern furrows.

>> **Tramp down snow.** In large, flat fields of snow these should be made very large. They're not optimal in overcast conditions or gray light.

>> **Make piles of branches, foliage, and rocks.** Make these large, obviously contrasting to the natural terrain, and with well-defined edges.

LEAVING DIRECTIONAL SIGNALS AND MESSAGES

If you have made the serious decision to move away from where you first became lost, it's important to mark your trail to help searchers find you. The trick is to leave obvious, unambiguous markers. Leave a big arrow at the place you first depart, pointing in the direction you intend to go. Then, intermittently leave clear signals; rather than just breaking one tree branch at eye height, break three.

Aside from breaking or bending vegetation, you can occasionally make a *cairn* (a pyramidal pile of stones) to indicate 'I was here.' The top cairn stone should be an oblong rock indicating your direction of travel.

Leave messages for rescuers (such as number in the party or medical condition) at the departure point and tucked in cairns. Write messages on paper and put them into a weatherproof container left somewhere visible.

Dye markers and flagging

Your survival kit (and many watercraft) may have a *dye marker*. These usually look like pouches of sand; they contain a solid dye that 'stains' large patches of water. Crush the dye to powder and use it to enhance shadow and other signal patterns if you're not on water.

A good way to signal is to fasten a bright piece of cloth to the end of a tree branch like a flag, and wave it vigorously when you hear potential rescuers. This is effective because it gives you motion and color.

Aerial flares

Aerial flares are effective day or night, on land and on water. However, most only last a few seconds, so use them sparingly and only when you're confident someone is near enough to see them. Wind can blow a flare back towards you, so be careful and follow the instructions.

Aerial flares usually come in one of two types:

>> **Pistol-fired flares:** These fly only a few hundred feet and burn only for a few seconds.

>> **Parachute-type flares, or rockets:** These flares are usually housed in their own cylinders and are sometimes labeled as *rockets*. Many reach 1,000 feet (305 meters) or more, and they usually burn up to a minute while descending on a parachute.

WARNING

Aerial flares are powerful; they can hit hard when shot and of course can cause fires. Hand-flares, like the type found in car trunks and highway emergency kits, have the tendency to drip pyrotechnics. Hold these well away from the body and keep them clear of flammable items. Some types of flares can sink an inflatable raft in the blink of an eye!

Electric lights

Use a flashlight, cellphone light, or some other light in a way that leaves no doubt that you're sending a distress signal. Flash in the SOS pattern, or using the pattern of three flashes, and do it deliberately, not haphazardly. Try to fasten a light to the end of a sturdy branch and wave it overhead. This gives the light a wide range of motion and makes you bigger, brighter, and different.

TIP

Pilots equipped with night-vision goggles see most electronic device lights as very bright points of light. If you hear aircraft approaching at night, consider moving to a clearing, turning a cellphone or laptop on so that the face lights up, and waving it vigorously in the direction you hear the aircraft.

Upside-down flags and other things out of place

You can simply put something where it doesn't belong to get attention. For example, raise the hood of your car, place a large piece of debris in a clearing, or hang flags upside down on a boat's flagpole or mast.

Signaling with Electronics

Electronics can give you peace of mind in the wilderness, but they have an important limitation: battery endurance. If you intend to rely on these in the wild, carry spare batteries and such battery supplements as solar panels.

TIP

Keep your batteries warm, dry, and protected from all fluids.

Radioing for help

Even in this era of cell- and satellite phones, ship, aircraft, and other radios can be very useful. Many of the folks who hear radio transmissions are amateur radio operators and ship captains, great allies when you're in trouble.

Tuning your radio into a distress frequency

In a survival situation you can legally use any radio transmitter set to any frequency to call for help. The best bet is to call for help on a *distress frequency*. Here's a list of the radios you're likely to run into and their respective distress frequencies:

» **VHF Radio — Channel 16:** VHF radios are common in watercraft and cars. They tend to be mounted on the overhead dash, with the microphone hanging on a hook at the unit's side. You can expect these radios to have a range of 25 to 40 miles (40 to 64 kilometers) if you're near a U.S. port or a U.S. Coast Guard installation and about a 10-mile (16-kilometer) range when transmitting to other boats on the sea. On land, the radio's range is dictated by hills and other obstacles that the radio can't transmit through. You may have a range of 40 miles or less than 1 mile.

TIP

Generally, distress signals on VHF are sent out on Channel 16. If you receive no response, try Channel 13, especially if you have a large vessel in your line-of-sight or if you find yourself in a shipping lane or near the inbound or outbound lanes near a large port. In some cases, large vessels are legally required to monitor 13.

» **CB Radio — Channel 9:** These are radios used by many long-haul truckers. These are short range, usually less than a few miles.

>> **Family Radio Service (FRS) UHF — Channel 1:** These are handheld units (walkie talkies) common worldwide. They have a very short range, usually less than a few miles.

>> **Single-sideband — 2,182 kHz:** These are long-range maritime radios found on better-equipped boats. They are for long-range communications, between 75 and 300 miles (120 and 480 kilometers), so they may send a signal that overshoots a nearby station.

>> **Shortwave (ham) radios — 2,182 kHz:** These can transmit hundreds to thousands of miles. In distress try 14.300 MHz or 14.313 MHz. These are the Maritime Networks for ham radio operators who will help you anytime you call.

If you don't have a powerful radio, you may be able to contact people who do; then they call help for you. Generally, the people who operate these types of radios are the most well-trained and experienced radio operators in the world. Distress signals sent on these radios get a very quick response.

>> **Airband Radios — 121.5 MHz and 243.0 MHz:** Use these frequencies on aircraft radios; they are monitored by many aircraft and amateurs.

Getting a clear signal

Whenever you use a radio, keep in mind that transmitting a clear signal requires a few physical actions:

>> Most radio transmitters are limited in range to *line of sight,* which means they can't send a signal around obstacles or over the horizon. Try to elevate the antenna as much as you can. If you're using a handheld radio, just getting a few feet up (standing atop a car or high on a boat) can help.

>> Make sure you know what kind of microphone the radio has: *push-to-talk* or *voice-activated*.

>> Be sure you are on the correct frequency (see the preceding section).

>> Be ready to report your position as precisely as you can; it's the most important information you can transmit in an emergency.

>> Try to keep your radio's antenna *perpendicular* to your intended receiver (not pointed at it).

TIP

If you have nothing in sight, try keeping the antenna at a right angle to the ground; Figure 12-2 shows how the signal is shaped in lobes, not straight lines.

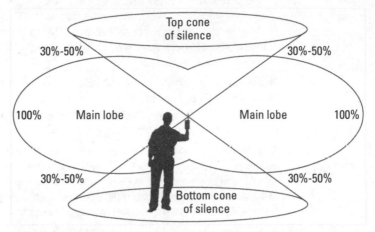

Top cone of silence

30%-50%   30%-50%

100%   Main lobe   Main lobe   100%

30%-50%   30%-50%

Bottom cone of silence

FIGURE 12-2: The shape of a signal for a radio lobe

Sending a distress call over the radio

Making a distress call over a radio is a significant event for many people. It will set in motion search-and-rescue units, volunteers, nearby vessels and aircraft, and law enforcement agencies. If you're satisfied that your situation is indeed grave, follow these directions:

1. Hold the microphone 4 inches (10 centimeters) away from your mouth and speak slowly and distinctly.

2. Call, "Mayday, Mayday, Mayday."

3. Say, "This is . . ." and then say the name of your boat or aircraft three times, or just say your name if you're not aboard a vessel.

4. Immediately give your position.

    If you don't know exactly where you are, say that you're giving an approximate position and then estimate how far you are from a prominent landmark and in what direction.

5. Give the nature of your emergency.

    For example, "My boat is sinking."

6. **Give the number of people in your party.**

7. **Give a very short description of your vessel, aircraft, or automobile if you're still near it.**

8. **Say, "Over," and then listen.**

   Try to be patient and wait for a response. Sometimes it takes a few moments.

Using cellphones

Cellphones function just like handheld radios. They can send and receive voice and text transmissions when they're in a *line of sight* of a transmission tower — in other words, they generally can't send signals around obstacles like hills or mountains or canyon walls.

There are some exceptions; cell signals can sometimes be reflected or refracted around obstacles. But gaining a clear line of sight to a distant cell tower should always be your goal when trying to call for help.

Cellphones normally have a range 5 to 25 miles when trying to reach a tower. However, many survivors have successfully sent a signal from farther than 25 miles, including your friendly authors. So, if you have the battery power, try calling even if you're far from a tower; you might get lucky.

When using a phone in a survival situation, protecting the phone and *battery discipline* are everything. The moment you become lost on land or at sea:

>> **Protect your phone in any way you can.** Wrapping it in plastic and/or cloth protect the phone from fluids and impacts.

>> **Turn down the screen brightness.** An unnecessarily bright screen drains the battery quickly. Turn off auto brightness and make sure the phone is in auto lock, which is like a screen-saver that prevents the phone from coming on and draining the battery inadvertently.

>> **Go into Settings and close all unnecessary apps that may be running in the background.** These use battery power, and you probably won't need them for a while.

>> **Watch the temperature of the phone.** Protect the phone from excessive cold or heat. Most cellphones automatically shut down once they reach 95 degrees F.

TIP

You can check the website https://www.fcc.gov/BroadbandData/ MobileMaps/mobile-mapwebappviewer to get an approximation of whether most phones will have service in the place you mean to travel. You can also call park rangers, harbor masters, and other personnel responsible for the area to ask about cellphone service before you head off into the wild.

Signaling with a charged cellphone that has reception

In a survival situation with a cell phone, dialing 911 is generally best. Even if you haven't paid your phone bill, the system will take this kind of call. (We list emergency numbers for various countries on the Cheat Sheet at www.dummies.com.) If you don't know your position and don't even have enough of a connection to talk, dialing 911 is still a good idea. *Most* modern phones transmit your location in a 911 call.

If your phone has reception but your calls are not getting through, text 911, and anyone you know who checks their texts frequently, anyway. For more on texting when you can't get through with voice, see "Signaling with a live phone that doesn't have reception" later in this chapter.

Signaling with a charged cellphone that doesn't have reception

Even if your phone indicates that it does not have a connection with a tower, keep in mind that reception indicators on cellphones measure the relative strength of the connection that your phone has with a nearby tower. That does not necessarily mean that you cannot successfully reach a tower with a text signal. There are numerous cases in which a text reached a tower when no reception was indicated on the phone. We know — we've done it!

If you are in a survival situation, but your phone is indicating that you don't have reception, you should do the following:

1. **Move to the highest place possible.**

   The higher the cell phone is, the more likely it will reach a tower. If you can't get to high ground, go to any area that gives you a better view of the horizon such as a clearing in the woods or an area in the desert that is free of large rocks.

2. **Remove anything that encases your phone.**

   Remove the phone from any case or protective wrappings; this improves your ability to send a signal.

3. **Attach your phone to a stick or other extension.** Use this to elevate the phone to the highest point possible. This can mean tying your phone to a canoe paddle, taping it to a long stick, or attaching it to some piece of debris.

4. **Prepare a short 911 text.**

   Explain your situation and give your location, as far as you know it. A 911 text will most likely communicate your location by accessing your GPS, but this should not be considered a guarantee. If you do have access to a mapping app, and you believe it to be accurate, you can take a screenshot of your location and include it in the text.

5. **When you're ready to send the text, hold the phone in your hand as high as possible (or use the stick or pole described in Step 3), and press Send.**

   If you're holding the phone in your hand, hold it with your fingertips rather than in the palm of your hand (which can impede the signal).

6. **Walk around if you can.**

   Walk in a large circle in a large open area, if possible, to increase the likelihood of reaching a tower.

7. **Repeat your text, but send it to someone who you know checks their texts often.**

   Even if you don't believe your 911 text was sent successfully, take this additional step.

When sending your texts, consider these situations to best optimize your chance of getting through:

>> **If you're moving and your phone is fully charged or nearly so, leave the phone on.** Your cellphone repeatedly tries to get through to a tower for as long as the phone is turned on, and at any time you may pass within range of a tower.

>> **If you're moving and the phone doesn't have much charge, text only at the most advantageous spots — like on the tops of hills or areas with wide visibility.** After you've texted, turn the phone off to conserve battery power. When you reach more open terrain turn the phone on and raise it as high as you can, so it can try to send the text again.

>> **If you're not moving, have no reception, and are low on battery power, shut off the phone.** Conserve your power and wait for as long as you can, then try your text again.

Signaling with a noncharged (or 'dead') cellphone

A dead cellphone can still be used to signal. The glass face of the phone, especially when polished with a clean cloth, makes an excellent reflective surface. For more on signaling with reflective surfaces, see "Mirrors and other reflectors," earlier in this chapter.

There are other uses for a dead cellphone, including using the case and/or circuit board as a sharp edge, which can be used as a cutting tool. We discuss making a cutting tool out of your dead cellphone in Chapter 14.

The battery of a cellphone can be used to start a fire. For more on starting fires with batteries, see Chapter 5.

Using satellite phones

Satellite phones (or *sat phones* for short) communicate with other telephones worldwide via satellites in Earth orbit rather than cell towers. You may travel far from towers in the wilderness, but satellites are nearly always overhead, making sat phones useful in remote areas. They are expensive and bulky, though, and are most often found on professional mountaineering and scientific expeditions.

Like any other electronic device, the sat phone requires a good battery. And they do sometimes have trouble getting reception when the sky is blocked by thick vegetation, or when you're in deep canyons. During times of large-scale calamity, like during tsunamis or hurricanes, sat phone networks can be overwhelmed by surges in traffic. Still, if you're going on a serious trip where there's no cellphone coverage, research the pros and cons of taking a sat phone.

Using radio beacons: EPIRBs, ELTs, and PLBs

Radio beacons may look like small, handheld radios, but you don't speak into them. Rather, they transmit a distress signal with your exact position to a low-orbiting satellite, which then relays this info to national search-and-rescue units. You register these devices so that when they're activated, search-and-rescue services receive info specifically about you (and/or your vessel) that could save your life.

Here are some of the most common types of beacons:

>> **Emergency position-indicating radio beacon (EPIRB):** This is a small radio beacon used for ships at sea. EPIRBs are usually yellow in color and have a simple activating mechanism that requires you to pull a small cord.

>> **Emergency locator transmitter (ELT):** Standard-issue equipment for all aircraft and similar to an EPIRB. Most people never come into contact with this type of transmitter because it's activated on impact.

>> **Personal locator beacon (PLB):** This personal, land-based equivalent of an EPIRB is usually very small, portable, and well-suited for terrestrial applications, such as backcountry hiking. Although PLBs are meant to be carried by a specific person, you can find them in small aircraft and sometimes on boats. Some outfitters now rent these units to hikers headed into backcountry.

If you buy a 406 MHz radio beacon, follow the instructions to legally register it with your country's search-and-rescue authorities.

Getting a Lift: What to Do When the Helicopter Comes

Helicopters can indeed hover and lower a basket to you, but this is a complicated process. Allowing the helicopter to land and then take you aboard is a safer option. This section discusses preparation for a landing and goes over some copter safety.

Preparing a landing zone

Your first action is to select a piece of ground suitable for landing. The following is a checklist for preparing a helicopter landing zone.

» **Choose an opening that's at least 100 feet (33 meters) across.** This is the *touchdown area,* and it's the bare minimum that most choppers can enter (see Figure 12-3). The wider the space, the better.

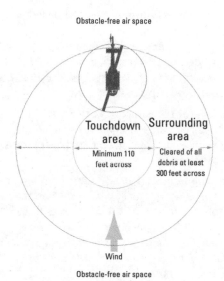

Obstacle-free air space

Touchdown area

Minimum 110 feet across

Surrounding area

Cleared of all debris at least 300 feet across

Wind

Obstacle-free air space

FIGURE 12-3: Minimum requirements for a helicopter landing zone

» **The *surrounding area*, the area near the touchdown area, needs to be wide, clear airspace if possible.** Though a helicopter can indeed hover, it's much safer for it to land and take off using forward motion.

» **Find the flattest ground you can.** Helicopters have trouble landing on slopes of more than 5 degrees to 10 degrees.

» **Clear the touchdown area.** Remove any object or plant that stands taller than 1.5 feet (0.5 meters) in the touchdown area.

>> **Remove or hold down all loose items in your landing zone, especially little things like plastic bags.** When the helicopter arrives, it can blow everything that isn't held down into the air.

Practicing helicopter safety

Here are basic points to keep in mind as the chopper lands:

>> **Stop signaling the moment you're sure the helicopter has seen you.** Pilots can be disoriented or blinded by signal lights.

>> **Put out any fires or smoke-producing devices.** The smoke can obscure the pilot's view.

>> **Be prepared to be winched if necessary.** If the helicopter can't safely land, one of two devices will be lowered to you:

- **A metal basket:** Climb into the basket, making sure nothing is hanging over the side that could get hung up during winching.

- **A strop:** This is a loop of very heavy cordage or webbing. Put both arms through the loop until it's under your armpits, and then hold your arms at your sides to prevent falling out.

    If you're at sea, static electricity builds around these devices, so when they're lowered, allow them to dip into the water first to discharge the static electricity.

>> **Try not to stand underneath a landing helicopter.** Stay well clear of the aircraft as it lands.

Here's what to do after a helicopter has landed:

>> **Wait until you're signaled to board the aircraft.**

>> **Always approach a helicopter from the front.** Remain in plain sight of the pilots or aircrew. Never approach the helicopter from the rear (check out Figure 12-4). If you do, you're walking into the pilot's blind spot and are at grave risk of injury. Stay clear of the tail and never go under the tail boom.

>> **Never approach a helicopter from higher ground.** If the aircraft is lower than you, stay well away from it until you've walked down to an even elevation.

>> **Keep long-handled objects out of the way.** Carry long-handled items like ice axes, ski poles, walking sticks, or digging implements low and parallel to the ground.

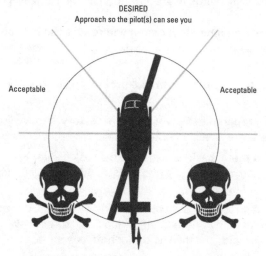

DESIRED
Approach so the pilot(s) can see you

Acceptable   Acceptable

Anywhere behind the midline is dangerous and must be avoided.

FIGURE 12-4: Safe helicopter approach zones

Chapter **13**
Administering First Aid

You can make a quantum leap in your ability to survive by knowing basic first aid. In this chapter, you find the step-by-step procedures you need to know when you face trauma in the field. We give you advice for dealing with injuries of all types, including animal attacks and insect stings.

Of course, how much first aid you can pick up from a book is limited, so consider taking a course on Basic Life Support or first aid.

Prioritizing First Aid Basics

Wilderness injuries come in many forms, from near-drowning to fire injuries, broken bones, and animal bites. It's vital to organize and prioritize your response to such injuries.

Various authorities provide a myriad of responses according to the environment, the resources available, and the training level of the people involved. We've distilled these ideas into a general-purpose set of priorities for immediate response to serious trauma, for people with little training and few resources in wilderness situations. Keep this system in mind, perhaps write it on a card to keep in your survival kit.

Responding to serious trauma, an overview

Medical crises in wilderness survival situations normally start with a 'person down' scenario, any situation in which someone is so injured that they cannot help themselves (and have normally fallen to the ground). We summarize the steps in this section, but never fear — they're discussed in more detail later in this chapter. First, become familiar with the recommended sequence of events, termed the *initial assessment*:

1. Move the injured person away from danger.

Be on guard for whatever may have caused the injury — rock falls, burning vehicles, poisonous gasses, and so on. Remove injured persons from danger using the *clothes drag* — grasp the shirt collar at the lowest point you can and, keeping your buttocks low, drag the subject gently out of danger (see Figure 13-1a).

WARNING

Moving someone with a neck or spinal injury can cause further damage. You must weigh the immediate danger against the danger of worsening an injury. If danger is imminent, support the neck with your hands or an improvised brace (see Figure 13-1b), then perform the clothes drag.

FIGURE 13-1: Performing the clothes drag (a) and immobilizing a neck injury (b)

2. **Quickly identify and treat major hemorrhage (bleeding).**

   Massive bleeding can kill in half a minute, so administering CPR may have to wait. Checking the body for such bleeding should only take about 10 seconds (though internal injuries probably won't be evident).

3. **Evaluate the subject's circulation, airway, and breathing (CAB) and begin CPR if needed.**

   This should also be done quickly with the methods we describe in the upcoming section.

4. **Protect wounds and immobilize fractures.**

5. **Treat for shock.**

Checking circulation, airway, and breathing

When an injured person is free of immediate danger and any massive bleeding is halted or slowed, you must check their circulation, airway, and breathing (CAB). Note that some outdoor medicine experts suggest checking CAB before even looking for and stopping massive bleeding; you'll have to decide for yourself, depending on the situation.

Circulation

Try to detect a pulse at the *carotid artery*, a large blood vessel in the neck. To find this vessel, place your first two fingers on the Adam's apple and then slide them over to where the windpipe meets the neck muscle (see Figure 13-2a).

To measure the heart rate per minute, count the pulses you feel in a 10-second period and then multiply by 6. Healthy rates vary, but adults should have more than about 60 beats per minute, children 90 or more.

A rapid pulse may be a sign of shock (see the later section "Treating Shock"). If you find no pulse, begin CPR (see the later section "Giving CPR"). Otherwise, if the person has a stable pulse and is breathing, put the subject in the recovery position, described in the "Using the recovery position" section later in this chapter.

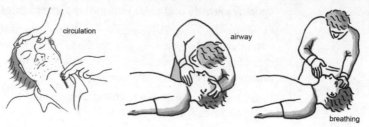

FIGURE 13-2: Checking circulation, airway, and breathing

Airway

Ensure a clear airway with these steps (see Figure 13-2b):

1. **Lay the palm of one hand on the subject's forehead and put two fingers of the other hand under their chin, pulling the jaw forward; then ease the subject's head back a couple of inches.**

   Skip this step if you suspect a broken neck.

2. **Open the mouth gently and examine the airway for obstruction.**

3. **If you can see anything blocking the airway (vomit, blood, broken teeth), use two fingers to reach in and pull it out.**

Breathing

Try to detect breathing by placing your cheek right next to the person's mouth (see Figure 13-2b). Listen for sucking noises coming from the upper body; these may indicate a punctured lung (see "Bandaging a sucking chest wound" later in this chapter).

If you can't detect breathing:

1. **Check for a pulse.**

   We describe how to take a pulse in the previous "Circulation" section.

2. **If you find a pulse but no breathing, the person is in respiratory arrest, which you address with _rescue breathing_.**

3. **To begin rescue breathing, pinch the person's nose completely shut, seal your mouth over theirs, and give them a one-second long, steady breath every 6 to 8 seconds.**

Watch for the chest to expand when you're administering these breaths.

4. **If the torso doesn't expand, check the person's airway again.**

If you can't find anything blocking the airway, try pushing three to five times forcefully on the subject's abdomen, halfway between the breastbone and belly button. This may eject the blockage.

5. **Continue rescue breathing until the person responds.**

People commonly vomit during mouth-to-mouth resuscitation; simply clear this away with your fingers.

Using the recovery position

If the person's circulation, airway, and breathing are fine but the subject is unconscious, place them in the *recovery position*, which allows fluids or vomit to drain from the mouth and keeps the tongue from blocking the airway. *Remember:* If you believe the injured person has a neck or spinal injury, don't place that person in the recovery position unless you've first immobilized the neck (refer to Figure 13-1b).

To place someone in the recovery position, reach across, grasp the subject's leg behind the knee, and pull the leg toward you. Place the leg at a 90-degree angle so that it props up the body (see Figure 13-3). You want the subject to end up with the following:

>> One leg and one arm raised

>> Head resting on an arm

>> Mouth free of obstruction

Ideally, you want to place the subject in the horizontal recovery position, with the head below the feet, to help treat shock. For info on shock, see "Treating Shock," later in this chapter.

FIGURE 13-3: The recovery position

Giving CPR

Anyone who plans to spend a good deal of time outdoors should know the principles of *cardiopulmonary resuscitation* (CPR), a method of supporting the heart and breathing until rescue crews arrive or until the subject is breathing on their own. CPR is best administered by someone who has received formal training. To find a CPR course near you, consult the Red Cross at www.redcross.org.

Here are the four main steps of CPR on adults; it is best to get training and practice them.

1. Kneel next to the patient so you can perform CPR without needing to moving around the body.

2. Place two fingers at the bottom of the person's breastbone and then place the heel of your hand just above the fingers; your hand should be near the center of the person's chest (nowhere near the abdomen) as shown in Figure 13-4a. Now interlock the fingers as shown in Figure 13-4b.

3. Using a straight-armed stance and a steady, smooth motion, lean forward to compress the breastbone down about 2 inches (5 centimeters), and then come back up, releasing pressure (see Figure 13-4c).

   You should try to do compressions at a rate of slightly more than one per second. The beat of the hit song 'Stayin' Alive' is considered ideal as a timekeeper for CPR rhythm.

4. **After every 15 compressions, pinch the person's nostrils together and give two slow breaths (see Figure 13-4d).**

Continue CPR until the person resuscitates (check the person's pulse and breathing on occasion) or until you're exhausted.

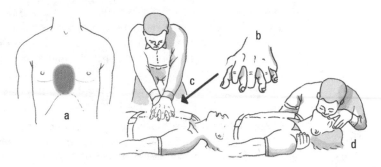

FIGURE 13-4: Administering CPR

Note: There's some debate about whether to give rescue breaths during CPR. In most wilderness survival cases, where help may be a long time coming, if at all, it's still recommended to provide more oxygen in hopes of reviving the unresponsive person.

Controlling Bleeding

There are three main types of bleeding: capillary, venous, and arterial. The following sections describe these types of visible bleeding and how to control them. Unfortunately there is no practical solution to internal bleeding in wilderness situations.

Treating common capillary and venous bleeding

Capillary and venous bleeding are the two most common types of bleeding. *Capillary* bleeding is usually not serious, coming from the small blood vessels near the skin. More serious is *venous* bleeding from larger blood vessels; this blood is darker and perhaps maroon.

A good way to stop serious bleeding is with a *blood clotting agent*; normally in the form of a powder or sponge kept in a first aid kit, these invaluable chemical treatments are applied to the bleeding site and rapidly clot the blood.

If you don't have a blood clotting agent on hand, use one of these methods instead:

>> **Direct pressure:** Apply pressure directly to the wound with a bandage or with your hand if you have nothing else. Apply pressure for 10 to 15 minutes or more and resist the urge to look at the wound during that time. If the blood doesn't coagulate, press for another 15 minutes and consider applying indirect pressure to a pressure point near the wound (see the next bullet point for details).

REMEMBER

Never apply direct pressure to a bleeding neck wound. This can interfere with breathing and circulation to the brain. In the case of a bleeding neck wound, try to carefully pinch the wound closed with your fingers and hold it until bleeding stops by coagulation.

TIP

If you need to continue applying pressure but are unable to do so manually, you can apply a pressure bandage. For more on applying a pressure bandage, see "Cleaning and covering wounds," later in this chapter.

>> **Indirect pressure:** As a desperate measure, apply pressure at one of the body's main *pressure points* (see Figure 13-5). If you can't locate an exact pressure point, experiment by exerting pressure at the joint just above the injury. Pressure points may be hard to find and use to control bleeding, but in a survival situation, you must try everything.

>> **Elevation:** When possible, simply raising the wound so that it's above the heart can slow the blood loss significantly.

Handling dangerous arterial bleeding

Arterial bleeding occurs when one of the body's arteries has been injured, resulting in large volumes of bright red blood spurting or pulsing from the body. When this happens, you can

>> Put one or two fingers into the wound (instead of over the wound) to stop the bleeding. This may be the only way to stay alive.

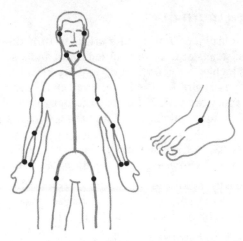

FIGURE 13-5: Pressure points where you can apply indirect pressure to help slow or stop bleeding

>> Try to staunch the flow of blood by exerting pressure on a pressure point above the wound. (Refer to Figure 13-5 for where the pressure points are.)

>> Apply a tourniquet if the situation is dire. A *tourniquet* is a band you apply with extreme compression to cut off circulation. Keep reading for more info on safely using a tourniquet.

Deciding to use a tourniquet

WARNING

Use a tourniquet only when the subject is in clear and immediate danger of bleeding to death. The tourniquet is an absolute last resort because it can cause severe tissue damage leading to loss of the limb later on; but this is preferable to bleeding to death, so a tourniquet is an option in life-or-death situations.

REMEMBER

Traumatic amputation, such as when a limb is severed or torn off as a result of an accident or an animal attack, doesn't necessarily warrant a tourniquet. The muscles in the remaining portion of the limb may spasm and close the blood vessels, reducing the flow of blood from the wound.

Applying a tourniquet

To make a tourniquet, you need a stick (to turn the tourniquet so that it constricts around the injured limb) and a strap or band preferably 3 inches (7.5 centimeters) or more in width. (*Tip:* If you must use rope or wire for the band, wrap cloth under or around the line to reduce the pain and damage from the tourniquet.) Follow these directions and check out Figure 13-6 for a visual.

1. Apply the tourniquet just above the bleeding site and tie it off only as much as is necessary to stop the arterial bleeding.

    To tighten the tourniquet, thread the stick under the band and then twist so the tourniquet constricts on the injured limb, cutting off or radically reducing blood loss.

2. If the bleeding hasn't stopped after an hour or so, and you know that no help is coming for at least 2 hours, loosen the tourniquet on occasion to see if blood has clotted significantly to reduce blood flow.

    After several hours of use, the chance of losing the limb is significantly increased — but this outcome is better than bleeding to death in the wild.

    Apply direct pressure to the wound as you loosen the tourniquet. If the bleeding is still severe, retighten. If the bleeding is manageable, leave the tourniquet in place but don't tighten. The bleeding could increase and you may have to retighten in a few minutes.

3. **If the person is breathing and has a pulse, and if the bleeding is either under control or absent, treat immediately for shock (covered in the following section).**

REMEMBER

Never cover a tourniquet. Leave it exposed so that emergency personnel can see it if they arrive to help. You can also write *TK* on the subject's forehead so that rescuers know this extreme treatment is in use. And, of course, never apply a tourniquet to a neck wound.

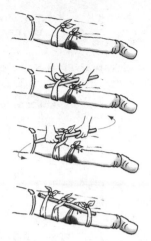

FIGURE 13-6: Applying a tourniquet

Treating Shock

Shock is a bodily response to inadequate blood flow. Low blood pressure effects all the body's functions, especially the brain, and they begin to shut down, which can be fatal. Shock can result from of a wide variety of traumas. The most common signs of shock are:

>> Cold, clammy skin

>> Acute anxiety, psychological distress, or disorientation

>> Bluish lips and extremities

>> Rapid pulse

>> Sensation of thirst

Because shock is a reaction to trauma, your first priority is to make sure that none of the subject's traumas are life-threatening. If the patient is breathing, has a heartbeat, and isn't severely bleeding, treatment for shock is as follows (see Figure 13-7; if you're alone, you must do these for yourself):

>> **Maintain the subject's body temperature.** Insulate the subject with blankets or other covers. If it's hot out, find shade and try pouring cool fluids onto a rag or sheet and then gently administering the cooling cloth to the subject's body.

>> **Try to calm the subject.** Stay near the subject and be reassuring, upbeat, and firm. People in shock can benefit greatly from reassurance.

>> **Lay the subject down and elevate the feet.** The proper position depends on whether the subject is conscious:

  • **Conscious:** Lay the person on his back and elevate the feet about 12 inches (30 centimeters) to improve the blood flow to the brain. Don't let the person smoke, eat, or drink.

  • **Unconscious:** Lay the person on their side, supporting the neck, and elevate the feet 12 inches. Make sure the airway is clear and that the subject is breathing. Do *not* attempt to give fluids to someone who's unconscious.

    If the subject has a head injury, don't elevate the feet. Just keep the subject warm and calm.

REMEMBER

>> **Continue to monitor the subject.** Be on guard and ready to treat for shock even if the subject is conscious and doesn't immediately feel pain or other discomfort. If the subject is unconscious, watch for changes in breathing, temperature, and circulation, and try to keep the subject in the recovery position (refer to Figure 13-3). Anything other than dry, healthy-pink skin and a normal body temperature can indicate the patient is still in shock.

FIGURE 13-7: Treating conscious and unconscious subjects for shock

Handling Breaks and Sprains

Any one of the common conditions that follow can debilitate you in the wilderness, and as we tell you at the beginning of this chapter, just knowing the basic procedures can mean the difference between life and death. In this section, we explain how to deal with broken bones, soft tissue injuries, and wounds.

Treating fractures

A *fracture* is a break in a bone, usually from some type of force-trauma. If you don't treat this type of injury, it can cause permanent damage and/or internal injuries. It can also seriously hamper your ability to travel, build fires and shelters, or otherwise move around without causing pain to the injury.

TIP

As soon as you believe you or someone else has sustained a fracture (or a sprain), you should assume the injured limb is going to swell. Remove wristwatches, jewelry, or any type of constrictive clothing near the injury.

In treating any fracture, strive to immobilize the part of the body that sustained the trauma. Immobilizing a fracture prevents the broken bone from doing more damage, and it makes transport of the subject possible.

There are two types of fractures, classified according to whether the bone breaks through skin: open and closed. The following sections explain how to treat them.

Closed fractures

Closed fractures, in which the broken bone doesn't break through skin, can be difficult to identify. Signs that a person has a closed fracture include the following:

>> Immediate swelling, usually in the form of a knot or lump

>> Tenderness at the site of the trauma

>> A grating sound when trying to move

>> An unnaturally bent or crooked limb or joint

To immobilize the fracture, apply a splint (see Figure 13-8). A *splint* is simply a rigid support, firmly attached above and below the fracture point. You can use poles, sticks, rolled newspapers, or anything else that's strong and firm as the support for your splint.

TIP

Try to use cloth to tie the splint and try to use square knots or bows that you can easily undo (go to Chapter 14 for more on knots). Always try to align all the knots on one side of the splint.

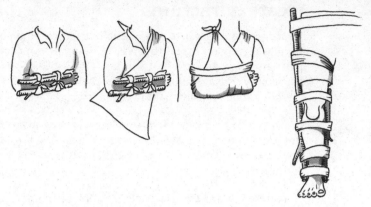

FIGURE 13-8: Splinting broken bones

If a limb is bent at such an angle that you can't immobilize the fracture, you can try applying *traction* — a gentle straightening of the limb — so you can apply a splint. Traction should be relatively painless, especially if you perform it before the swelling becomes excessive. To apply traction, gently pull the misaligned part of the limb away from the fracture and move it slowly toward alignment. If this causes any appreciable pain in the subject, stop. Sometimes you can perform traction only in small movements.

REMEMBER

After you perform traction on a fracture, you need to check for circulation at the extremity of the limb. If you feel no pulses, or if the skin is discolored beyond a fracture, you may have to realign the fracture to restore circulation. If circulation is okay, go ahead and apply the splint.

Open fractures

You can quickly identify *open fractures* because when the bone breaks, it pierces the skin.

WARNING

Open fractures are exceedingly susceptible to infection, so now's the time to put on sterile gloves, wash your hands, wear a mask — do whatever you can to keep things sterile with the supplies you have. Try not to breathe on the wound, and don't touch the protruding bone directly.

Here's how to treat an open fracture in the wild (see Figure 13-9a):

1. **Apply traction if necessary (as we explain in the preceding section).**

2. **If bleeding is severe, apply direct pressure to the wound or skin near the break.**

   Try pushing downward on either side of the bone to stop the bleeding, but don't put any pressure directly on the bone (refer to Figure 13-9b). For more on applying direct pressure to stop bleeding, see "Treating capillary and venous bleeding."

3. **Pad around and protect the bone before bandaging.**

   You can do this by putting a protective housing over it, such as a clean plastic cup, or you can use rolled gauze (Figure 13-9c). Afterward, apply the proper dressing and bandage. For more on that, see "Cleaning and covering wounds," later in this chapter.

4. **Bandage firmly (Figure 13-9d) and then pinch the limb's extremity to make sure circulation is adequate.**

   For more on checking for blood flow by pinching the skin, see the upcoming section, "Treating sprains."

   The limb is now ready to splint, as we explain in the preceding section.

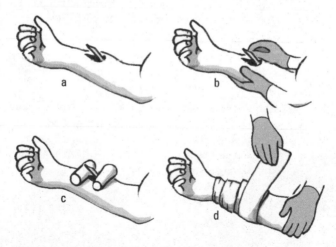

FIGURE 13-9: Padding and bandaging an open fracture

Treating sprains

You can think of sprains and pulled muscles as *soft tissue injuries*, which means that the bone hasn't been damaged. You suffer these types of injuries because of stresses on joints, muscles, and damage to tendons. They can be just as debilitating and painful as fractures. In the field, you may not be able to tell the difference between a fracture and a sprain. If you can't tell, put a splint on the damaged site to immobilize it.

To treat a sprain, use the memory tool RICES:

TIP

>> **Rest:** Give the limb at least 72 hours rest, if you can, or it won't heal. Rest can mean simply minimizing motion, although no motion at all is the best.

>> **Ice (cold therapy):** Apply cold to the injury for 15 to 20 minutes every 3 to 4 hours. Do not apply continuous cold therapy, and don't apply ice directly to the skin; always wrap the ice in cloth.

>> **Compression:** After applying cold, wrap the injury in a *compression bandage* (any bandage that applies pressure), like an elastic Ace bandage (see Figure 13-10a). The bandage should be snug but not constricting.

After you apply the bandage, pinch a finger or toe on the injured limb to see whether the blood is circulating properly. If you don't see a noticeable flood of blood under the skin after you pinch it, you've put the bandage on too tightly, and you have to rewrap the injury.

>> **Elevation:** Elevate the limb by propping it up about 6 inches to 1 foot (15 to 30.5 centimeters) on something soft. This cuts down on swelling and throbbing.

>> **Stabilization:** Don't move the injury and take precautions to prevent an object or person from bumping into or striking the damaged limb. In the case of a sprained wrist or arm, you can use a sling to immobilize it, or you can simply tie the limb to the person's body.

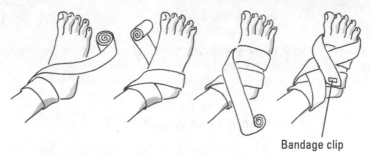

Bandage clip

FIGURE 13-10: Wrapping a sprained ankle

Cleaning and Covering Wounds

You should bandage any wound, no matter how small, to protect it from infection. Take three important steps: clean the wound, dress it, and then bandage the wound. This section explains how to do all three.

Cleaning wounds to reduce infection

Before you start to dress or cover the wound, take a moment to clean it. Cleaning the wound reduces the risk of infection, which could slowly incapacitate you. When cleaning the wound, keep in mind these basic guidelines:

>> **Operate cleanly.** Try to use sterile gloves when handling a wound. If you don't have them, wash your hands thoroughly with soap and water if possible, or use alcohol or hand sanitizer.

>> **Irrigate the wound to remove debris.** Use a flow of clean water to wash debris out of a wound instead of removing it with your hands or with a cloth, because your hands usually have unwanted bacteria on them. If clean water is unavailable, you may need to remove grit and dirt with tweezers (make sure your first aid kit has a set).

>> **Use soap and water.** Washing a wound with common soap and then rinsing it with clean water can do more to prevent infection than anything else. The iodine or antiseptic wipes in most first aid kits are fine, but you should use them only if you don't have soap and water.

Don't use antiseptics on deep wounds. Antiseptics are for small, shallow wounds.

>> **Clean the wound from the center, outward.** If you clean from the outside toward the center, you risk bringing in dirt and germs from the surrounding skin.

Dressing the wound

Cleaned wounds are ready for a *dressing*, such as sterile gauze or some other clean, lint-free material, that protects the injured area. Remember the following points:

>> **Make sure the dressing is the right size.** It should be large enough to extend well beyond the wound's edges.

>> **Without touching any of the surrounding skin, place the dressing directly on the injured site.** Skin isn't sterile, so avoid sliding or dragging the dressing over the wound.

>> **If blood soaks through your dressing, don't take the dressing off.** Instead, put another one directly over the first.

Bandaging the wound

With your dressing in place, you're ready to apply a *bandage*, which holds the dressing on the wound. When you bandage, keep the following guidelines in mind:

>> **Use nonfluffy cloth, such as fabric from a shirt, as your first option.** If you don't have any, then you can use almost anything else.

>> **Make your bandages wide.** Roll the bandage in a wide area to spread the friction and force, and tape the bandage to itself, not to the skin.

>> **Apply bandages firmly and secure them with tape or safety pins or tie them with a square knot directly over the dressing.** To see how to tie a square knot, see Chapter 14.

>> **Monitor the circulation.** Keep an eye on circulation, because cutting off the blood flow with a bandage is all too easy. If blood is flowing properly, you should see a rapid return of blood under the skin after you pinch it.

Periodically check bandages, and the wounds under them, to make sure infection isn't setting in. For more on infections, see the later section "Treating infections in wounds."

Closing open wounds

If you encounter a clean, open wound (free of dirt or debris), try to close it to avoid infection. There's little reason to sew up wounds in most outdoor situations, but you can essentially tape a wound shut:

>> **Butterfly bandages:** This is an adhesive strip shaped like a butterfly--when applying, make sure that the wide parts (the 'wings') grab the skin on either side of the injury, with the thin part stretched across the closed wound.

>> **Tape:** If you're desperate, you can use strong tape to close a wound. Bring the edges of the flesh *loosely* together with adhesive tape or, in dire circumstances, a safety pin.

Bandaging a sucking chest wound

A *sucking chest wound* is evident if the patient has trouble breathing, and/or there are bubbles and a sucking sound at the chest. Left untreated this causes lung collapse. Take action immediately:

1. **Put the palm of your hand over the wound to seal it shut.**

   This can prevent the lung from collapsing.

2. **Quickly bandage the wound on only three sides.**

   Place sterile gauze over the puncture and then tape it in so that one side is left unattached. In a pinch, you can tape plastic wrap over the puncture.

   The gauze or dressing should lie down snugly over the hole. When the subject inhales, you want the bandage to close tightly over the puncture, like a one-way valve; when the subject exhales, you want the air to escape.

Treating infected wounds

Despite cleaning and washing, some wounds still become infected. While not as dramatic as broken limbs or massive bleeding, we know from gruesome experience in jungles, and at sea, that infection can be just as debilitating as any broken bone. Symptoms of infection include:

>> Inflammation, redness, and pain at the wound

>> Elevated temperature at the wound (the skin feels hot)

>> Reduction of mobility in the limb

>> Presence of fluid discharge (pus) from the wound

Treatments include:

>> **Rest:** This may not be possible in a wilderness survival situation, but if you can't rest the whole body, try to rest the infected area so the body's defenses can go to work.

>> **Heat therapy:** Apply very warm, moist bandages over the wound for half an hour, three times daily. A clean, sterile cloth soaked in hot water is ideal.

>> **Daily wound cleaning:** If you collect foreign matter in the wound, or if it appears infected, wash the wound with soap and water.

>> **Antibiotics:** Antibiotics can fight infection, but in many survival situations, broad-range antibiotics aren't always effective. Before going into the field, check with your doctor to find which antibiotics have proven effective for treating infections in the area you're planning to travel in.

Treating Burns

Burns threaten your life in two major ways: shock and infection.

When you're burned, your body leaks fluid in response, which you can think of as "clear bleeding." Burns also damage the body's protective layer, making you more susceptible to infection.

In this section, we tell you how to treat burns, both minor and severe. (For information on treating sunburn, see Chapter 17.)

Handling minor burns

Superficial burns and scalds can be treated by following these directions:

1. **Remove jewelry and clothing.**

You don't want anything to impede the swelling that accompanies all burns.

2. **Pour cool liquid over the burn site for at least 10 minutes.**

Other clean fluids will help to soothe the pain and prevent excessive inflammation

3. **Bandage the wound according to the guidelines in the "Cleaning and covering wounds" section, earlier in this chapter.**

Try to be as clean and sterile as you can, because burns invite infection.

REMEMBER

Don't break or burst blisters; this interferes with the healing process and could introduce infection. Cover blisters with a protective bandage, like the type used to protect an open fracture (see the earlier section "Treating fractures").

Dealing with more-severe burns

Severe burns char and otherwise disfigure the skin. Treat with these steps:

1. **Lay the subject on a clean patch of ground, taking special care that the burned area doesn't come into contact with the ground.**

2. **Douse the burn with cool liquid immediately to stop the burning process.**

TIP

If you're short on water, put some kind of receptacle or dish underneath the subject so that you can catch the poured water and recycle it over the wound. Continuously pour water over the wound as needed for pain.

3. **Check the subject's airway, breathing, and circulation and treat as needed.**

4. **Remove constricting jewelry or smoldering clothing near the burn site.**

5. **Apply a sterile bandage.**

See "Cleaning and Covering Wounds," earlier in this chapter.

Treating Hypothermia

In this section, we discuss a common outdoor condition, hypothermia (the cooling of the body). We cover extreme environment maladies in other chapters, such as dehydration in hot regions (Chapters 7 and 17) and preventing frostbite in cold conditions (Chapter 16).

When your body cools below the optimal temperature of 97–98.6°F (36.1–37°C), you begin to feel the effects of *hypothermia*. This shuts down bodily systems and can be lethal. (Chapters 4, 5, and 6 have tips on how clothing, fire, and shelter can help you avoid hypothermia.)

Hypothermia is a *progressive condition*; the longer it's left untreated, the more dangerous it becomes. If you notice initial symptoms, such as shivering, do something immediately, such as putting on an extra layer of clothing. Signs of hypothermia include:

>> Vigorous shivering

>> Bluish coloring

>> Apathy and the desire to lie down or give up

>> Dizziness, disorientation, slurred speech

>> A total cessation of shivering even though the patient is very cold (very dangerous)

The basic treatment for hypothermia is as follows:

1. **Try to keep the hypothermic subject horizontal.**

   When dealing with water casualties, try to hoist the subject out of the water horizontally rather than head first. In any case, try to keep the subject's heart level with the head. In extreme circumstances, turning the subject vertical can cause cardiac arrest.

2. **Remove wet clothing.**

If possible, replace wet clothing with dry clothing.

3. **Rewarm slowly and steadily, monitoring the subject very closely.**

Rewarming a hypothermia subject too fast can cause shock or cardiac arrest, so watch closely and be ready to perform CPR. Rewarm the patient slowly, following these steps:

1. **Apply sources of warmth slowly, gently, and steadily, starting with the chest.**

   Work steadily by applying warm rocks, hot water bottles, warm hands, or anything else you can to warm the skin of the upper torso.

2. **Warm the neck and crotch.**

   Don't rewarm the limbs; this causes the subject's body to divert precious blood to those areas, which can cause shock, stroke, or cardiac arrest.

3. **Insulate the subject with a blanket, sleeping bag, and/or your survival kit's space blanket.**

   Always use some insulation to keep them insulated from the ground; this could be a sleeping mat or a pile of vegetation. Modern wilderness medicine points out that getting into a sleeping bag with a severe hypothermia patient is ineffective.

Never assume that a hypothermia subject is out of trouble after being rewarmed. All hypothermia subjects are at risk for *afterdrop*, a continued cooling of the body even after exposure to heat. Don't take your eyes off your subject. Stay with the person and treat for shock and exhaustion.

Treating Bites, Stings, and Poisonings

In case of an animal attack, your first priority is to make sure that you and the subject are no longer in danger. Your second priority is to record accurate information that you can pass on to the medical team when you reach professional help. Specifically note the following:

>> **The type of creature or source of poisoning:** For instance, record the color and shape of the spider. Most effective treatments are specially designed for a particular species or substance.

>> **The condition an animal was in:** Notes on obviously sick animals can help doctors choose treatments or watch for specific signs of disease.

>> **When the incident occurred:** Some treatments depend on the time that has expired since the bite, sting, or poisoning.

This section provides some basic advice for treating bites, stings, and poisonings when medical help isn't nearby.

Mammal bites

If you're attacked by a mammal, follow these steps:

>> **For superficial bites:** These are basic punctures and scratches. Clean and bandage the wound as we describe earlier in this chapter.

>> **For serious bites and attacks:** In case of a deep punctures, gouging or dismembering, concentrate on stopping the bleeding even before worrying about infection. Tightly bandage the wound and then get help or transport the subject out of the wild as soon as possible. If that is not possible, try to keep the wound properly dressed and bandaged. Deep bites carry the risk of rabies or tetanus infection, but you cannot do anything about this in the wild.

Snakebites

Lethal snake venom usually takes several hours to kill a person. However, venomous snakes usually don't inject enough toxin during a strike to kill an adult human. In fact, bite marks don't necessarily mean that the snake has discharged venom at all. Still, any snakebite can cause infections, so take all snake bites seriously.

Monitor the subject for at least 2 hours after they've been bitten. Watch for the signs of envenomation:

>> Continuous extreme pain at the bite site

>> Head and muscle aches

>> Dizziness, nausea, and sweating

>> Difficulty breathing and shock

The main concern after an envenomation is to slow the spread of poison. Here are the steps you should take after envenomation (*Note:* In some countries the advice for treating snakebites varies from what we provide here, so check with local experts about the specific snake hazards):

1. **Try to identify the snake.**

   Most antivenins (also called antivenoms) are engineered to work against venom from only one type of snake, so knowing exactly which type of snake bit the subject is critical.

   When trying to identify or catch the snake, keep in mind that a dead snake can still strike from reflex and that the venom is still just as potent.

REMEMBER

2. **Make sure the bite is lower than the subject's heart at all times.**

3. **Work to calm the subject.**

   Anxiety raises heart rate, distributing the poison faster. Try to remain calm, which helps the patient to be calm.

4. **Wash the wound.**

   Soak up any venom that may be near the fang marks, wash the site (with soap and water if possible) and pat it dry.

5. **Apply a pressure bandage.**

   This is a simply a compression bandage that starts below the wound, winds tightly toward the bite site, and then continues above it as high as possible. For example, if you're bitten on the ankle, you start bandaging at the toes, winding tightly upwards, covering the bite and continuing up all the way to the knee or higher. Binding as tightly as you would for a sprained ankle helps slow or stop the flow of toxin through the body. *Remember:* Don't wind so tight as to cut off circulation.

6. Immobilize the limb.

This prevents movement and reduces poison circulation. Be ready to treat for shock and to perform CPR (covered earlier in this chapter).

REMEMBER

The best treatment for a venomous snakebite is the administration of antivenin, so get to the hospital as soon as you can. In a wilderness survival situation of course, this may not be possible, in which case you must let the victim rest and hope their body can handle the bite.

Spider bites and insect stings

Most spider bites and insect stings are merely itchy or painful, but others can cause allergic reactions, paralysis, tissue damage, or death. Avoidance, of course, is the best course of action. (For more on avoiding spider bites and insect stings, see Chapter 15.)

Of the dangerous spiders, black widows, brown recluses, and tarantulas tend to cause the most harm. Brown recluse bites are usually the worst; they are painful and normally result in a large pustule at the bite site. This usually ruptures and the dead tissue around it falls away in 10 to 14 days. Black widow bites usually cause pain and even partial paralysis, usually for no more than 24 hours; bites are rarely fatal. Tarantula bites are painful but rarely fatal.

In any bite or sting situation, follow these instructions:

1. Try to identify the insect or spider.

Try to catch or photograph the animal, or at least its shape and coloring.

2. Check the subject's Circulation, Airway, and Breathing.

Use the methods described earlier in this chapter. Also watch for difficulties swallowing and choking, which are signs of anaphylactic shock.

3. Try to calm and reassure the person who's been stung.

Anxiety and high heart rate only amplify the symptoms.

4. **Remove the stinger or mouthparts if they're still in the skin.**

   If the stinger has been left in, scrape it off with a piece of paper, the edge of a knife, or a similar tool. Don't use tweezers for this procedure, which can squeeze the poison sac and just inject more venom.

TIP

   Ticks anchor to the skin with barbed mouthparts that break off and stay inside you if you remove them the wrong way. To force a tick to release, grasp it at the precise point where it enters the skin, preferably with tweezers, and pull slowly and steadily. Your skin should rise slightly with the pull; hold this pressure anywhere from 10 seconds to 2 or 3 minutes, but it should release. Don't crush or twist the tick's body, you want it to stay alive so it can disengage cleanly.

5. **Wash the sting or bite site with soap and water, and then apply cold compresses.**

6. **Monitor the subject for an allergic reaction or shock, and be ready to give CPR.**

   Insects pose the greatest threat when they inflict multiple stings. Even if you're not allergic, multiple hornet stings or ant bites can cause you to go into anaphylactic shock. Always take multiple sting situations seriously.

Poisoning

Unlike venom, which critters inject, a *poison* is a substance you ingest through your food or water. You can avoid eating poisonous plants by performing the Universal Plant Edibility Test, which we outline in Chapter 8.

The common symptoms of poisoning are

>> Nausea, vomiting, abdominal cramps, and/or diarrhea

>> Weakness

>> Sweating

>> Seizures

If the subject has lost consciousness due to suspected poisoning, put them in the recovery position (Figure 13-3) and monitor their airway. The subject may vomit, which can obstruct the breathing.

Try to identify what caused the poisoning; what have they recently eaten? Did they drink unprocessed water? Treatment depends on the nature of the poisoning, so you may have to make a judgment call. If someone has recently eaten a poisonous plant — and is conscious and coherent — that person can put a finger down their throat to induce vomiting and attempt to get it out of their system. However, note that vomiting up caustic substances can burn the throat. Many times, food- and water-related poisonings result in cramps and/or diarrhea, for which the main wilderness treatment is rest and hydration, allowing the body to fight the infection.

Chapter **14**

Survive or Thrive? Advanced Methods and Tools

The skills in this chapter supplement the basics we have covered so far, and can help change you from an intruder in the wild to more of a natural. But remember — nothing beats practice, so try these ideas out at home before you really need them.

In this chapter, we give you a basic primer on rope, knots, and lashings, we show you how to make tools, weapons, and rope, and we tell you about a few medicinal plants.

Keeping It Together: Ropes and Knots

Even possessing just a few skills with rope (also referred to as *cordage*) can give you tremendous confidence in the wild. This section introduces the main types of rope and shows you the essential knots and lashings for wilderness survival.

Understanding rope strength

Rope is often used to bear a load, so it's important to be familiar with how strong your rope is. Various factors effect rope strength, however, including the following:

>> **Shock puts tremendous strain on rope.** When you're estimating whether your rope can hold a certain amount of weight, you will generally want thicker rope if you expect sudden snaps or shocks than if you are applying the load slowly.

>> **Ropes lose strength over time.** Ropes that are bleached by sun, are flakey or powdery, and/or are nicked, fuzzy, or covered with burrs should be considered of suspect strength.

>> **Knots weaken rope.** Knots weaken rope strength by 30 to 60 percent.

>> **Braided rope is stronger than laid rope.** Ropes that are *braided,* or woven together, are stronger than ropes of the same size and material but are *laid* (twisted).

The following list names the main types of rope you're likely to use in your travels, from strongest to weakest:

>> **Spectra/Dyneema:** Modern synthetic ropes are many times stronger than steel, and come in diameters from a few millimeters to about 10 millimeters. They hold knots well and don't stretch, so a sudden load on them can be very jarring.

>> **Nylon:** This fiber is used for climbing ropes and boat anchor lines because it's both strong and somewhat elastic, acting something like a shock absorber. Nylon doesn't float. *Kernmantle* ropes (common in mountaineering) have a nylon core inside a smooth woven covering.

>> **Dacron:** Often found on sailboats, dacron doesn't stretch or float.

>> **Polypropylene:** Often a shiny blue color, polypropylene floats and is slow to rot, so it's common on fishing boats. It stretches slightly, although nothing like nylon.

>> **Polyethylene:** This is what you find in most hardware stores; a shiny, smooth-to-the-touch rope often yellow and usually braided. It does not stretch much, is slow to rot, and floats. On the downside, it can be slippery and not hold knots well,

>> **Manila and sisal:** Hairy yellow or brown ropes, these feel raspy in the hands. They are made of natural fibers, so they rot quickly, and they stretch a good deal. They don't float and they swell when wetted. For these reasons they are rarely sold for outdoor use these days.

>> **Cotton:** Soft to the touch, but hopelessly weak for outdoor activities, cotton rope is normally used as clothesline.

Tying some essential knots

Knots are simply the use of friction to make the rope perform a certain type of job for you. There are hundreds of types of knots. Here, we list what we consider the most practical knots for survival purposes. Learn to tie these knots securely, so that you would trust your life to them. Learn these knots with rope in your hands, following the text and figures; soon they'll all be easy.

Square knot

A square knot is useful for tying the ends of two similar ropes together (see Figure 14-1):

1. **Take two ends of a rope, lay the right end over the left, and wrap it around in an overhand knot.**

    This is the same way you start to tie your shoelaces or any other bow, for that matter; just fold the rope around itself.

2. **Take the end in your left hand, lay it over the right, and fold it over once again.**

    You know you have a square knot when it looks symmetrical.

FIGURE 14-1: A square knot

Sheet bend

The sheet bend is good for joining two different types of rope. To tie the sheet bend, follow these steps (see Figure 14-2):

FIGURE 14-2: Tying a sheet bend

1. Take the thicker of the two ropes and make a *bight* or loop.

2. Thread the thin line (white line in Figure 14-2) up through the bight and then wrap it around the head of the bight.

3. Thread the thin rope between itself and the bight; then tighten.

Sheet bend double (Beckett bend)

The sheet bend double is the exact same knot as the sheet bend from the previous section with one extra step at the end: you just wrap another loop of rope around the bight to increase its gripping strength. Use this knot (see Figure 14-3) when you join wet, slippery ropes; we've used it for everything from making a longer rope from two lengths of different rope to towing watercraft.

Anchor bend

Use the anchor bend knot (see Figure 14-4) whenever you want to attach a rope to a pole, log, or ring. To tie this knot, follow these simple steps:

1. Wrap your rope twice around whatever you want it to hold so you end up with a circle of rope around your object.

2. Bring the free end around and thread it through the circle; then tighten.

3. Loop the free end under the tightened knot, and tighten again for security.

FIGURE 14-3: Making a sheet bend double

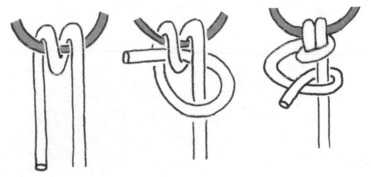

FIGURE 14-4: Tying an anchor bend

Bowline knot

The bowline knot (see Figure 14-5) instantly gives you a loop that won't slip. It's great as a foot loop, for example, to stand higher, or as an improvised loop around the chest when scrambling on high ground. To make this knot:

1. **Hold the palm of your left hand up and lay your rope on top of it so that you're grasping the rope about 3 feet (0.9 meters) from the end.**

The 3 feet of line should be hanging down from the heel of your upturned palm.

2. **Take the hanging bit of line in your right hand, reach up, and lay a loop over the line in your left, forming a design that looks like the numeral 6.**

   You should now have a loop of line in your left hand, with about 2 feet (0.6 meters) hanging down from the heel of your upturned palm.

3. **Take the point of the rope, which is called the *rabbit*, in your right hand; thread the point up through the bottom of the loop, snake it around the rope on the other side of your left hand, and then thread it straight back down into the loop.**

   This saying can help you remember what to do: *The rabbit comes up through the hole, runs around the tree, and goes back down the hole.*

4. **After you thread the end of the line back into the loop, pull on it to tighten the knot.**

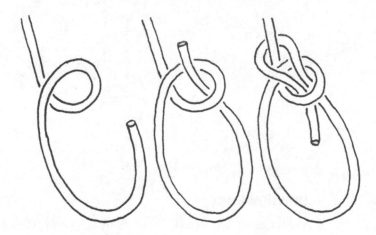

FIGURE 14-5: A bowline knot doesn't slip

Clove hitch

The clove hitch (see Figure 14-6) is the knot that begins and ends most lashings on wood. To make this knot, do the following:

1. **Wrap your rope around a pole; then wrap it a second time, laying the first wrap over the second to form an X.**

2. **Thread the point of the line underneath the X and tighten.**

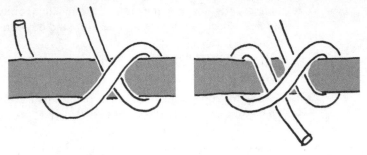

FIGURE 14-6: Tying a clove hitch

Two half hitches

You use this quick knot when tying a rope to a standing pole. To tie two half hitches, do the following (see Figure 14-7):

1. **Wrap your rope around a pole and then lay the loose end over the line.**

2. **Thread the loose end under the line lying over the pole; tighten.**

3. **Lay the loose end over the line and thread it through the loop underneath; tighten.**

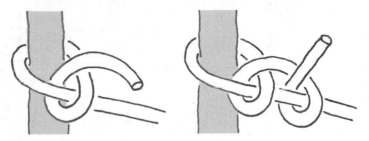

FIGURE 14-7: Tying two half hitches

Lashing down a load

If you ever need to secure a *load* (cargo on a boat or raft, for example), you can use this simple and reliable method to hold it down securely. This lashing, sometimes called a *trucker's hitch*, is simply a loop and a tensioner. This lashing gives you the ability to regulate exactly how much or how little tension you want to put on the line. Check out Figure 14-8 as you read these instructions:

1. **Tie an anchor bend to one pole.**

   We show anchor bend earlier in Figure 14-4.

2. **Grasp the rope in the middle and pull it up until it forms a bight; then double the bight over itself so that it forms a knot.**

   This step gives you a loop in the center of your line.

3. **Wrap the line around the second pole and then return it to feed through your loop.**

   This is your tensioner.

4. **Pull the line through the loop until you have the amount of tension you want; then pinch the neck of the loop with your hand to hold the tension.**

5. **Finish with two half hitches.**

   Tie two half hitches (refer to Figure 14-7) at the neck while holding the tension.

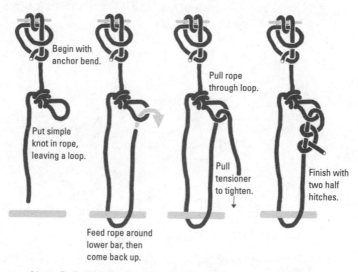

Note: Pull all knots tight! These are shown loose for clarity.

FIGURE 14-8: Lashing a load down

That's a wrap: Making a tripod

A *tripod* is three poles tied together by a lashing, useful for a wide variety of purposes in the wild, including making an improvised shelter frame and suspending pots for cooking over a fire. Refer to Figure 14-9 as you follow these instructions:

1. **Start with three thin poles of the same length; place two on the ground, with a space between them, and place the end of the third pole between them.**

   The poles can be of any length, depending on what you're using the tripod for, but they should be sturdy.

2. **Tie a clove hitch (refer to Figure 14-6) to the end of one of the outer poles.**

3. **Wrap your rope tightly around all three poles securely.**

   Knead and work each of these wraps so that all the slack comes out and you get a good, firm bond on the poles. Make sure you leave a good deal of rope to finish the lashing.

4. **Tighten the entire lashing with fraps.**

   A *frap* is a wrap that goes between the logs and gathers the ropes into a tight bunch. Take time and care to really tighten your fraps.

5. **Finish with a clove hitch on the pole opposite your first clove hitch.**

Making a square lashing

You can use a square lashing to bind one pole to another at a right angle, which is useful when joining poles to make shelters. Look to Figure 14-10 as you follow these steps:

1. **Put a clove hitch (refer to Figure 14-6) on one pole; then wrap the rope around that pole once to get the lashing started.**

2. **Mount the tied pole at a right angle to the new pole you want to attach it to; wrap the free end of the rope behind the new pole.**

3. **Bring the rope around, pass it over the original pole, and then wrap it around the new pole once again.**

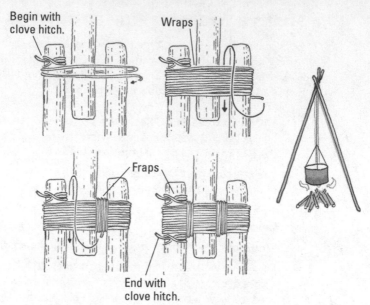

FIGURE 14-9: Making a tripod

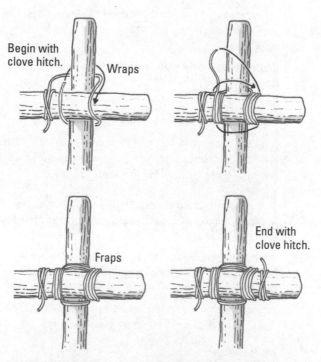

FIGURE 14-10: Creating a square lashing

4. **Continue this binding process until you have about four or five wraps; then frap.**

   To frap, take the rope and go between the poles, wrapping up only the rope — not the poles. Fraps are for tightening the wraps.

5. **After you get about three fraps squeezing the wraps, finish tightly with a clove hitch on the pole that doesn't have one yet.**

Crafting Your Own Tools

With just a few raw materials, such as stone, wood, and cordage of some sort, you can fashion tools to build shelters, fire-making equipment, and weapons for defense and catching food.

This section introduces how to make such tools. They will be much easier to make if you have a survival kit, containing at least a knife and some cordage (for more on kits, see Chapter 2).

Making cordage in the wild

The simplest cordage requires no fabrication at all. Just cut vines or other tough plant parts to use as rope. Strip these of bark or other outer coats so that anything you have tied doesn't loosen as the outer parts dry and crumble away.

If you need to make your own survival cordage, you can do so by twisting together the plant fibers from a variety of plants and then twisting multiple strands you've completed into larger diameter cordage.

In deserts, the leaves of yucca-like plants can be beaten to separate them into fibers (see Figure 14-11a), whereas in more temperate regions, plants such as stinging nettle have tough stalks that can also supply fibers. You can split these longitudinally using your thumbnail or a knife (see Figure 14-11b). Note that nettles have wicked spines so you have to strip these off first by running the length of the plant through a pair of gloves or some other hand protection.

TIP

To test vegetation for suitability for making cordage, try tying some into a simple overhand knot. If the vegetation doesn't crack or split too badly, it's probably suitable.

Once you have suitable fibers, you can make simple cordage just by twisting strands together. For heavier cordage, this method works well:

1. **Tie two cleaned fiber ends together (see Figure 14-11c).**

   These will be combined to make a single string, so plan the diameter you want accordingly. Hang these cords vertically so you can work them with both hands.

2. **Separately twist each of the strands below the knot in the same direction to make the cordage a little denser and stronger (see Figure 14-11d).**

3. **Now tightly twist one of the strands around the other in the direction *opposite* of the initial twists (see Figure 14-11e); tie off at the bottom.**

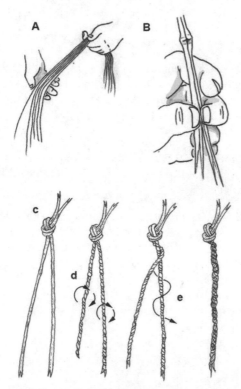

FIGURE 14-11: Twisting fibers into cordage

For (finer) cordage, the same method is used, but it's a little more controlled and done in your lap (see Figure 14-12):

1. **Twist the upper fiber away from you (see Figure 14-12a).**

2. **Bring the lower fiber up and over the upper fiber but toward you (see Figure 14-12b).**

3. **Repeat by twisting the upper fiber away from you again (see Figure 14-12c).**

   The resulting cordage is composed of two fibers, each individually twisted, and then twisted around one another for greater strength (see Figure 14-12d).

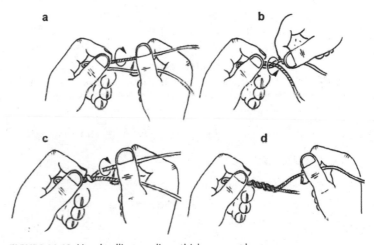

FIGURE 14-12: Hand-rolling medium-thickness cordage

TIP

To make longer cordage, you simply lay in or splice additional lengths of cordage, twisting them into the original length while rolling them on your thigh. Try wetting the ends of the original and lengthening the cordage to get them to "mate" better. Splices like this will probably be weak points in your cordage, so try to use the longest fibers you can from the start to minimize splicing.

TIP

Split vegetation will dry out quickly, making fibers resistant to adhering to one another. Shade pre-prepared lengths of fibers while working, and/or wet them occasionally.

You can make even better-quality cordage with the thigh-rolling method. This takes an hour or so of practice to learn and depends on good initial fibers, patience, persistence, and a good rolling surface:

1. **Twist a length of fibers into an initial string, and at the center, twist until a loop forms (see Figure 14-13a).**

2. **In a seated position, hold the looped end with one hand (see Figure 14-13b), and with the other hand pushing forward, roll the two separate fibers, coming off of the looped end like a V, on the top of your thigh (see Figure 14-13c).**

   You are not trying to roll or twist these fibers together in this stage. You are twisting both away from you at the same time.

3. **Work the hand holding the looped end back and forth, which tends to bring the two legs of the V of fibers together, somewhat parallel (see Figure 14-13d).**

4. **Keeping a good hold of the looped end, press down and vigorously draw the hand toward you on the thigh, twisting and rolling both twisted fibers together (see Figure 14-13e).**

   This is the step where the two fibers are being twisted into a single piece of cordage.

FIGURE 14-13: Thigh-rolling fine cordage

TIP

The surface you are rolling on needs to "grab" the cordage strands as you roll them. Wet trouser or bare skin (the top of your thigh) can improve this grip, although using bare skin will initially pull hairs out of the top of your leg — but in a survival situation, that is the least of your worries!

Improvised cordage will not look like rope in the movies — it will be irregular and sort of hairy — but you only need it to work. Also, it will wear out pretty quickly, so keep your eyes open for replacement fiber material. Making cordage is a good way to spend free time at camp, for example, after eating. You never know when it will be handy and staying productive is good for morale.

TIP

You can run lengths of improvised cordage through sticky substances, such as tree sap, to keep them holding together a bit longer. Treating them with wax slows rot from water if you use them as fishing line.

Making stone tools

If you lose your knife, never fear — a stone tool will do in a pinch. This section explains how you can break a stone to determine its type. After you know the type, you can shape it into a tool for various tasks.

Splitting a stone to assess its type

Before you can craft your own stone tool, you need to know about the different stones available and what they can do for you. Superficially, river or beach *cobbles* (baseball to softball–size round rocks) all seem the same: round, boring, gray rocks. But if you split them open, you find some differences.

To split a stone, take it in two hands and slam it down on another rock. (*Warning:* At the moment of the blow, close your eyes to prevent being injured by a chip of flying stone. Better yet, wear glasses or sunglasses.) You can simply throw the stone at a cliff wall if you don't want to risk smashing your fingers, but holding the rock can give you a little more control over what you're doing.

TIP

After you open the stone, you can assess its grain size and identify what the stone is useful for. Run your thumb over the exposed surface of the rock to feel its grain size. The following are common rock types listed in order of increasing grain size, along with some ways you can use them:

>> **Obsidian:** Obsidian is volcanic glass. It's often black, and when chipped, the edges come off razor-sharp, which is useful for cutting.

>> **Flint and chert:** Flint and chert are smooth, fine-grained stones; the edges are sharp but not as sharp or brittle as obsidian. Chert is ideal for making *armatures*, the sharp ends

of hunting tools. (If you have access to steel, you may want to save a piece of flint or chert for starting fires — see Chapter 5 for details.)

>> **Basalt:** Basalt is a dense, dark rock that doesn't shatter as easily as chert or obsidian. Its edges aren't razor sharp but they are durable and ideal for heavy-duty work like scraping or chopping.

>> **Pumice and sandstone:** Pumice, an igneous rock, and sandstone, a sedimentary rock, are the sandpaper of the natural world. They're both ideal for abrading wood, bone, and antler into various shapes.

Shaping the stone into a tool

After you have an idea of how fine the grain is, you can begin to shape the stone into the tool you want. Here are the two main tools you need so you can work stone into useful shapes:

>> **Hammerstone:** A *hammerstone* is a rock you use to break open another rock. Larger hammers (about the size of a baseball; see Figure 14-14a) are useful for breaking the rock to get good slivers and splinters of rock; smaller hammers (see Figure 14-14c) can be the size of a peach pit or a large marble and are used to trim the edge of a splinter of rock with a little more control. In either case, the point is to break the *core* (the main rock) with the hammer and produce *shatter* (see Figure 14-14b) useful for woodworking or other tasks.

TIP

Smash the hammerstone against the edge of a core stone. Holding the core in the hand gives you more control over where your strike lands. This bashing often results in sharp flakes of stone that you can easily use as knives without any further shaping. In most survival situations, you can get what you need just by breaking open lots of rock and picking through the debris to find just the right shape — no pressure flaker required.

>> **Pressure flaker:** A *pressure flaker* is a piece of metal, bone, or antler, about the size of a pen or pencil, with a robust but sharpened tip (see Figure 14-14d); you use it to press hard on the very edge of a piece of shatter. This allows fine control of the shape of the rock you're working on (see Figure 14-14e) after some practice.

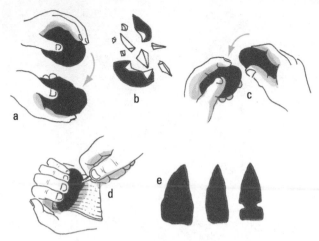

FIGURE 14-14: Breaking and shaping stone for tools and weapons

To learn more advanced stone toolmaking, get a book on *flint-knapping* and practice, practice, practice.

TIP

Carving bone and antler tools

You can carve bone and antler into tools you can use in the wild. These materials flex under impact instead of shattering (like some stone), making them very durable survival tools.

You can harvest bone and antler from the carcasses of many large mammals. Figure 14-15a shows an elk, highlighting (in white) the very useful antlers and the *metapodials*, the lower leg bones. Always collect such resources in a survival situation. Soaking bone and antler in water for 24 to 48 hours can make them easier to work with.

Here are the main ways to shape bone and antler:

>> **Smash them with a hammerstone on an anvil to produce splinters.** Use a baseball-size stone or even drive a small wedge of stone into the bone with a hammerstone, as in Figure 14-15b. Many bones (and antlers, see Figure 14-15c) are very hard to break, especially if the animal died recently.

>> **Abrade the splinters with a coarse stone.** Grind away the surface with sandstone, pumice, or any coarse rock, just as if you were using sandpaper (see Figure 14-15d).

FIGURE 14-15: Making tools from bone and antler

> » **Perforate the abraded splinters with a hard item, such as the awl on your knife or a splinter of stone.**
> Perforations allow you to thread cordage through a hole, for example as an improvised sewing needle.

Making Natural Remedies

When you're in the wild, you may encounter sickness, infection, and other ailments. If you're in a bind and don't have certain treatments in your first aid kit, you can improvise by making your own remedies. This section introduces a few medicinal plants.

Using salicin, nature's aspirin

Salicin, or salicylic acid, is one of the main ingredients in aspirin, and you can use it for light relief of pains, swelling, and inflammation. You can find it in aspen and willow trees. To extract salicin, peel away some bark and scrape off the soft tissue between the bark and the wood. Figure 14-16 shows an example.

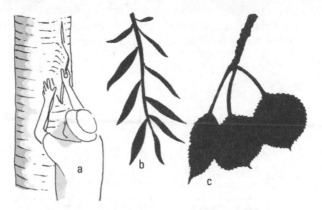

FIGURE 14-16: Extracting salicin from an aspen tree (a); recognizing willow leaves (b); and aspen leaves (c)

To use salicin, prepare a tea by boiling twigs, buds, or scrapings from the moist layer of wood between the bark and the tree. Steep the materials for an hour, then mash them into a liquid pudding for consumption. You can also chew on the twigs and use the resulting solution as a topical reliever by smearing it on an inflamed area.

Preparing medicines for wounds, burns, and bowels

You can apply any of the substances in this section to your skin to treat a wound or burn, or depending on the plant, you can ingest them to treat bowel problems or satisfy your hunger.

Tannin

Tannin, or tannic acid, is useful for preventing infection, for treating burns and other skin problems, and for treating diarrhea. You can draw tannin from all types of sources, including just about any tree bark, especially brown tree bark (see Figure 14-17), acorns, strawberry leaves, blackberry stems, and banana plants.

To use tannin, prepare a tea by boiling or soaking crushed bark, especially moist, brown, inner bark, acorns, or leaves. Steep for an hour, and then add more of these ingredients to steep until you have dense tea. Treat burns or wounds by applying cool compresses soaked in the tea.

If you're desperate and suffering from a debilitating bout of diarrhea, try drinking a small portion of tea made from white oak bark or other hardwood barks known to contain tannin.

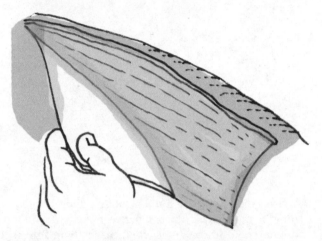

FIGURE 14-17: The bark from just about any tree contains tannin

Plantains

Plantain plants, which come in more than 200 varieties in the tropics, are good for treating wounds of all kinds, itching, and problems in the bowels, such as diarrhea and dysentery. A plantain (see Figure 14-18) is a little banana-like fruit, usually green, flat, and hard like wood.

To use plantain plants, brew a tea of plantain leaves or seeds. Drink it for diarrhea, or mash up the boiled or soaked leaves in the tea and then apply it to irritated skin.

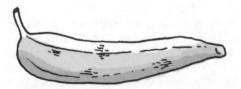

FIGURE 14-18: Plantain fruit

Common cattail

Cattail grows at the edge of water sources and is good for treating wounds, sores, and burns because it is a natural antiseptic. It's also a food source. Check out Figure 14-19 to see a cattail and its roots.

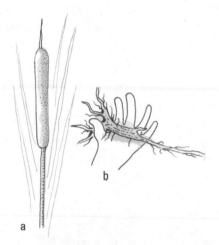

FIGURE 14-19: Common cattail (a) and cattail roots (b)

To prepare cattail for medicinal use, pound the roots into a mash and then apply the mash to wounds or sores. To eat, cook the green bloom spikes, or peel and eat the shoots raw.

3

Surviving in Extreme Land Environments

Deal with hazards, disease, and survival in jungles and forests

Stay warm and dry when surviving in snowy environments

Find water and stay cool in deserts

Chapter **15**

Special Considerations for Forests and Jungles

emperate forests offer many resources that make survival a little easier than it is on the open sea or in the desert. More tropical forests (also known as jungles) present many problems for the survivor because they harbor so many diseases and parasites. Before entering either type of forest — temperate or tropical — make sure you're ready for these situations.

In this chapter, we cover bear safety, insect and parasite awareness, and the dangers of tropical disease. We also give special instructions for dealing with the problem of getting up off the floor of the jungle (often wet, muddy, and crawling with insect life) and explain how to use your best friend in the tropics, the machete.

Identifying Hazardous Wildlife in Dry Forests

Knowing what kinds of animal life are nearby helps you know where to set traps for food, where to make camp, and where you shouldn't tread. This section points out some dangerous wildlife you may encounter in temperate forests.

Preventing bear attacks

Many times, bear attacks occur because a person accidentally stumbles upon the animal when it's feeling vulnerable or territorial. Knowing the signs that bears are nearby can help you remain safe in the wild.

Bear paw prints (check out Figure 15-1a) are about the size of a large human hand, and their claw marks are unmistakable on trees — just make sure you're looking in the right place for these marks. Bear claw marks on trees are frequently 8 to 9 feet (2.4 to 2.7 meters) up the side of the trunk.

TIP

Whenever traveling in bear country, take the following proper precautions:

>> **Carry bear spray or bear pepper spray.** You can buy it in most National Parks and outfitter stores. Make sure you read the label and follow the instructions. Recent studies suggest that bear pepper spray really works, and you should have it handy — not buried in your pack.

>> **Be careful about food smells.** Never keep food in your shelter, not even a morsel. Perfumed soaps and deodorants fall into this category, too. Always place your food at least 100 yards (91 meters) downwind from your shelter. Also, don't sleep in the same clothes you wear when you cook your food.

>> **Make plenty of noise as you travel.** Many experienced hikers in bear country make constant noise as they hike. Singing, banging metal, or making other such noises lets bears know that you're approaching. Making a noise often causes the bear to move away long before you get there.

>> **Remember which way the wind is blowing.** If the wind is at your back, bears can smell you coming and usually get out of the way. But if the wind is in your face, you're in danger of startling a bear because your smell is flowing behind you. Make a lot of noise when the wind is in your face.

WARNING

You should also keep an eye out for three important scenarios in which bear attack is likely:

>> **Cubs:** If you see bear cubs in the wild, consider yourself in peril. Locate the mother bear as quickly as you can and

move away from her. Female bears are known to attack anything near their young.

>> **Fresh kills:** If you come across a freshly killed animal that has been covered up with some freshly flung dirt, a tree branch, or some leaves (see Figure 15-1b), you may have run across a bear's cache, and the animal may be nearby. Get away from this kill site as quickly as possible.

>> **Hibernation dens:** A large hole that faces away from the wind or at an angle to the wind — especially one that allows snow to build up around its face — may be a hibernation den, especially if you're in bear country between the months of September and April.

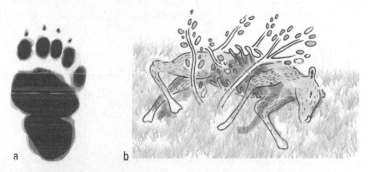

a   b

FIGURE 15-1: Keep an eye open for bear paw prints (a) and kill sites (b)

TIP

If you do encounter a bear, freeze. Talk calmly in a monotone and try to back away slowly. For more on what to do when a bear attacks, see Chapter 24.

Avoiding mountain lions

Mountain lions *(Puma concolor)*, or cougars, are big cats that stand about 3 feet (0.9 meters) tall and weigh anywhere from 100 to 250 pounds (45 to 115 kilograms). They rarely attack humans, but in survival situations they should always be considered a threat. Mountain lions usually attack children or the elderly, and they usually do so by lunging for the neck.

Keep in mind that big cats of all kinds hunt for the weakest of the species and that many times, they can tell when you're infirm, especially if you have a limp. (Animal trainers sometimes feign limps or infirmity to draw big cats' attention.) If you're infirm and traveling in big-cat country, stay off trails near dusk and dawn and always try to travel with a companion.

If you encounter a mountain lion, don't run. Make yourself appear to be as large as possible and hold your ground. Running will trigger the lion's instinct to chase and kill. For more on mountain lion encounters, see Chapter 24.

Steering clear of woodland snakes

TIP

You can avoid snakebite almost indefinitely if you use your head. You should always expect snakes to be under any rock or log. The best way to prevent snakebite is to practice the following:

>> **Wear stout boots.** The taller, the better. Most snakes can't bite through good boots, and most bites occur below the knee.

>> **Watch your step.** Stepping on snakes is a common problem in the wild.

>> **Use a stick and look closely.** Always use a stick or pole to part foliage or turn over rocks or boards.

>> **Check bedding and clothes.** Snakes like to curl up in warm, dark places.

If necessary, you can kill a snake with blows to the head or immobilize the head by using a forked stick to pin the snake's neck to the ground. For information on treating snakebite, see Chapter 13.

In a survival situation, all snakes should be considered dangerous and potentially deadly. Unless you're hunting them for food, there is no reason to approach snakes. All snakes killed as food in a survival situation should have the head cut off (removing poison glands) and buried away from the camping site so they are not accidentally stepped on later.

Evading spiders and ticks

Thankfully, some methods of protecting yourself from insects, spiders, and other creepy-crawlies are easy. The problem arises when your mind wanders and you forget the following precautions:

>> Always wear a hat.

>> Thoroughly shake out all clothing — especially shoes — and bedding.

>> Try not to put your hands in dark places or holes.

>> Use whatever animal repellents you have (research these before travelling) particularly on your ankles and wrists, where spiders and ticks often crawl into clothing.

Here are some troublesome eight–legged creatures you may encounter — note that they prefer dark, sheltered areas, so be careful when moving logs or rocks:

>> **Brown recluse:** This spider is brown, with thin legs and a body in the shape of a violin. The bite causes fever, chills, and vomiting for up to 48 hours. It's rarely fatal, but it can cause disfigurement and even lead to limb amputation from tissue death.

>> **Black widow:** The notorious black widow is generally black with a distinctive red or orange hourglass design on the body. This spider is usually found in warmer environments. The bite, which is rarely fatal, is very painful and can cause temporary paralysis, sometimes up to a week.

WARNING

Most spider bites appear as a red, circular welt. If someone is envenomed by a brown recluse or black widow, treat for shock and be prepared to administer CPR (see Chapter 13). Seek medical help as soon as possible.

>> **Ticks:** You can find varieties of these tiny arachnids in most temperate forests. They prefer thick vegetation. Ticks carry a wide variety of diseases, including Lyme disease. In areas with many ticks, it's important to check your body thoroughly every day, particularly after traveling through tall or thick vegetation; it's almost impossible to avoid them entirely. See Chapter 13 for tips on removing ticks.

Laws of the Jungle: Surviving in the Tropics

We wish we could tell you that you should prepare yourself to fight off a stealthy jaguar or swing from a vine, but unfortunately, the main problem you face in jungle survival is disease. Jungles are dense, warm/tropical forests. While they pose plenty of hazards, it's the microscopic creatures that are problem number one in a survival situation.

This section gives you a heads-up on how to survive in the tropics, including info on how to prevent tropical diseases; obtain safe drinking water, clothing, and shelter; and travel specifically in the jungle.

Preventing jungle diseases

REMEMBER

Taking necessary precautions is the best way to avoid jungle disease. The following are the top four things you can do to stay healthy in jungle environments. If you do them all, the chances of being infected drop significantly.

>> **Disinfect water and cook food thoroughly.** Many tropical diseases come from contaminated water and food. Chapter 7 thoroughly explains how to filter and purify water (or collect rainwater, which is usually fresh if your collecting surface is clean).

>> **Wear proper clothing, sleep up off the ground, and use insect repellents.** Bug bites can infect you with microbes carried by the bug, and uncleaned bites themselves can be infected.

>> **Wash and bathe often.** Soap and water can do a surprisingly good job of stripping away harmful bacteria and other parasites. Watch for red bite marks and welt-like bumps, and keep these spots especially clean.

>> **Use vaccines and preventive medication (prophylactics):** These, of course, must be specific for the environment. Consult with a doctor before your trip as some vaccines and preventative medications need to be taken weeks before travelling.

TIP

We highly recommend visiting the Centers for Disease Control (CDC) website at https://wwwnc.cdc.gov/travel/page/travel-vaccines for travelers' info well in advance of your journey.

Diseases from contaminated water or food

Unfortunately, if you're out there long enough, you eventually pick up something — it is, after all, the tropics. Knowing the signs of disease, when combined with prevention, gives you the best defense. The following tropical diseases are usually contracted from contaminated food or water:

>> **Bilharzia (or schistosomiasis):** You contract bilharzia from contaminated water, either from drinking it or through a break in the skin. A microscopic worm grows in the liver, causing illness, rash, and, worst of all, a dehydrating case of diarrhea. Medication is needed to kill the worms.

>> **Cholera:** You contract cholera from contaminated food or water. It causes very runny "rice water" diarrhea, which causes rapid dehydration. It's fatal in the very young, the very old, and the sick. Treatment is large quantities of clean water. A vaccine is available.

>> **Dysentery:** This comes from contaminated water. Dysentery causes severe and persistent bloody diarrhea. Treatment is rest and rehydration; antibiotics may help.

>> **Giardia:** Giardia also results from contaminated water. This parasite causes severe and persistent diarrhea, stomach cramps, and unpleasant burps. Treatment is rest and rehydration. The disease responds to antibiotics, but no vaccine is available.

>> **Hepatitis:** Jungle hepatitis is also caused by consuming untreated water, resulting in nausea, loss of appetite, abdominal pain, and yellowing of the skin *(jaundice)*. There are many variations of this disease; some have vaccines, others don't. Treatment is rest and prevention of catching it again, which is mainly ensuring that drinking water is disinfected. Ask a doctor about hepatitis risk before travelling to tropical areas.

>> **Lung flukes (paragonimiasis):** This parasitic disease, which is prevalent in Southeast Asia, occurs when a fluke worm grows in the lungs. It comes from undercooked food, especially shellfish. Symptoms include fatigue, coughing, and abdominal cramps. Paragonimiasis responds to antiparasitic medicines.

>> **Traveler's diarrhea:** This is the commonest complaint in travelers to the tropics, and it may be caused by bacteria, viruses, or parasites. Avoiding contaminated food and water is important. Maintaining fluid intake is very important. Symptoms can be reduced by antidiarrheal drugs, and antibiotics might kill the infecting microbe.

>> **Typhoid fever:** Typhoid results from a bacterium found most often in undercooked food. It causes severe intestinal disturbances, pink spots on the torso, and fever. Treatment is antibiotics, rehydration, and rest. A vaccine is available.

Diseases from insect and animal bites

Here are the identifying characteristics of the most common tropical diseases that are passed on through insect and animal bites (for more on protection from bug bites, see the later section "Identifying jungle insects and other buggy creatures"):

>> **Bubonic plague:** You contract this disease from fleas, and it causes fever, persistent vomiting, and painful swelling in the lymph nodes. It's fatal if not treated, but it responds to antibiotics if diagnosed early.

>> **Dengue fever:** Dengue fever, contracted by mosquito bites, causes flu-like symptoms and sometimes rashes, especially on the face and neck. It usually lasts a week and is sometimes fatal. There's no vaccine. Treatment is rest. It is not advised to take over-the-counter medicines such as aspirin or ibuprofen if you think you have dengue, because these can cause bleeding complications. Before travel, research the hazards of dengue fever in the region you mean to visit.

>> **Malaria:** Malaria is also contracted from mosquito bites and it causes weakness, fever and chills, violent shivering, nausea, and sometimes coma and death. Preventive medications are effective, but they must be taken up to one week before exposure to the disease and several weeks afterward. Malaria can't be cured, but treatment can reduce the severity of the symptoms during the lifelong outbreaks that come after infection.

WARNING

Malaria is a constantly evolving disease, and older medications become ineffective over time. You must take an up-to-date prophylactic — one that's engineered to cope with new strains. No vaccine is available.

>> **Leishmaniasis:** This disease is passed on through sand flies. It causes large sores on the face, neck, and arms that can last for months and frequently disfigure the victim. This condition can lie dormant in the body for months or even years before rising to the surface. It's very difficult to treat, and there's no vaccine.

>> **River blindness (onchocerciasis):** Bites from black flies cause worm larvae to infest the victim, which causes tissue damage and blindness. It responds to worm-killing drugs and antibiotic courses. No vaccine is available.

>> **Rabies:** This viral disease comes from bites from infected mammals, including bats. It causes madness and death. Rabies may respond to a vaccine after the bite, but, of course, you will have to be at a hospital for that treatment; try to prevent it in the first place by staying away from bats and other mammals in the wilderness. Cooking an infected animal as food would be risky, but will likely kill the virus.

>> **Yellow fever:** Yellow fever is another mosquito-borne illness. It causes headaches, pain in the limbs, high fever, constipation, vomiting, and yellowing skin after about four to five days. It's sometimes fatal. Treatment is rest and rehydration. A vaccine is available.

Obtaining safe water

In a survival situation, consider all bodies of water deadly, and be sure to treat all water before consumption (see Chapter 7). The clarity of the water in a particular stream means absolutely nothing. Rainwater may be healthy to drink, but it can pick up microbes as it contacts vegetation during rain. Treat rainwater before consumption as well.

TIP

If you don't have the equipment or fire to boil water, start a rain-catching operation. Even a brief rain shower — like the type that comes almost every day in the tropics — can give you more than enough water. You can use broad leaves, like those on plantain and banana plants, as water–catching planes and receptacles, but remember, even water collected this way requires treatment before drinking. For more on the finer points of catching rainwater, see Chapter 7. Because the tropical jungle is often very wet, you may not have the option of making fire to disinfect water. In this case, you will have to drink untreated rainwater; not great, but much better than untreated lake or river water.

The jungle cover-up: Dressing for the tropics

When you're in a jungle environment, you can think about clothing in terms of *coverage*. You want to cover as much of your skin as possible to prevent bites from insects. Make sure you wear the following pieces of clothing (and check out Chapter 4 for a basic overview of clothing needs in a survival situation):

>> **Hat:** An important piece of clothing in a tropical forest is a hat. Keep your head covered as often as you can because spiders and insects can drop from foliage and into your hair and scalp, or climb aboard your head as you move through thick vegetation.

REMEMBER

Wear a hat even inside a tropical house or hut, even if it has a metal roof. Many insects dwell in the roof of a tropical house or hut, where they have the nasty habit of dropping down from the ceiling.

>> **Lightweight long-sleeved shirt and long pants:** Look for breathable textiles like ripstop nylon, nylon blends, and cotton. Cuffs, both at the wrists and the ankles, should be snug.

TIP

Ideally, you want adjustable cuffs so you can loosen them during the day and tighten them at dusk. Many outfitters sell lightweight pants and shirts with Velcro on the cuffs just for this purpose.

>> **Boots:** A boot that rises up and meets the pant legs, combined with a snug cuff on the pants at the ankle, can do much to protect you from mosquitoes, fleas, and mites. Drainage holes allow water to drain from the boot, important to prevent trench foot and other jungle maladies.

WARNING

In any tropical environment, mold and mildew are serious threats. Mold appears as small black and gray dots on fabric, and it eats through clothing, backpacks, and webbing in just a few days. The best way to defend against this is to hang all fabrics to dry every chance you get. If you've ever wondered why castaways' clothes are always so shredded, now you know.

Avoiding mud flats, sand traps, and other dangerous terrain

When you're moving through the jungle, or whenever you're deciding where to camp, be aware of these undesirable types of terrain and move away as quickly as you can:

>> **Stagnant water and mud flats:** Avoid large, open patches of mud and/or stagnant water. They're home to millions of mosquitoes, and when the sun sets, those mosquitoes swarm. They attack by the thousands, and they can cause convulsions, shock, and malaria.

Consider the afternoon sun to be like an alarm: If you're still near mud flats or stagnant water at dusk, you're going to have a problem with mosquito swarms. Don't get caught out in the open at dusk or dark near a mud flat or stagnant pool — try to get away or under a net or some other protection.

>> **Mud holes and quicksand:** These areas are small holes in the ground, usually less than 50 feet (15 meters) across, filled with mud or sand so soft that it can't support your weight. Sometimes you can see these areas, but many times you can't. Quicksand and mud holes won't suck you down and suffocate you, but they can leave you quite stuck. There are many cases of strong people who walked into mud holes and couldn't extract themselves.

You should carry a large walking stick to probe the ground in front of you — especially if you leave the trail. This can seem cumbersome, but in remote areas, especially if you're alone, you have little choice. Whenever you begin to sink, especially if you sink past your calf, don't struggle — turn around immediately and go back. For techniques for extracting yourself, see Chapter 24.

>> **Beaches near rivers:** Beaches near tropical rivers are inviting, but you should camp on them only as a last resort. Tropical rivers have a bad habit of rising quickly. If you do camp on the beach, you have to maintain a good watch at night.

Using a machete

A machete is a critical tool for jungle survival, as important as warm clothing in the Arctic. A *machete* is a long metal blade with a plastic or wooden handle. They're found in practically every house, bus, and car in the tropics. Sometimes they're called *cutlasses*, or *cuchillos* (knives). Because the vegetation in the jungle is soft and it grows over the trails quickly, you need the unique cutting ability of a machete, as opposed to the harder, blunter cutting ability of an ax. (Sorry, but that beautiful ax you bought at the outfitter starts to lose its value the moment you head off into the Great Green Tangle.)

Choosing and using the right blade

A variety of types of machetes are available. Just know that they can be divided into two categories: those you use to travel with and those you use to work with. If you can, carry both types. Here's when and how to use them:

>> **Use the long blades when you're traveling.** To travel a trail with this type of machete, you use a lazy forehand swing to reach down low and strike the stalks of the plants standing in your way. Try not to flail away at the leaves or stems hanging in your face. Cut the foliage low, at the stalk, using a reaching motion. Done well, you shouldn't have to bend over all day — which is precisely why the blade is made so long.

>> **Use the short blades for work.** When chopping, making shelters, or preparing rafts, use the shortest blade you can. Attempting to use a long blade for work — like when you're doing a lot of chopping — causes fatigue and injury, and it destroys the wood. Always use the short, cleaver-type of machete for work.

WARNING

A machete isn't a baseball bat or tennis racket; it's not designed to be swung with enormous speed. When working your way through tangled foliage, make your low cuts with a controlled medium-speed motion (which isn't very Hollywood, we know, but there's nothing we can do about it). Wide and fast swings made with a machete eventually result in the blade's coming back and striking you. Even the most experienced jungle people occasionally miss what they're aiming at and strike themselves or someone nearby. Practically everybody we know has a machete scar on their leg.

Cutting bamboo

Bamboo is common in many, but not all, tropical forests. Where it's available, local people make just about everything from this versatile resource. Cutting bamboo cane is a fine art that requires a lot of technique. Generally speaking, you cut at an angle. If you deliver the blow straight down — at a 90-degree angle to the wood — you just splinter the cane, and as soon as bamboo begins to splinter, it becomes exceedingly difficult to cut through. (If you're in the mood for a bout of hair-pulling frustration, just try cutting bamboo cane the wrong way.) Here's the right way to make the cut:

1. **Deliver the first blow at an angle slightly higher than 45 degrees.**

   Cut just below the joint, and cut away from the joint, not toward it. The farther you move away from the joint, the harder cutting the cane becomes.

2. **Rotate the cane slightly and deliver another blow, at the same angle, so that the cuts are joined.**

   You want to form one continuous incision. If the cane is standing, you need to move your body around it to make this continuous incision.

3. **Continue cutting around the joint, lengthening the incision until you've severed the cane.**

TIP

Firm blows made with a slight flick of the wrist at the end of the motion — not heavy or hard blows — are the best. Don't rear back and slam the machete into the cane. This just causes it to splinter. Most of the cutting should come from your wrist at the end of the motion. Experienced jungle people cut cane with a subtle wrist motion at the end of the chop.

Making camp and shelters

WARNING

When you're in a tropical environment, making camp well before dark is absolutely critical. Keep in mind that there's almost no dusk in tropical areas, especially in the jungle. When the sun starts to drop in the late afternoon stop what you're doing and set up camp.

When making camp, take extra precautions to get off the ground. Even if you're really in trouble and have no equipment at all, you can make a platform. The platform is an essential tool in the jungle or swamp (see Figure 15-2a). To make one, you want to find three or more stout trees that you can tie poles to. The best poles are usually bamboo canes that are around 6 inches (15 centimeters) thick. Tie the poles to the trees so you have a rough triangle, and then use branches or other poles as crossbeams. You may have to use vines to make your platform if you don't have rope. When building a platform, use square lashings. (To see how to make a square lashing, go to Chapter 14.)

If you can stand it, consider building a smoldering fire below your platform. The smoke can do much to drive away insects. If you can't build a platform, try to get off the ground with a hammock (see Figure 15-2b). A hammock is lightweight and packs down small, so it should be in your pack any time you travel in tropical forest.

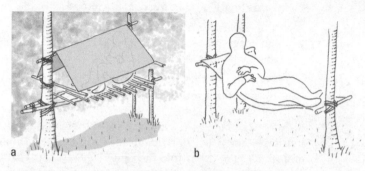

a   b

FIGURE 15-2: Get off the ground with a platform or hammock

Identifying dangerous animals

Like so many other dangerous animals, those in the tropics can be surprisingly hard to see. You can do a lot to protect yourself by using a long stick (or your machete) to part foliage or probe dense vegetation; this almost always flushes out these animals. This section identifies some of the most dangerous critters in the tropics.

Insects and other buggy creatures

To avoid many tropical diseases — as well as some unpleasant bites and stings — you must try to avoid contact with bugs, spiders, and other multi-legged creatures. The best line of defense is to wear a hat and not to expose your skin, but to be realistic, it's hard to be completely protected.

Jungles are home to millions of species of life including all manner of bugs, many of which are giant, fairly hideous, and fascinating in a creepy sort of way. But the critters that are most likely to cause you trouble in the tropics are relatively mundane. Here are the usual culprits:

>> **Mosquitoes:** Common in all tropical regions, they're generally more severe at dusk and then through the night. Never go into a tropical region without a proper net and antimalarial drugs. For info on mosquito swarms, see "Avoiding mud flats, sand traps, and other dangerous terrain," earlier in this chapter.

>> **Botflies:** Botflies are small, hairy flies found mostly in the tropics of the Western Hemisphere. They deposit their eggs under your skin, which hatch and grow into a larval sack about the size of a thumbnail. The sacks must be drained in a sterile environment, and a course of antibiotics is advised. Infestation usually isn't fatal, but it's sometimes debilitating.

>> **Black flies:** These are small black or multicolored insects with bulbous bodies often found in tropical America and Africa. They bite hard and spread river blindness (see earlier section "Preventing jungle diseases").

>> **Tarantulas (and other spiders):** Large, furry spiders can be found throughout the world, not just in the tropics. The bite is painful but rarely fatal.

>> **Centipedes, millipedes, and stinging caterpillars:** These crawling creatures administer painful stings that are rarely fatal. They often have small spine-like hairs on their backs that can seriously irritate the skin and can be next to impossible to get out. Always sweep these animals off your skin in the direction they're crawling.

>> **Ticks:** Ticks are widespread in all environments. Always wear a hat to keep them off your scalp, and always inspect yourself each evening. For more on ticks, see Chapter 13.

Jungle snakes

Like snakes everywhere, tropical snakes prefer dark holes or other tucked-away places. However, keep in mind that snakes in tropical areas can be *arboreal* — which means they're fonder of trees than their dry-forest counterparts are. As we mention for the temperate forests, we suggest treating all snakes found in the tropics as potentially lethal. Do not approach them unless specifically hunting for them as food. For more on treating a snakebite, see Chapter 13.

Gators, crocs, and caimans

Alligators, crocodiles, and caimans are *ambush predators*. Generally, they strike at short range, trying to catch you unaware. The most dangerous areas are near water's edge, where these animals wait to make their ambush. Also keep an eye out for large clumps of bushes near rivers; these are sometimes used as nests for females laying eggs.

These animals usually don't chase their prey long distances. However, they have been known to chase people in the water, and to capsize boats. Black caimans in the Amazon and saltwater crocodiles in Australia are the most dangerous. Give these animals a wide berth.

Leeches

Leeches are small wormlike parasites, usually black in color, that live in tropical and temperate waters. They attach themselves to your skin when you swim in streams and rivers; they suck your blood until they've had their fill, and then they fall off. Sometimes leeches can be found on the ground, too, or in dense, water-covered vegetation.

TIP

The best way to avoid leeches is to stay out of the water as much as you can. If you do go into the water, even if you're just crossing a stream, keep your skin covered and the cuffs of your pants cinched tightly around your boots. Leeches can also find their way into the water supply, so as always, strain and boil your water thoroughly. Leeches can make you quite ill in the bowels if accidentally swallowed.

Like ticks, leeches have a way of working into strange places on your body, so take a moment each night to examine yourself thoroughly. You can remove a leech by applying salt, alcohol, kerosene, or gasoline to the body of the leech, burn it off by holding a burning ember to its body, or scrape it off carefully with a knife. The key is not to let the mouth and head break off in your flesh, so be careful, and clean the wound when the leech is removed. Leeches excrete an anticoagulant to the bite area, so you may bleed for some time from a bite.

Piranhas

Piranhas are small fish, ranging from 8 inches to 1.5 feet (20 centimeters to 0.5 meters) in length. They're found in South America, largely in and south of the Amazon basin. Though they're nowhere near as dangerous as their legendary reputation suggests, they do nevertheless bite humans with their large, razor-sharp teeth, which causes infection.

Piranhas have developed a reputation of being especially dangerous when water levels are low and when the victim is bleeding. Stay out of waters where locals say piranhas live and be careful crossing shallow streams. Like elsewhere in the wild, we recommend you wear tall, stout boots and long pants in tropical forests, even when venturing into water in a survival situation.

IN THIS CHAPTER

» Staying warm when it's cold out

» Building survival shelters from nothing but snow

» Avoiding avalanches, crevasses, and thin ice

» Finding water when you're surrounded by snow and ice

» Making tools (like snowshoes) to survive in snowy environments

Chapter **16**
The Big Chill: Enduring in Snowy Places

C old is simply an absence of heat energy, and you can feel cold in just about any environment on Earth. In this chapter, we focus on snowy environments, which you can encounter in around half of all the land masses in the Northern Hemisphere and somewhat less in the Southern Hemisphere. You can find snow even in unexpected places — both Hawaii and Australia offer snow skiing — so being prepared for cold is always a good idea. In this chapter, we cover methods for surviving in cold, snowy wilderness.

REMEMBER

When you're cold, you must act. Don't try to just force your way through the sensation of cold — it's your body's signal that something is wrong, and you may not have much time to solve the problem. Take action.

Staying Warm in Extreme Cold

Keeping your body warm is your first priority in a cold-weather survival situation. If you become hypothermic — undergo a debilitating reduction in body temperature — in extreme cold or wind chill, survival becomes an epic battle. Use the following principles to stay warm outdoors (also be sure to check out Chapter 4 for important info on cold-weather dressing):

» **Breathe through your nose and wear a scarf.** Breathing through your nose conserves body moisture and wrapping a scarf or other cloth across your nose and mouth can cut the chill so that the coldest air doesn't hit your lungs directly.

» **Stay dry.** Wet clothing cools your body faster than just about anything else, so if you get wet, get under some shelter, make a fire, and dry out your clothes. If you don't have the option of making a fire, try to keep moving — moving generates body heat, and if you stop moving in cold, wet clothes, you will soon become hypothermic.

» **Eat and drink.** Keeping the body fueled and hydrated can prevent most cold injuries! If you have food, eat some to keep the body's fires stoked. From your food supply, choose the food that has the most calories. Drinking lots of liquid keeps your body hydrated, which can forestall hypothermia.

» **Get out of the wind.** Wind rapidly sucks heat away from the body, so take shelter when there's wind; if you can't take shelter, try to improvise a windproof layer for your clothing (see Chapter 4).

» **Loosen your footwear.** Tighter footwear constrains the blood vessels that would normally carry warm blood to the feet, leading to frostbite. So when it gets cold, *loosen your laces.* But be careful to keep the top of your footwear sealed around your calves so that cold air, snow, and ice can't get in.

» **Protect your hands and feet.** These are the first to go when your body gets cold, and because you can't really travel with frozen feet or do anything at all with frozen hands, you must protect them. Mittens are normally warmer than gloves, something to keep in mind when you prepare to go outdoors in the first place. Gloves worn under windproof mittens is an ideal combination for really cold weather.

>> **Stay active.** If your clothes aren't providing enough warmth, you can temporarily stay active to warm up; but don't do so much that you sweat, which dampens your clothes. Even confined in a small snow cave or something similar, you can do *isometric exercises* that tense the muscles without lengthening them. You just flex the muscles, for example, pressing the palms together tightly and then releasing the tension.

Cold Comfort: Making Your Shelter in a Snowy Environment

When you're cold, the benefit of a shelter is as much psychological as physical. One of the first things you notice in a snow shelter is how quiet it is. Coming in out of wind and storm is a tremendous relief. This section first walks you through some general building principles. We then describe three main ways to use snow to make a shelter.

Snow shelter basics

Snowy landscapes can look unsurvivable, but snow itself can provide a home. Snow is composed of frozen water crystals that can trap air, which is a good insulator. You can use snow as a building material and take advantage of this insulating capacity. Just remember these important tips, whatever shelter you build:

>> **Build your shelter in a safe location.** Stay away from avalanche slopes, and if you're on a frozen lake or sea surface, build on thick ice.

>> **Keep the shelter as small as is practical.** A large shelter takes more heat (from your body or fire) to keep warm than a smaller shelter, and takes more time and energy to build. Make your shelter roomy enough to be practical, but no bigger.

>> **Keep your shelter ventilated (see Figure 16-1a).** Burning a camp stove or other fuel in your shelter can lead to an excess of carbon monoxide (a colorless, odorless gas that leads to lethargy and then death), so carefully poke several

ventilation holes in the shelter's roof with a long pole. A ski pole is thin, so you may need more than eight or ten holes.

Keep your eyes open for the signs of *carbon monoxide poisoning*, which include a splitting headache, nausea, dizziness, and weakness — if you notice these, get outside fast and then vent that shelter! Periodically check ventilation holes to be sure they're not filling with snow.

>> **Keep a digging-out tool inside your shelter (see Figure 16-1b).** Heavy snow — or in the worst case, avalanche — can trap you inside a snow shelter, so always store a digging tool inside. You can improvise a digging tool from several stout branches lashed together with cordage (see Chapter 14 for tips on lashing), or you can use a helmet, a license plate, or even a cooking pot.

>> **Block the entrance of your shelter (see Figure 16-1c).** Just covering the entrance/exit hole of your shelter with your backpack and perhaps some heavy brush helps to trap warm air inside; a snow shelter with an open door isn't much better than a refrigerator. But don't block the door until the shelter is ventilated.

>> **Make a cold trap in your shelter (see Figure 16-1d).** Warm air rises and cold air sinks. A *cold trap* is simply a basin, trench, or other hole in the snow floor of your shelter that traps the coldest air in the shelter; don't stand in the cold trap unless you want to chill your feet.

FIGURE 16-1: Snow shelter basics

>> **Make your shelter visible.** Snow shelters can blend right into the landscape, so make your position visible to rescue personnel. For example, lay out giant symbols in the snow using dye markers, charcoal from your fire, or sod from beneath the snow. Or securely peg a brightly colored piece of cloth or tarp to the top of the shelter. See Chapter 12 for more on signaling.

>> **Insulate yourself from the snow.** Never sit or sleep directly on snow; use anything — such as pine boughs, a bed of moss, seat cushions, the fireproof hood liner from a car — to stay off the snow (see Figure 16-1f). Similarly, when you're sitting, place a backpack or other insulating object between your back and the wall of the shelter.

>> **Keep your shelter organized.** At the very least, designate a place to store the first aid kit, your wilderness survival kit (see Chapter 2), and any items you have for signaling passing aircraft or other potential rescuers. Keep these items in their designated places; you don't want to be scrambling around in the dark interior of a snow shelter for your signal mirror when you hear the sweet sound of a helicopter!

Making a simple snow-cave

A snow-cave is the simplest snow shelter, and it's entirely capable of keeping you warm enough to stay alive indefinitely. A *snow-cave* is basically a burrow inside a snowdrift or a pile of snow. You can either burrow into a naturally occurring snowdrift or build your own mound of snow.

To make a snow-cave shelter, you need a digging tool, such as a helmet, ski, snowshoe, cooking pot, several strong green sticks (cut from a tree) lashed together, or even the glove-compartment door from a car. The best tool, of course, is a *mountaineer's snow shovel*, which is small enough to strap to a backpack (the handle telescopes out) and very strongly built — we won't even travel in snow country without one. The best have metal blades that don't break. Plastic shovel blades eventually do.

TIP

Consider stripping off a layer of clothing before you start working. Making any kind of snow shelter is heavy work that can make you sweat, and wet clothing quickly cools your body. Also, you'll probably be covered in snow after all the digging that's involved, and that snow can melt from your body heat, leaving you wet.

GAS POISONING IN THE ARCTIC

Many winters back, I (Cameron) was the sole inhabitant of a remote glaciological research hut on Iceland's Vatnajökull glacier. One night, I heard a machine turn on behind a locked door — an electrical engine activated by satellite control. It was hard to sleep, but finally I did. I'm lucky I ever woke up.

About the incident, I wrote, "A few hours later, I woke with stinging eyes and aching lungs. It felt like someone was standing on my chest. I coughed and hacked and lunged out the door leading to the ante-chamber. A fierce migraine was slowly slicing my brain in two. Without consciously thinking about it, I was suiting up, and soon I was crawling dizzily out the hatch and gulping fresh air. The first gasps I took in the blast of storm outside collared me and tugged me back from the brink.

"Crouched in the storm just outside the hatch, I realized that the machine behind the locked door was gasoline-powered! The exhaust fumes had filled the hut. My symptoms were those of carbon monoxide poisoning. I breathed for a minute or so before climbing back in and opening the door to the living compartment. This let in piles of blowing snow, but I didn't care. I had to breathe."

Creating shelters from natural snow drifts

Wind often blows snow into dunes or drifts, which you may be able to use as a shelter. Before you use a natural snowdrift as a shelter, verify that the snow is compact enough to hold its shape when you burrow inside.

Dig horizontally into the drift for about a body-length before burrowing left for half a body length and then right for half a body length, making an L-shaped burrow (see Figure 16-2). You can use the entrance tunnel to store your gear and food and the perpendicular tunnel as your sleeping and resting area.

REMEMBER

The L-shape of the natural-drift burrow is a strategy for the fact that many drifts aren't deep enough to make a large, round burrow inside. If the drift is large enough, you can make the shelter roomy enough to sit upright — but remember, larger means colder and takes more energy to build.

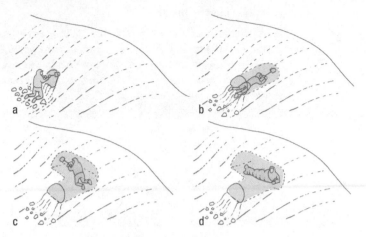

FIGURE 16-2: Building an L-shaped burrow in a natural snowdrift

Making your own snow-heap shelter

If you can't find a natural drift, or if the snow is too loose in any drift you find, you can make your own snow heap. This is a lot of work, but may be your only option in a survival situation. To make a snow-heap shelter, just follow these steps:

1. **Strip off a layer of clothing and — using any tool you can — scoop up snow and pile it in a giant mound, up to 6 feet (1.8 meters) wide and 6 feet high (see Figure 16-3a).**

2. **Put your layer back on while you let the heap settle for an hour or so.**

   Go and do something else, such as finding a heavy pole or other tool that you can use in the next step.

3. **When you're back at your heap, start to compact the snow by tamping it down hard.**

   Use a large pole or a snow shovel, or even climb onto the heap and jump up and down. You're trying to make the heap as dense as you can, so it may be only 4 feet (1.2 meters) high when you're done.

4. **Strip off a layer of clothing again and start burrowing into the side (see Figure 16-3b).**

   TIP

   Make the door of your shelter face east or a little southeast so you can see the sky lighten with sunrise; this is very good for morale after a cold night.

5. Hollow out the inside.

As you dig in, assess the compaction. Is the roof holding its shape? Is the tunnel collapsing? If not, burrow on! Your shelter is taking shape. After a foot or so, start excavating the interior so you have a round chamber with a flat floor and a dome-shaped roof (see Figure 16-3c).

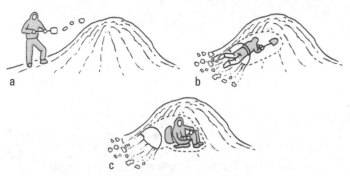

FIGURE 16-3: Building a shelter from your own snowdrift

Lighting a Fire in Cold, Snowy Environments

Cold itself doesn't interfere with making fire. If you can ignite it, fire fuel (such as wood or animal fat) will burn no matter how cold it is. The main fire-making challenge in the cold is finding fuel and getting it to burn without your fire melting into the snow. But don't worry — you can build a fire in a cold, snowy environment with the pointers in this section.

Finding fuel in snowy places

Wooded areas provide plenty of fuel to burn. High in the mountains, though, or on open Arctic tundra, wood may be scarce or absent. You may be able to use the following as fuel:

>> **Driftwood:** It may be frozen into a beach, but if you can pry or chop it free, it'll probably burn.

>> **Tundra grasses or mosses:** These are under a blanket of snow for much of the year, but by burrowing down, you can

find them even in winter; twist them into compact "sticks" or even thick bundles — they burn better than loose clods.

>> **Dried animal dung:** Herbivorous mammal droppings, often composed of dense dry vegetable fibers, may burn if they dried out before freezing.

>> **Animal fats:** Fats such as seal blubber burn well. If you have the luxury of such a resource, use it sparingly — for example, only to cook or dry clothes but not for warmth unless you really need it. It burns quickly.

Getting any fuel to burn requires the fire-making skills we introduce in Chapter 5.

Protecting a fire from the snow

TIP

If you build a fire on a snowy surface, the heat quickly melts the snow and your fire collapses into a wet, smoky snow crater — not what you were after. Building a fire directly on ground you've cleared of snow and ice doesn't work well, either; in the Arctic regions, this ground is usually interlaced with ice, and the heat of the fire melts it into a soggy mess. But you can make fire in these situations:

>> **In or on a piece of metal:** You can use a cooking pot (see Figure 16-4a); any sheet of metal stripped from a car, snowmobile, or airplane wreck (be sure to burn off potentially toxic plastics and paints before cooking over such a fire); or even a piece of tin foil (double it a few times to be sure you don't burn right through it). If you have only one pot, you'll have to find some other container to boil water, but if you're just cooking food, you can roast it above the flames.

>> **On a wood platform:** Build a flat platform of several layers of branches, each layer laid out at 90 degrees to the last (as in Figure 16-4b). The log platform will catch fire eventually, but by using lots of logs, you can keep a small fire going well enough.

>> **On a slab or bed of rock:** Exposed rock slabs work fine. You can make a bed of rock by setting small rocks together on a flat snow surface, as in Figure 16-4c.

FIGURE 16-4: Making a fire on a platform in snowy environments

Don't Eat the Yellow Snow: Safe-to-Drink Snow and Ice

Locating clean drinking water is essential in any wilderness setting. You may be in a cold tundra with pristine white snow everywhere, but before you grab a big handful and start eating, take a moment to read this section.

Choosing and treating frozen water sources

Microbes can live in the coldest places on Earth, so before you eat snow or drink melted ice, make sure you disinfect it (see Chapter 7). Whatever method you use, keep these points in mind:

>> **Select clean snow.** You don't want snow that has been discolored by urine or feces (either yours or that of other animals). Snow can be discolored pink *(watermelon snow)*, black, brown, or yellow by cold-climate algae. Some people feel nauseous after consuming these.

>> **Select non-salt ice.** If you're near a frozen seashore, remember that sea ice is salty, but over a period of years, the salt leaches out. Salty ice is gray or white, but blue or glassy ice should be safe to melt and drink.

Melting snow and ice

Never eat snow in extreme cold unless you're in a warm shelter or have other ways to keep warm besides just your body heat. A mouthful of snow on a hot day can be refreshing, but to stay hydrated you will need to melt snow in truly drinkable quantities.

REMEMBER

Ice is denser than snow, so it yields more water than snow when melted. If you can't find ice, choose densely packed snow over looser snow for melting. Here are several main methods to melt snow or ice:

>> **In a pot over a fire:** Always use a lid to keep as much heat in the pot as possible.

>> **In a cloth bag next to a fire:** Hang snow or ice in a bundle of porous (nonwaterproof) cloth next to a fire and catch the melt in a container. This works if you have, for example, a plastic container (such as a milk jug or soda bottle) but no metal pan to melt in.

>> **In a container you keep next to your body:** Packing some snow into a bottle that you keep next to your body overnight (inside your sleeping bag or blankets) will be chilly, but it can yield some liquid and keeps it from freezing.

>> **In the sun:** If you have a black or dark-colored plastic bag and the temperature isn't too cold, you can pack snow into the bag and leave it out in the sun.

Steering Clear of Cold-Environment Terrain Hazards

Cold, snowy environments present a number of special hazards for the survivor. With the basic information in this section, however, you can avoid this dangerous terrain altogether.

If you encounter a whiteout and your visibility drops to nearly zero in the blowing snow, you need to stop moving and wait it out. See Chapter 24 for tips on surviving a whiteout.

Avoiding avalanche terrain

REMEMBER

Avoid avalanche terrain at all times. Nobody can fight tons of snow moving according to the laws of gravity! You don't want to set your camp up near or under avalanche slopes. Luckily, it's often pretty easy to assess whether your campsite is safe and whether the snow–slope you're about to try to cross is at risk of avalanching.

An *avalanche* is a mass of sliding snow (and ice, tree trunks, mountaineers, and anything else it picks up) that moves down mountainsides unstoppably, whether fast or slow. It occurs when a new layer of snow doesn't bond well with the snow it settles on. After accumulating for a while, the new layer simply slips off the old layer, headed downhill.

People caught in avalanche are normally killed either by trauma (while being tumbled in the snow) or suffocation, after the snow stops moving and settles tightly around the body.

The following avalanche-hazard notes apply worldwide (and Figure 16-5 shows these points visually):

>> Avalanches *normally* occur on slopes from 30° to 40° in steepness, but some occur on slopes as low as 20°.

>> Most avalanches occur within a day or two after a heavy snowfall (anything more than a few inches).

>> Many people killed in avalanches trigger the avalanches themselves by walking or skiing in avalanche-prone snow.

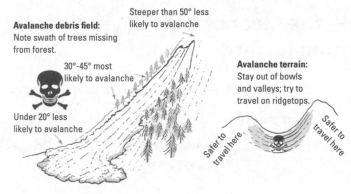

FIGURE 16-5: Avalanche hazards

TIP

If you can't avoid avalanche terrain and you find yourself having to cross a snow slope that you think may avalanche, take some precautions:

>> Unfasten your backpack buckles so you can cast aside your backpack if needed (it can drag you down in an avalanche).

WARNING

>> Zip up all your clothes and pockets (these can fill with snow and drag you down).

>> Test the slope by listening to the snow under your boot. Is there a *crump* or *whump* sound? If so, get out of there! This may well indicate that one layer is settling on top of another to which it is poorly bonded — extreme hazard!

>> Trail a long rope or string so that if you're buried, someone may be able to follow the string to you.

>> Cross the slope one at a time so that if the slope avalanches, not everyone is endangered at the same time.

Make your way across the slope. Try not to panic; this is very scary. After you reach more solid terrain on the other side, the next person should come across in your footsteps, or a little higher up the slope. As soon as everyone is across, get out of there and don't come back!

Avalanche transceivers are devices carried by many backcountry skiers and others in snowy terrain; they broadcast a signal that friends can use to locate you under snow. These are specialized tools that you should research if you're going to spend a lot of time in snowy terrain.

For advice on surviving an avalanche, flip to Chapter 24. Finding and digging people out of avalanches is a topic for a whole other book; you can start with detailed advice in *Mountaineering: The Freedom of the Hills* (The Mountaineers Books).

Staying off thin ice

Falling through thin ice (ice over a stream or lake, for example) is a terrible survival scenario. The definitive studies of Dr. Gordon Giesbrecht, at the University of Manitoba, have identified exactly what happens: The body goes into *cold shock*, leading to hyperventilation, gasping reflex, and possible cardiac overload, panic, and death. Every person is different, though. The cold shock response may not come for a few minutes, so use those minutes wisely to get out of the situation (check out Chapter 22 for more on cold shock response).

Do your best not to fall through the ice in the first place. Here's how to avoid this terrible fate:

>> **When traveling on ice, be aware of the following measurements:**

- **If you are walking:** Lake or river ice needs to be at least 4 inches (10 centimeters) thick; saltwater ice needs to be 6 inches (15 centimeters) thick.

- **If you are driving a snowmobile:** Lake or river ice needs to be at least 6 inches (15 centimeters) thick, and sea ice needs to be at least 1 foot (30.5 centimeters) thick.

- **If you are driving a car or truck:** Don't venture onto any ice less than 1 foot (30 centimeters) thick.

>> **Keep an eye on the color of the ice.** In Wisconsin, where people spend a lot of time ice-fishing (and therefore wandering around on the surface of frozen lakes), folks say, *"Thick and blue, tried and true; thin and crispy, way too risky."*

>> **Be extra-careful when the ice is covered with snow, which hides the ice's true color or texture.** On sea ice, stay away from dark, smooth ice that forms thin plates directly over seawater.

>> **Don't walk on ice without using a probe.** Use a hard pole to test the ice ahead every few steps.

If you need to get someone else out of ice, don't rush to their aid! Take a second to think through the situation and make a plan. Here's what to do:

>> **Calm down.** Take a deep breath. Look for any long item — a rope or pole or branch for example — that you can use to reach the victim. If you have a rope, tie something to the end (to give it a little weight) and throw it to the victim or slide it to that person across the ice. If you don't have a rope and your stick is too short to reach, consider lashing together branches or poles.

>> **If you have to go for the person, get on your belly and slither to distribute your weight over a larger area.** Remember that the two of you are at risk of death, so be extra careful.

> **≫ If you have several people available, you can reach out to the victim like a human chain.** Each person holds the next person's ankles, all spread out on their bellies on the ice.

After getting out of the ice, get the victim out of wet clothes and warm them up immediately. Make a shelter and a fire and treat the victim for hypothermia and shock (see Chapter 13 for treatment details).

Avoiding cornices

When you're traveling in snowy mountains, you want to stay on *ridges,* the spines connecting mountain peaks. That's because avalanches slide down the sides of mountains, not the ridge tops. However, when you're on ridges, you must avoid *cornices,* which are unstable ledges of snow that form on the downwind side of the ridge. Figure 16-6 shows where cornices form and how to avoid them. Even experienced mountaineers sometimes misjudge the cornice break line, so always stay back from the edge.

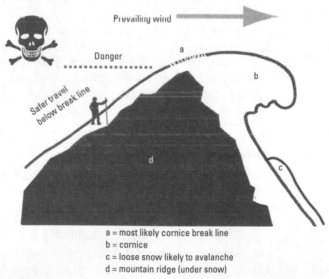

a = most likely cornice break line
b = cornice
c = loose snow likely to avalanche
d = mountain ridge (under snow)

FIGURE 16-6: Cornices are dangerous places, so steer clear of them at all costs

Glacial cracks: Avoiding crevasses

Crevasses are cracks in *glaciers,* which are vast rivers of ice that creep down from mountainous terrain. Crevasses are normally V-shaped, so if you fall in, you continue to fall until your body wedges in tightly at the bottom. Obviously, you want to stay out of crevasses in the first place, and the best way to do that is to stay off glaciers.

If you find yourself trapped on a glacier — for example, if you've crashed a plane on one — your best bet is to stay put and signal for help — you'll stand out against the snow and ice. If you decide to move for some reason, keep the following in mind:

>> **Try to get off the glacier.** Estimate the distance to the surrounding ridges and other rocky terrain and head for them.

>> **Avoid snow bridges if possible.** A *snow bridge* is a natural bridge of snow across a crevasse. They may look sturdy but many aren't. If you see no other way, wait until night, when the snow is frozen more solidly. Go across on your belly to spread out your weight.

WARNING

>> **Don't use a rope to make a bridge crossing "secure."** Tying a rope to someone else while that person crosses a snow bridge will probably (if the snow bridge collapses) just result in both people falling into the crevasse; the first will drag the second in unless you have specialized mountaineering gear and training.

Dealing with snow slopes

If you're in a snowy survival situation and you have to deal with a steep slope, you can use the following pointers to give you a little edge:

>> **Ascend or descend steeper slopes by step-kicking.** Kick the first third of your boot into the snow with each step; see Figure 16-7a. Face the slope and keep three points of contact at all times (at least one foot and both hands). Move deliberately, not in a panic.

>> **Descend a very low-angle slope by *glissading.*** If you slip and start sliding down, stopping can be tough — you may fall

thousands of feet. So *glissade*, or slide downslope on your rear end, with great care. Here are two ideas to keep in mind:

- **Control your speed with a very heavy wooden pole.** A metal rod or a ski pole works fine. Just grasp it firmly (fit it with a wrist loop) and lean on it as you descend, as Figure 16-7b shows. Go slowly while glissading — you may be headed for a cliff!

- **Stop sliding if the terrain gets steeper.** Dig in hard with the pole. If you're going fast, whatever you do, don't dig in your heels — that just catapults you forward!

WARNING

a   Keep feet wide for balance   b

FIGURE 16-7: Dealing with steep snow slopes by step-kicking (a) and glissading (b)

Making Wearable Tools for Cold-Weather Survival

The special tools in this section, which are all clothing–based, can really help you in cold environments and stack the odds in your favor.

Creating footwear

You can't travel if your feet are frozen, and sinking into the snow makes walking a cold, wet, exhausting ordeal. In this section, we explain how to assemble footwear to protect your feet and help you make tracks.

Making your own snow boots

If you can't loosen your shoes to increase circulation and you constantly feel your feet are frozen, taking off your shoes and making your own boots from heavy cloth or any other flexible material is a good idea. To make your own boots, follow these steps:

1. **Lay out a square or rectangle of any heavy cloth (see Figure 16-8a).**

2. **Place a slab of bark, plastic, or other semirigid material on the cloth (see Figure 16-8b.)**

    This is the *footbed;* if your shoes really are useless in the situation, you can cut your shoes down to supply the footbed only.

3. **Wearing the warmest socks you have, place your foot on the footbed; then put dried grass, crumpled newspaper, padding from a car cushion, or any other insulating material under, on, and around your foot (see Figure 16-8c).**

    You need a lot of this insulating material to stay warm, so don't be skimpy. Depending on which material you use, you may have to change this insulation frequently as it gets wet or squashed flat.

4. **Draw the sides of the boot up and around your ankle, and tie off with a cord (see Figure 16-8d).**

    Don't tie so tight that you constrict blood flow.

FIGURE 16-8: Making your own snow boots

These boots are better than nothing, but stay out of water while wearing them, because they fall apart more easily than normal boots.

Making a pair of snowshoes

Snowshoes spread your weight over a large area, allowing you to walk on top of the snow instead of punching through it at each step. Functional snowshoes are easy to fashion from a few sturdy branches, some good, strong cordage, and some persistence and creativity. To make your own pair of snowshoes, follow these steps:

1. **Cut two sturdy, green branches from a tree to use as the frame; strip them of bark.**

These should be about 3 feet (0.9 meters) long and at least 1 inch (2.5 centimeters) in diameter. Cut the wood from living trees, because dry wood breaks.

2. **Assemble the frame as Figure 16-9a shows.**

3. **Select a number of sturdy green branches (at least ¾ -inch [2-centimeters] diameter) as crossbars and lash them across the frame.**

Use natural places where the sticks branch off to more securely socket the crossbeams to the frame (see Figure 16-9b).

4. **Using heavy cordage (parachute cord is ideal), begin lacing across the frame, adding crossbars as needed (see Figure 16-9c).**

Make a kind of web across the crossbeams. This web and the snowshoe frame distribute your body weight across the snow.

5. **Using heavy cordage, make a kind of sling to tie your boot to the frame.**

A sturdy loop over the toe section may be all you need (see Figure 16-9d). Keeping the heel free allows for a more natural walking motion, though while getting used to snowshoes, shuffling your feet is easier. Don't tie your boot so tightly to the snowshoe that it cuts off your circulation — this causes frostbite.

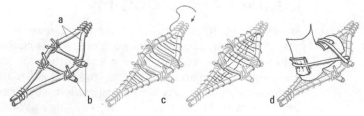

FIGURE 16-9: Making your own snowshoes

TIP

Snowshoes can be difficult to get used to, but they're worth it; half an hour of *postholing* in deep snow, going thigh–deep at each step, makes that clear. You can use a pair of wooden poles like ski sticks to help keep your balance as you learn to walk in them.

Boot wraps: Making and wearing gaiters

Gaiters are boot covers that prevent gravel, snow, and ice from getting into your boots; in snowy environments, this can be particularly important because you really want to keep your feet dry and warm. You can make your own by following these steps:

1. **Cut a piece of heavy cloth, flexible plastic, or even cardboard to the shape and size in Figure 16-10a; puncture two holes in the tabs on the lower margin.**

2. **Roll the fabric into a tube and sew up the loose ends.**

   Make sure the tube is big enough around that you can slide it up to your knee and that it fits over the top of your boot (see Figure 16-10b).

3. **Take off your boot and slip the gaiter up your leg; then put your boot back on.**

4. **Slip the gaiter down and over the boot-top; tie a length of cordage under the boot, connecting the two tabs, to keep the gaiter from coming off (see Figure 16-10c.)**

FIGURE 16-10: Making your own gaiters

Insulating your clothing

Air is a good insulator, and anything that you can use to trap air next to your body can keep you warmer. Insulate clothing by adding a second layer to any garment and stuffing the gap between them with loose material, such as crumpled paper (though this becomes useless if it gets wet) or vegetation. These hold the layers of the garment apart, just a little, allowing a pocket of air to be warmed between them.

Protecting your face and eyes

Snow reflects a lot of light that can burn skin and damage your eyes. In this section, we tell you how to make tools that reduce the glare and protect your face from the sun, wind, and cold.

Making a balaclava

A *balaclava* is ideal for cold environments because it insulates the head and neck. You can make one from the leg of a spare pair of pants or stitch together any textile, as we show you in Figure 16-11.

FIGURE 16-11: An improvised balaclava

Carving snow-glare goggles

WARNING

Even on an overcast day, wear eye protection in snowy terrain. *Snow blindness* (retinal sunburn) is very painful, feeling as though hot sand grains have been packed under your eyelids. The cure is to rest with the eyes closed, perhaps wearing a blindfold. Two days of rest normally restores vision.

If you don't have eye protection, improvise goggles from a piece of cardboard, leather, heavy cloth, or pliable plastic, using the following steps:

1. Cut a slab of bark, plastic, cardboard, or other semi-pliable material into a bar about 8 inches (20 centimeters) across and 1 to 2 inches (2.5 to 5 centimeters) high (see Figure 16-12a).

2. Cut slits into the material, about eye distance apart (see Figure 16-12b).

3. Tie a headband onto the goggles by perforating the ends and tying cordage through them (see Figure 16-12c).

FIGURE 16-12: Improvising snow goggles

Chapter **17**

Staying Alive under the Desert Sun

You face unique challenges in hot regions, especially deserts, which are characterized by sparse vegetation and little rain. Dehydration is always a threat because water is scarce and the heat makes you sweat. Complicating things for a survivor, you have to be ready for very cold nights in such regions, so hypothermia is also a threat. These regions are also home to some hard-to-see animals that strike quickly with dangerous, sometimes lethal, poisons.

In this chapter, we show you how to protect yourself from the sun, make shelter, find food and water, and avoid certain critters. We also show you how to hike your way safely across desert terrain in the dark, when it's cooler.

Dangers Posed by Sun and Heat

Your body reacts to overheating by sweating and dilating your blood vessels to expel more heat from your system. If the body becomes so hot that these methods can no longer dump excessive heat, injury can occur. Overheating can be just as deadly as hypothermia (or excessive cold).

The heat and sun can threaten your well-being in three ways: sunburn, heat exhaustion, and heat stroke. This section helps you grasp what the sun and heat can do to you if you don't take action.

TIP

If you have a good supply of water, you can prevent most heat injuries simply by remaining hydrated. A good indicator of hydration level is the color of urine; anything darker than a wheat color is a signal to drink more.

Going skin deep with sunburn

Sunburn isn't just an annoyance, it can become debilitatingly painful. You can easily prevent sunburn by wearing the correct clothing and using sunblock (see the later section titled "Wearing Sun Shields").

Overheating: Heat exhaustion and heat stroke

Heat exhaustion and heat stroke are forms of *hyperthermia*, an excessive heating of the body. These lead to brain damage and death. Here's how to recognize and treat these problems.

Recognizing the symptoms of hyperthermia

Heat exhaustion is indicated by one or all of these symptoms:

>> Pale and perhaps clammy skin

>> Racing pulse

>> Dizziness and/or headache

>> Nausea and/or diarrhea

REMEMBER

A person with heat exhaustion isn't always sweating profusely; the body may have already used up its water supply prior to reaching heat exhaustion.

Heat stroke is a more dire condition than heat exhaustion, and it's indicated by the following:

>> A red, flushed look to the skin

>> Shock

>> Extreme mental disorientation or unconsciousness

>> Very dark urine

>> Body temperature over 103°F (39.4°C)

Use your first aid kit thermometer to take a rectal temperature and monitor it carefully; anything over 103°F (39.4°C) is potentially life-threatening, so keeping the body cool, wet, and rested is critical.

Cooling off

If the person has heat exhaustion or heat stroke:

>> Get the person out of the sun.

>> Loosen the clothing.

>> Cool the body with liquid. Applying warm to tepid water to the skin and then fanning it may be the best course of action. You can substitute alcohol or soda if water is scarce.

>> Fan the body vigorously, or if you're the victim, fan gently to avoid overexerting yourself.

>> Massage the body to keep the blood circulating.

>> Rehydrate the exhausted person with cool water.

When the body temperature is below 102°F (38.9°C), you can stop the cooling with water treatments (both applying it to the skin and drinking it), but be sure to monitor temperature carefully, because a person may go back into heat stroke.

If your survival situation doesn't allow you copious amounts of water to cool a heat-stressed person, you have to decide what's more important: long-term water conservation or saving the person right now.

Wearing Sun Shields

The first step in protecting your body from the sun is to dress appropriately. You should also cover your exposed skin with some kind of sunblock, whether you've packed some SPF 50 lotion or have to improvise some from your surroundings. This section tells you how to wear your sun defenses.

Cool clothes for hot times: Dressing for desert survival

Your first thought may be to strip down while in a desert to avoid overheating, but actually, you have to shield yourself from the sun's rays.

TIP

Dress yourself from head to toe in clothing that shields you from the sun. You can find out how in Chapter 4 and with the tips we show you here (see Figure 17-1):

>> **Hat or head covering:** To improvise a head covering to keep your brain from cooking, you can use a t-shirt: Simply put the neck of the upturned t-shirt on your head and drop the rest of the t-shirt behind your head, fully protecting your neck and ears. Alternately, you can sew stiff fabric, cardboard, or even pliable plastic, cut to shape with a knife, into a ball cap.

>> **Sunglasses or goggles and a mask:** Sunglasses or even goggles protect you from becoming sunblind. If you don't have sunglasses or goggles, you can improvise them (see Chapter 16). You can also improvise a cloth mask to keep the dust and sand out of your lungs (see Chapter 4).

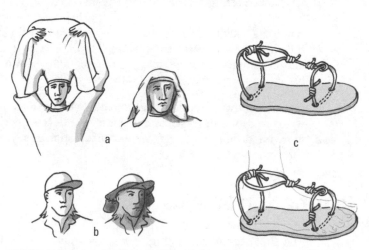

FIGURE 17-1: Improvised hot-weather clothing for your head and feet

>> **Shoes or sandals:** These protect your feet from hard stones, sharp thorns, cactus spines, and hot sand and rocks. You can improvise footwear from many materials, such as wood, hard plastic, or rubber. You may be able to protect your legs from snakebite by making a pair of gaiters (that come to the calf) from heavy cloth or even cardboard (see Chapter 16 for more on making gaiters).

REMEMBER

Don't ditch your warm clothes! Deserts get cold at night (or they can), and then you face the risk of hypothermia.

TIP

If you have the luxury of extra water, keeping a wet cloth wrapped around your head can keep your brain cool. If you're short on water, you may as well use urine's cooling potential. Yes, that's right: *The next time you need to urinate, urinate on your hat and then put it back on.* Urine is sterile when you first urinate, and in a desert survival situation, it evaporates before bacteria become problematic.

Slathering on the sunblock

You can protect yourself from the sun with any cream or other paste that stands between your skin and the rays of the sun. If you're venturing into hot terrain, always carry a tube of sunblock.

TIP

If you don't have any on you, you can improvise sunblock from the following:

>> **Mud or clay:** Pigs and rhinos have the right idea when they wallow in the mud. Smear either mud or clay on the skin.

>> **Charcoal:** Grind it up (after you've made a fire) and smear it on your face, mixing it first, if possible, with water or some kind of oil.

>> **Used motor oil or axle grease:** These substances will block some sunlight, but they contain toxins and may cause discomfort.

Securing Shelter in the Desert

Sheltering from the sun is particularly important in a desert to avoid sunburn and dehydration. Shaded areas may not feel particularly cool, but they're normally 10 to 20°F (5 to 10°C) cooler than areas in direct sunlight.

Building a sunshade

You can fashion a basic desert shelter from two large sheets of cloth or plastic (such as a tarp and a space blanket from your wilderness survival kit — see Chapter 2). To make this shelter, follow these steps and check out Figure 17-2:

1. **Using a sturdy stick or flat rock, dig a trench in the ground, at least 1 foot (0.3 meters) deep, to get below the hot surface.**

   This trench needs to be big enough to lie in; you must never rest directly on the hot surface.

2. **Pile rocks to hold up the corners of your sheets.**

   Pile the rocks so they hold the sheets off the ground and trap a layer of air between the two sheets. With this construction, the sun beats on only the upper sheet, and the space below it keeps the heat from blasting through and reaching you.

   TIP

   Using a space blanket as your top layer both deflects the sun's rays and creates a bright, reflective signal to passing vehicles.

3. **Pile up sand and/or rocks to make a shelter against wind.**

   Wind can be strong and prolonged in desert areas, so weigh down your tarps to prevent them from blowing away.

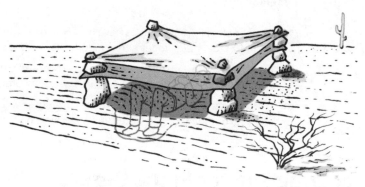

FIGURE 17-2: A desert shelter

Looking for shady places

If you don't have the resources to make the desert shelter we show in Figure 17-2, look for the following shady spots:

TIP

>> **Bushes and rock overhangs:** First evict snakes, scorpions, or other critters by first pelting the area with rocks or prodding vigorously with a stick. Animals want that shade as much as you do.

The animals you find, such as rabbits or snakes, may be edible, so always be prepared to kill with a club (see Chapter 8).

>> **Wrecked vehicles:** Make sure all the doors and windows are open so breezes can blow through. Otherwise, they act like ovens.

REMEMBER

The surface of a desert is usually much hotter than the air just a foot (30.5 centimeters) above it, so sitting up on a rock or even bundled clothing is a good idea.

Warming shelters overnight

Whatever shelter you use, be sure to make a fire in the late afternoon if you're staying put for the night. Collect wood, brush, and other fuel before it gets dark, so you can see what you're doing.

WARNING

Do not burn wood from species of the genus *Euphorbia* (milk bush or pencil-tree) — the smoke is toxic. Before venturing into desert terrain, look up the milk bush and see what they look like — there are many kinds!

Pile on heavy fuel throughout the night so you have embers to keep the fire going in the morning. As always, keep embers and spare fuel ready to make a smoke signal (see Chapter 12). For more on making fires, see Chapter 5.

TIP

If you can't make a fire — for whatever reason — you can slip sun-warmed rocks inside your clothes before you turn in. As soon as they cool down, though, toss them out so they don't suck heat from your body.

Finding Water in the Desert

Though deserts may lack flowing water, every desert does have some moisture — moisture you need to keep cool and slake your thirst. You just need to know where and how to find it. This section gives you some water-finding methods that are particularly useful in deserts. Chapter 7 covers general methods to collect and purify water (including info on gathering dew, which can work in a desert).

REMEMBER

Dehydration can kill you in hours. You must prevent it at all costs, even at the risk of getting a water-borne disease. You should filter and purify all water you find in the wild, but if you're on the verge of perishing from dehydration and you have nothing to purify your water with, you will have to drink unpurified water. This can easily can cause diarrhea that dehydrates you quickly, but if you're facing death by dehydration *right now*, you'd better just take your chances. This will be a serious judgement call in a survival situation.

Discovering standing water

When looking for water, one of the best places to start with is standing water. *Huecos* are holes in rocks or the ground that contain standing water. Even in the driest-appearing deserts, you can usually find such water in four main areas:

>> **River courses:** Wet mud or sand, and even pools of water, can stand for a long time wherever rock or canyon walls hang over the riverbed. ("Squeezing water from mud or sand," later in this chapter, shows how to extract water from mud or sand.)

>> **Under the shade of boulders and in caves, where shade may prevent evaporation:** Don't venture too far into a dark cave, though, or you could get lost or fall into a hole.

>> **In solution pockets:** Solution pockets are bowl-like depressions in rocks that catch rain and may contain anything from a cup of water to hundreds of gallons.

>> **Snow patches:** Not exactly standing water, but still useful; in winter and even into spring, patches of snow can sometimes be found in shaded areas, such as under dense bushes.

A *mirage* is an illusion created by heat rising from the ground, and you can see plenty in desert terrain. A common — and frustrating — desert mirage is that of a distant pool of water, shimmering on the horizon. Don't head for one of these unless it is accompanied by dense green vegetation.

Locating water underground

You may be able to find water in river courses that appear dry, as seen in Figure 17-3. Dig in the outside bends of riverbeds where undercuts provide shade that sometimes prevents water from evaporating. Digging may be hard work, yet again leading to dehydration; you will have to make the call, depending on the situation.

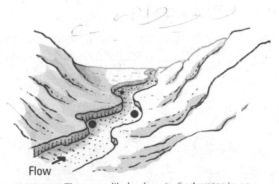

Flow

FIGURE 17-3: The most likely place to find water in an apparently dry riverbed

Sometimes, palm trees can indicate the presence of water as well. You can often find water about 3 feet (0.9 meters) below a palm tree of any type.

TIP

To access underground water, dig down several feet using a stick, a flat rock, or some other tool to preserve your hands. If you find wet sand, wait awhile; water may seep into your excavation, filling it like a basin. If the water doesn't seep into the excavation, you can either try digging deeper or in another spot, or you can try to squeeze water from damp sand or mud.

Squeezing water from mud or sand

Water trapped in sand or mud can be extracted by squeezing it with a twisted cloth (such as a shirt) as seen in Figure 17-4.

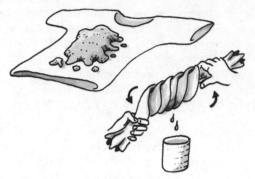

FIGURE 17-4: Squeezing water from wet mud or sand

Accessing water from cracks and shallow pools

You can suck water from narrow cracks in rocks, or very shallow pools, with some kind of tube, such as surgical tubing (good to carry in a survival kit) or a long straw or reed (see Figure 17-5).

FIGURE 17-5: Using a tube to get water from a rock cranny

You may have to suck vigorously a few times to get the water going. Don't drink the water when you suck it with the tube unless you're on the verge of succumbing to dehydration; spit it into a receptacle and then use some method to filter and purify it if you can.

Making a desert solar still

You can use a solar still to process urine (or any water of questionable cleanliness) into drinkable water. Chapter 7 discusses how to make a solar still. To repurpose your urine, place a receptacle of urine in the bottom of the still, next to the collection receptacle (see Figure 17-6). The heat evaporates the water from the urine, leaving behind the impurities; the clean water condenses on the plastic and drips into your water collector, from which you can suck up the water with a tube or straw. Microorganisms can live even in distilled water droplets, so you should boil or filter water obtained from a still, if possible.

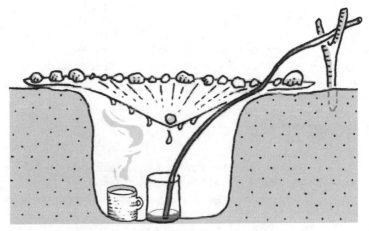

FIGURE 17-6: A desert solar still for distilling pure water from urine

Collecting water from a cactus

Hollywood cowboys often cut open cacti to drink, but there's quite a bit more to it than that.

To get water from a cactus (such as the fishhook cactus shown in Figure 17-7), cut it open with a heavy knife, mash the inside with a stick, and scoop out the fleshy tissue onto a piece of cloth. You can then squeeze the water out using the method we describe in the earlier section "Squeezing water from mud or sand." This may only provide drops of water, and you must judge the effort needed against your level of dehydration.

FIGURE 17-7: The safe fishhook cactus

When drinking the fluid out of a barrel cactus, take your time and make sure you can digest it; if the taste is really bad, seek other sources of water. Some cacti are very alkaline, which can make you ill, even if you put the fluid through a solar still. For more on solar stills, see Chapter 7.

Foraging for Food in Dry Places

Only after you've protected your body from the sun with clothing and shelter and have secured some water (or thought out how you're going to get it) can you turn your thoughts to food. You can go weeks without food, so water always comes first.

Food requires water to digest, so if you don't have water, too, don't eat. Some experts even recommend throwing away or destroying your food if you don't have water to help you avoid the temptation of eating! This is a pretty extreme measure, though — a decision best left to the circumstances and your judgment.

This section considers the different types of food sources you may find in the desert as well as some to avoid at all costs.

Insects

Insects are excellent survival foods. Here's how to prepare them:

>> **Ants and termites:** Ants and termites are one of the few survival foods that are safe without cooking.

- **>> Grasshoppers and beetles:** The wings and legs of grasshoppers and beetles are a choking hazard, so remove them before cooking. You can boil these animals in water to make a soup, or to save water, broil them next to a fire.

- **>> Larvae:** If you find beetles, you may find beetle larvae — white, grub-like animals — under or inside logs or other pieces of wood. Simply cook and eat them as you do for beetles.

Stay away from bees and hornets because of their painful stings — you may be allergic, leading to a serious and sometimes life-threatening reaction.

Cacti and other plants

The fruit of any cactus is edible. The fruit is usually red, purple, or yellow, and found growing from the furthest extremity of the cactus plant. Some of the fruit can be simply plucked and eaten, like the soft yellow fruit of a fishhook cactus. But with the hard red fruit of prickly pear cactus, you will need to remove the peel first. To do this, cut off the ends of the fruit bulb and then make a single incision lengthwise down the fruit. The peal will come off easily and leave the fruit, which is juice-filled.

REMEMBER

Some fruit has spines, some of which are as fine as peach fuzz. Whenever possible, handle cactus fruit with gloves or some type of hand protection.

You can eat the inner meat of the body of many cacti; the problem is getting past the thorns. There are two main ways to do this (gloves or other hand protection are recommended):

- **>>** Impale the cactus on a stick or knife and then grill it over a fire. This chars many of the spines which can then be scraped off with a stone. Be thorough!

- **>>** For a tube-shaped cactus, select one about the size of a salami and cut the ends off. Insert a knife longwise into the flesh of the cactus and cut outward to slice open the cactus without driving the spines into the flesh of the cactus. Once you have a lengthwise incision you can open it like a book and slice up the cucumber-like interior for eating.

The leaves, stems, roots, and flowers of many desert plants are safe to eat, but many species can sicken or kill you. For instance, species of the genus *Euphorbia* (commonly known as milk bush or pencil-tree) are poisonous. So before you eat any plants, check them with the Universal Plant Edibility Test in Chapter 8.

Some fungi do grow in the desert, but don't eat them or use the Universal Plant Edibility Test on them (see Chapter 8) — they can be toxic even in small amounts.

Poultry and eggs

All birds and their eggs are edible. Remember that birds don't just nest in tree branches; they may occupy a cavity in a cactus or tree trunk, or their nests may be under a bush on the ground, in a cave, or on a rock ledge. Boil the eggs and broil the birds after plucking off the feathers.

Desert mammals

Small mammals, such as mice, are common in many deserts. They can be tough to catch, though — they're so small that snaring them would require a very small, delicate snare. You can sometimes trap mice by placing a can of water or other bait in the bottom of a 2-foot (0.6-meter) deep, steep-sided hole. At night, mice are attracted by the smell of food or water, and as soon as they fall into the hole, they can't get out.

Larger desert mammals include foxes and various herbivores, such as antelope. You may be able to snare these animals as well, but insects, snakes, or small mammals are much easier to catch. If you do catch a mammal, you can butcher and cook it in ways we cover in Chapter 8.

Lizards and snakes

Many lizards and snakes are harmless and edible. If you do decide to hunt them, make sure you know what you're hunting. We don't recommend hunting desert snakes because some have lethal bites, but if you do come across one and feel the situation is manageable, there's no reason not to kill and eat it. What is a manageable situation, with respect to a potential killer (like a rattlesnake), will depend on how hungry, well-armed, energetic, and confident you are.

If you choose to eat snakes and lizards, here's how to process them:

1. **Cut off the head by cutting at the neck, several inches down from the base of the skull.**

   The poison glands of snakes and lizards are in the head, and this gets them out of your way. A forked stick can be used to pin down the head during the cut.

   Snake heads can still bite 24 hours after death, and lizard mouths are breeding grounds for bacteria. Bury the head away from your butchery and eating spot and mark the burial spot with a pile of stones so you don't accidentally dig it up.

2. **Strip off the skin.**

   Start an incision, lengthwise, down the body from where you removed the head, and then pull the skin off like a sheath.

3. **Cook it properly.**

   Broil the carcass next to a fire or bake it under hot coals. When the meat is flaky, white, and dry, it is edible.

Avoiding Dangerous Desert Animals

In deserts, keep your eyes out for the following creatures, especially in shaded areas or at night, when desert animals are most active.

Gila monsters and slithering snakes

Most desert lizards aren't toxic, but beware of the bite of the large Gila monster (see Figure 17-8) and Mexico's very similar beaded lizard. Both lizards are around 1 foot (30.5 centimeters) long and are unlikely to attack unless provoked. Unless you have a weapon that you can use to kill the lizard so you can eat it, your safest move is to just walk away.

Many desert species of snakes can sicken or kill you with a lightning-fast bite. Especially stay away from the rattlesnake, which has a diamond-shaped head that's fatter than the neck, as in Figure 17-8. These snakes have a lethal bite, and they make a distinctive *sssss* sound with their tail-rattles as a warning. Many poisonous snakes don't have diamond-shaped heads, though, so in a survival situation treat all snakes as though they are lethal.

FIGURE 17-8: The distinctive head of a rattlesnake and a Gila monster

You can sometimes scare snakes away by making plenty of noise as you walk. Sturdy boots and heavy trousers can protect you from a bite. You can also use *gaiters*, which are fabric covers that seal the space between the trousers and the boots. To see how to improvise these, take a look at Chapter 16.

Stinging scorpions, centipedes, and spiders

Arthropods are critters with hard shells and lots of little jointed legs — and sometimes some pretty nasty bites and stings. You do have to watch out for wasps and ticks as you do in temperate environments (see Chapter 11), but you may also run into some scorpions, centipedes, and desert spiders. In this section, we tell you what to watch out for.

Scorpions and centipedes

What they say in the movies is true: The big, burly scorpions sting hard, but the small ones can be lethal. Meanwhile, centipedes can deliver a very painful and occasionally debilitating bite, to which some people can have a severe allergic reaction.

REMEMBER

Scorpions (see Figure 17-9a) and centipedes (see Figure 17-9b) are tough to avoid in deserts, but you can take some precautions:

» Be vigilant with every rock you turn over — use a stick.

» Never put on a piece of clothing (such as a shirt or a shoe) without first checking it for scorpions and centipedes. Shake all your clothing and foot gear before putting it on — and we mean shake it vigorously so the fabric makes a *pop!* sound.

>> Be especially careful between sundown and the next noon — that's when most scorpion stings occur.

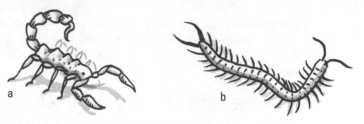

FIGURE 17-9: Watch out for scorpions (a) and centipedes (b)

Scorpion stings feel like bee stings, and less than 1 percent of scorpion stings in the U.S. are fatal. The symptoms of a serious sting, however, include the following:

>> Dilation of the pupil and twitching of the eye
>> Difficulty swallowing
>> Heart palpitations and sweating

Treat scorpion stings and centipede bites simply by washing and then keeping the wound clean. Painkillers may ease the pain. There are antivenoms for scorpion venom, but they must be administered by a doctor.

Spiders

The world is home to over 40,000 spider species, some of which live in the desert. Most are harmless to humans, but some can be lethal. Dangerous spider bite symptoms include

>> Dizziness, nausea, and vomiting
>> Fever
>> Cramps, especially in the abdomen

Chapter 13 covers spider bite treatment. Avoid spiders by checking under rocks and shaking out clothing.

Wind and Water: Watching Out for Desert Weather

Deserts seem so calm most of the time — little wind, not much weather to speak of other than the relentless sun. But there are two real dangers you have to keep an eye out for, outlined in this section.

Staying high and dry during flash floods

A *flash flood* is any unexpected arrival of water on a landscape, and strangely enough, this is a big danger in deserts. A big storm can drop millions of gallons of water 100 miles away — while you're being blistered by the sun — and suddenly the dry riverbed you're staggering along or sleeping in turns into a raging river!

To avoid flash flood dangers, walk along the rim of a dry river while you assess the danger, remembering a few tips:

>> **Look for high-water marks.** High-water marks (refer to Figure 17-10) include stains on rock walls or piles of vegetation snagged in tree limbs adjacent to watercourses, where vegetation floating on a prior flash flood rose up and got caught. Stripes in the rock may not be high-water marks — they may be natural rock layers — so look for stranded vegetation and other signs of flooding.

>> **Before venturing into a canyon or dry riverbed, look at the horizon all around for clouds.** If you see low, dark clouds that look rainy, get back up on higher ground. The flash-flood water may be pouring down way over there, right now — just an hour from where you are.

Taking shelter from sandstorms

High winds can pick up mass quantities of sand and blow them across deserts with tremendous force in what's called a *sandstorm*. Some sandstorms can actually strip the paint off a car. If you see a giant, sand–colored wall on the horizon (for once, it looks just like it does in the movies!), prepare yourself by covering your mouth with a cloth (to filter out some sand) and finding some shelter. If you have to, build a wind–shelter from rocks. A circle or semicircle of stones large enough to lie behind may be enough to break some of the wind, but you still get covered by sand every few hours. Don't put a tarp over the shelter if the wind is strong — it'll just blow away.

FIGURE 17-10: High-water marks in a dry riverbed mark this canyon as a dangerous place to walk.

TIP

Dense, blowing sand can interfere with radio transmissions, and will ground rescue aircraft anyway, so if you have a radio, save your batteries and wait until the storm ends to begin signaling again. Sandstorms can last for days.

Finding Your Way in the Desert

The decision to travel in a survival situation is a big one that we cover in Chapter 11. If you do decide to move in desert terrain, one thing going for you is that you can normally see a long way, allowing you to navigate more efficiently than in, say, a dense jungle. Also, night skies are visible, so the stars can be used to find your way (see Chapters 9 and 10 for more on navigating). This section helps you travel in the desert both during the day and night.

If you travel away from where you became lost, be sure to leave a note or signal when you begin, and leave messages in trees or under conspicuous piles of stone so people can find them easily. Indicate the following:

>> Who you are and what happened to you

>> What direction you're headed and why

>> What supplies you have

>> The date and time that you're departing

Traveling at night

If you've committed to traveling to get out of your wilderness survival situation, traveling at night is a good tactic for dealing with hot country. Temperatures are cooler and often downright cold in deserts at night, so your body uses less water — about half the water it needs when traveling in daylight.

For navigation, you can use the stars, which — after you know a few basics — are nothing less than a vast compass in the sky (and the stars never lie, thankfully). Chapter 10 tells you how to navigate by the stars.

Spend plenty of time during the day making your plans before traveling at night. Get to the highest point you can safely reach to give you a better vantage point, and then study the terrain, locating the features that can act as landmarks.

Seeing in the dark

To travel at night, you have to use night vision, which you can acquire by letting your eyes adjust to darkness. In the space of an hour of sitting in darkness — with no campfire or any other artificial light — your pupils dilate to their maximum, which allows your eyes to gather more light.

When using night vision, you have to maintain strict light discipline. Don't use a flashlight or even light a match after you start traveling, because these lights will ruin your night vision.

TIP

If you have a red lens filter on your flashlight, you can use it to read maps at night without destroying your night vision. A *red filter* is simply a red-colored translucent plastic cap that fits over your flashlight bulb housing. If you don't have a red filter, improvise one by taping red fabric over your flashlight.

Using a staff to probe ahead in darkness

When traveling at night, make sure you use a walking stick or staff to feel the ground in the darkness and help you keep your balance on uneven terrain. Using one in each hand, like ski poles, is also effective.

You can also use a walking stick or staff to prod bushes or other obstacles (or better yet, go around them) when you suspect they may be home to a snake or other potentially dangerous animal. Remember, a lot of desert animals come out at night, when it's cooler.

Confronting drop-offs

Walking at night can pose potential dangers, such as the inability to see that canyon in front of you. If you're on rocky ground, beware of sudden drop-offs.

TIP

If the ground goes completely black in front of you, stop and feel with your walking stick or staff. You may have to go around an obstacle, or you may be able to judge how far a drop-off is by probing with a walking staff. If you can feel that solid ground is just a few feet down (and, by throwing a stone into the darkness, you can tell that it's not just a little ledge leading to a high cliff!), you can proceed. But don't jump down the drop-off — that's crazy! To clamber down a 3-foot (0.9-meter) cliff, do the following and see Figure 17-11:

1. Probe the ground at the bottom of the drop-off with your walking stick.

2. Turn to face the land you're walking on and kneel down.

3. Hold onto the edge and shove your legs over.

4. Slide/lower yourself down, using your arms for support.

FIGURE 17-11: Checking height and clambering down a 3-foot drop-off

Traveling in daylight

REMEMBER

We don't believe there's any good reason to travel significant distances in deserts in daylight in a real survival situation. You may as well wait for cooler hours of dusk till dawn, when you'll consume less water and you're at less risk of heat exhaustion or heat stroke. However, if you're forced to travel in the day (we can't really think why, but it may happen):

>> **Watch yourself and your companions for the symptoms of heat exhaustion and dehydration.** We discuss these earlier in "Dangers Posed by Sun and Heat."

>> **Protect yourself from the sun with the proper clothing.** See the earlier section "Wearing Sun Shields."

>> **Drink plenty of water.** If you have the water, drink at least 1 gallon (4 liters) a day. You may need up to 5 gallons (19 liters) a day.

>> **Rest in shade and up off the ground for at least 10 minutes every hour.** This gives you a few moments to cool off.

>> **Breathe through your nose rather than your mouth.** You want to minimize water loss from exhaled vapor.

Better yet, avoid all these problems by traveling at night.

Crossing Desert Terrain

The vast, open terrain of deserts can be deceptive, making distant hills look three times closer than they really are. Don't get frustrated. Stick to your plan even as you encounter these obstacles:

» **Sand dunes:** The wind can blow sand into mountainous heaps. Dunes present no real immediate dangers, but they're dangerously exhausting to climb. You either have to slog over them — sinking back with each step — or go around them, which may cost miles. Tough call.

» **Rocky terrain:** Wear or improvise good footwear to protect you from heat, sharp rock, and thorns; high cuffs or gaiters may stop a snake attack, and a somewhat stiff boot can help prevent a twisted ankle. In any case, travel with care to prevent injury.

» **Wadis and lagas:** Dry watercourses — termed *wadis* in Arabia and *lagas* in East Africa — are riverbeds that flow in the spring (when mountain snows melt) but are dry the rest of the year. They can be the home of flash floods in the springtime, so beware of this danger.

» **Gallery forests:** These are vegetation stands that run along riverbanks, whether the river is dry or flowing. They can be a great source of water — because tree roots and other vegetation trap water in their vicinity — but remember that a lot of nonhuman animals (such as African lions) like to take shelter in the shade of gallery forests, just like you do.

4

Surviving on the Seas, Oceans, and Great Lakes

Chapter **18**
Staying Afloat and Warm

Most survival situations on water begin in either of two ways: people somehow get separated from their vessel or their vessel sinks. Neither are pleasant thoughts, but it's good to know that there are plenty of strategies to help you survive such disasters.

In this chapter, we introduce scenarios in which life rafts aren't involved. (Chapter 19 covers life raft procedures as well as what to do if your vessel is disabled.) For now, we show you how to recognize that watercraft are in trouble, how to cope with that situation, and how to stay alive in the minutes and hours after the sinking — with or without a life jacket.

Recognizing When Your Vessel Is in Trouble

If you spend any time studying the harrowing history of tragedies at sea, you quickly see a clear pattern: Those who recognize what's happening immediately — as it's happening — usually have the highest rate of survival. This section discusses some of the causes of sinking and the warning signs that the vessel you're aboard, whether large or small, may be in danger.

Overloading

If you find yourself aboard a vessel that you feel is overloaded, strive to stay above deck; go below only if you have to. If danger comes — such as heavy weather — an overloaded vessel is going to get into trouble quickly.

Island-to-island ferries and river ferries are often overloaded, causing many tragic *capsizes* (overturning). But danger from overloading can happen anytime and anywhere — even with canoes and rowboats on lakes and ponds.

If you haven't yet boarded the boat, here's how you can tell whether it's overloaded:

>> **Check the *freeboard*.** This is the amount of the boat's hull that's above the surface of the water. If the rim *(gunwale)* of the vessel is too close to the water, even a small wave could sink it. Check out Figure 18-1.

Note that some vessels have intentionally low freeboards, especially on the big rivers including the Amazon and the Mekong. In these cases, compare the freeboard of the vessel you're about to board with other vessels, loaded and unloaded.

>> **Look for empty spaces.** All vessels should have empty spaces in them, places where no person stands, no equipment rests, no cargo is stored. Few boats are designed to be stuffed to the brim, so if a vessel is absolutely packed, be on guard.

Overloaded

FIGURE 18-1: An overloaded vessel

Poor trim or listing

Watercraft should sit level in the water, not *list* which is a sort of leaning from side to side. If your vessel is listing you should be planning your escape, especially if the vessel is rolling with water motion. If the vessel rolls one way and doesn't roll back upright, something is seriously wrong.

Generally, all water vessels should be *trimmed* (balanced) in the water. Even sailboats, which lean over (*heel*) naturally, should still be trim — in other words, they should lean over in an organized fashion. Figure 18-2 shows trimmed and poorly trimmed boats. If your vessel leans over so hard that it is swamped or flooded, you may sink; see "Knowing what to do if your boat beings to sink" later in this chapter.

Out of trim

Trim and not
overloaded

FIGURE 18-2: An out-of-trim vessel and a trimmed vessel

REMEMBER

Small boats swamp quickly. *Swamping* means that the boat floods almost to the brim. This happens when an enormous mass of water comes over the side, or over the back (*transom*) of the boat.

Bad weather and big waves

Properly trimmed and operated vessels normally come through bad weather, though it can be uncomfortable and scary for passengers to see and feel big waves and high winds working over the boat. In such conditions, be proactive by ensuring that you know where the life jackets, rafts, and other survival equipment are located.

If the vessel you're aboard *labors* (has a hard time recovering from pitching and rolling, or has more water coming aboard than draining off) in rough water, especially if the boat loses power, start working on a concrete plan for survival.

When you're in any boat, but especially a small boat, you're vulnerable to the *plunging breaker,* a wave that flings water in front of it. A perfect example is seen near the shore because the surf is often made up of plunging breakers — but these can develop in open water as well. Remember, size isn't the main factor here; a wave can be only about 6 feet tall, but if it plunges, it's dangerous (see Figure 18-3).

FIGURE 18-3: A plunging breaker

Whenever you see plunging breakers, be prepared for serious problems like flooding and capsize — another reason to wear your life jacket in rough conditions, or even better, a good reason to avoid the surf altogether! Note that while weather may be fine ashore, even just some miles off, on open water, things may be rough. Ask experienced people about what to expect offshore; if they're not going out that day, it's a good idea to do the same.

Collisions

Rivers, lakes, and especially oceans are big bodies of water, but ships and boats still find ways to run into each other, or submerged objects, every day. Knowing how collisions occur can give you the added edge of a few extra seconds or minutes to plan your survival. Below we introduce how to avoid running into things on open water.

Understanding collision courses with other vessels

Collisions between boats usually occur in marinas, ports, entrances to ports, or places with bad visibility and congested conditions, but they *can* occur almost anywhere. Here's what to do whenever you see another vessel (check out Figure 18-4).

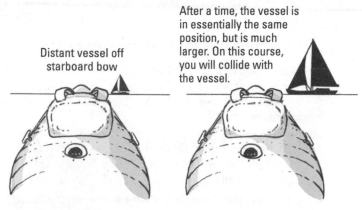

Distant vessel off starboard bow

After a time, the vessel is in essentially the same position, but is much larger. On this course, you will collide with the vessel.

FIGURE 18-4: A collision course

1. **Align your view of the other vessel with some object of reference on your vessel.**

   Line up a nearby object with the faraway vessel, just like looking down a gun sight. In Figure 18-4, a distant sailboat is lined up off your kayak's *starboard* (right) *bow* (front).

2. **After a few seconds, check the alignment again.**

   In this case, if the sailboat is still aligned with the same place on your sea kayak (just off the starboard bow), but the sailboat is much larger — in other words, much closer — the two of you are moving toward the same point.

   In a few more seconds take your sighting again. In this case, if the sailboat is so large that you can see the person who's steering it — but it's still at the same sighting point (the starboard bow), you're on a *collision course*.

3. If you're on a collision course, turn sharply away.

If you have no control of the vessel — such as when you're on a charter or ferry and someone else is piloting and they will not listen to your warning of an imminent collision — begin taking the steps we show you in "Knowing What to Do If Your Boat Starts to Sink," later in this chapter. If you have control of the vessel but can't turn soon enough, signal the other vessel using sound (such as a whistle) and/or shouting and waving to warn them of the collision course.

WARNING

In waters where there are Jet Skis, Sea-Doos, or any other sort of personal water crafts (PWC), be especially vigilant. These small motorcycles-on-water are involved in a lot of collisions.

Watching out for underwater obstacles

The second type of collision is the type that occurs when the boat you're on strikes a fixed object, or a submerged one, like a reef, rock, or large tree trunk. Maintain a very sharp lookout for the following:

>> **Any signs or buoys bearing large red diamonds:** These signs can vary from country to country, but in North America, they mark danger.

>> **Any foam (especially near the shore):** This usually means that a rock (or other obstacle) is just right under the surface (*awash*).

>> **Any long lines of rocks extending from land:** Where these long, rocky peninsulas stop is only the start of danger. These rocks usually continue just under the surface.

Fire

Watercraft often burn fiercely because on open water there is often a breeze, and there is often fuel aboard. Concentrated flames, smoke, and heat often make it impossible for the crew to function, so the fire is hard to extinguish, putting everyone at the mercy of the winds and waves.

If you see a fire on a cruise or charter, notify the crew immediately. Though you should always try to let the crew put out the fire, be aware that fire extinguishers are available on most vessels larger than a canoe.

Hatch failure and ship damage

A *hatch failure* is when water enters a vessel through normally-closed openings such as doors and windows. Larger vessels have automatic *bilge pumps* that pump out such *shipped water*, but they may not be working. Keep hatches secure and always watch for shipped water inside a vessel.

REMEMBER

Many tragedies at sea are forewarned by sounds or bad vibrations. Water itself can make horrendous noises against a boat's hull without causing any damage, but when a ship strains, the sound is different; there is groaning, metal twisting on metal. All ships make these sounds when laboring, but listen for them, and try to develop a sense of what's unusual. The best way to react to loud or violent noise is to be vigilant, but not panicked.

Knowing What to Do If Your Vessel Starts to Sink

If your vessel starts to sink, remain calm and take decisive action. Doing so greatly increases your chance of survival. This section introduces the immediate steps to take if your ship is in trouble and starting to sink.

Radioing for help

It is legal for anyone, regardless of experience or license, to operate *any* radio if sending a distress signal. A serious stipulation is that to signal SOS or Mayday, you must be in "grave and immediate danger" of death or loss of significant property. If your situation isn't that bad, consider signaling *Pan*, which is for smaller problems. (For directions on how to send a Mayday or Pan signal, check out Chapter 12.)

If you've made radio contact with someone and your distress signal has been sent and completely received, make a schedule. Tell the radio operator on the other end that if you lose contact, they should listen again at a specific time for another signal. If radio contact is very good, and you have the schedule worked out, shut off your transmitter or cellphone. Good battery discipline can give you the upper hand on your surroundings.

If you know you're going to leave the vessel — in other words, if the boat is sinking and you know there won't be a second radio contact — tape down the button on the microphone so that the radio continues to transmit for as long as possible. An alternative to this is to press the DSC button, the *Digital Selective Calling* button, a red button on the face of some VHF radios. This activates a distress signal that automatically alerts authorities. For more on DSC, see Chapter 12.

Putting on a life jacket

Never leave shore without knowing where the life jackets are, and as a precaution, put them on in any unusual situation in the water. If life jackets aren't offered by the crew, you may have to find them yourself. Life jackets often 'live in the dark,' so if they're not readily found, look in the darkest places of a vessel — in closets, under seats, in the *forepeak* (storage space under the front of the vessel), the *lazarette* (a storage trunk at the rear), and in closets in the *bridge* (where the vessel is steered).

If you have time and the water is cold, put on as much clothing as you can before putting on your life jacket, because clothing traps water near your body, which is then warmed by your body, forming a protective layer. With a life jacket, the extra clothing won't be a hindrance.

Always choose the thickest life jacket you can find, but don't select an *oversized* life jacket. Put the life jacket on *before* you go into the water. If you're wearing an inflatable life jacket, don't inflate it until you are in the water.

Snug up life jacket adjustment straps so it fits well, but not so much that it will interfere with swimming. Often if you have to jump overboard, the life jacket's buoyancy keeps it at the surface while your body plunges down in the water; you might slip right out of it! The crotch strap is the most effective way to prevent this, so anytime a jacket has a crotch strap, use it.

The only exception to the rule of putting on your life jacket before you go into the water is if your surrounded by burning fuel or if you have to submerge your body to swim to safety. If you face this type of situation, try throwing your jacket beyond the flames and then make your underwater escape.

Preparing to abandon ship

If the vessel is sinking, make abandoning it cleanly your first priority — you don't want to be pulled down with the sinking vessel.

When your life jacket is securely on, take these steps to prepare to abandon ship:

>> **Protect your cellphone or radio.** Protect electronic devices from water damage by putting them in any kind of container, such as a handbag or plastic bag. For advice on signaling for help with a cellphone, see Chapter 12.

>> **Gather signaling materials.** You must be able to signal for help after the sinking. Chapter 12 lists items you can grab to make signals.

>> **Put on a hat.** If you have access to wool, grab it. A hat can double your survival time in some cases.

>> **Collect water and/or containers.** Even just a small amount of water can help. Your ability to survive long term on the sea might well come down to your ability to catch and store rainwater. (For more on fresh water at sea, see Chapter 20.)

TIP

If you can, make sure water containers have a little air inside them so that they'll float well in water.

Abandoning ship: The how-to

Stay on the vessel for as long as you think it's safe (even if 'on' means clinging to the side of a mostly-sunk vessel). Any vessel is easier for rescuers to see than a life raft or just your body floating in the water. Many 'sunk' vessels stay partially floating for a long time. If, however, the vessel is decisively and rapidly leaving the surface, and you can step straight into a life raft, boarding a life raft is preferable to swimming for it. (For more on using life rafts, see Chapter 19.) The rest of this chapter deals with situations in which you *don't* have a life raft.

REMEMBER

A sinking vessel is a body in motion. Just because the boat is oriented one way right now doesn't mean it's going to stay that way. Expect the boat to roll or pitch heavily. If you must abandon, keep these ideas in mind:

>> **Leave from the side on which the wind is blowing (upwind).** If you jump off the boat on the other side (downwind), you run the risk of having the boat blown over you.

>> **Enter at the point closest to the water.** Ideally, you want to slip smoothly into the water — slowly. Doing so can help to prevent cold shock (see Chapter 22). Jumping can cause injuries as you hit the water or items floating in it.

>> **If you must jump into the water, assume the following position:**

- **Fold your arms across your chest and grasp the lapels of your life jacket with your fingers before you jump.** Hold your jacket down securely. Remember, when people lose their life jackets, they usually lose them over their heads because the buoyancy makes the device shoot up while the body is plunging down.

- **Cross your legs tightly at the ankles.** Jump feet first and with crossed ankles to prevent your legs from becoming entangled in rope or other items in the water.

- **Above all things, part company cleanly.** Stray lines and fishing gear, cables and railing, masts — all these things can grab you. Abandon decisively and swim away quickly. Stay clear of propellers, turning or not!

COPING WITH COLD SHOCK RESPONSE

Members of 'polar bear clubs' get a thrill out of the gasping breaths and racing pulses that come from plunging into cold water, but cold water is no friend to the survivor. Unlike hypothermia, *cold shock response* kills by causing cardiac arrest, stroke, or by incapacitating you physically so that you cannot do such tasks as climbing into a life raft.

Entering the water gradually — if you have that luxury — goes a long way toward preventing cold shock response. Another way to help yourself is to cling to floating objects, or just float in your life jacket, and wait until your heart rate normalizes. This usually takes from 7 to 10 minutes.

Immersion in cold water can make it hard to hold your breath for any length of time. Before trying to hold your breath for some reason in cold water, wait until your heart rate returns to a more normal pace.

TIP

After you are sure the vessel has gone down for good, return to the sinking site to retrieve useful items from the *debris field*, which is the scatter of floating objects that have come off of the sunken vessel. Remember that debris disperses quickly. Recover jugs, bottles, sheets of fabric — just about any floating item will have some survival value.

Shark!

In the oceans, practice shark attack prevention and safety. You're not trying to be cruel to sharks; you're trying to save your life. Keep the following pointers in mind:

» **Reduce the amount of blood in the water.** Tend to any wounds as best you can.

» **Don't swim erratically.** Swim in smooth powerful strokes. Avoid weak or fluttering strokes, and don't thrash about in the water.

» **Don't urinate or defecate in the water if sharks are nearby.** Sharks have a keen sense of smell and may be attracted to the scent.

» **Stay in a group.** Most sharks are scavengers and are looking for easy targets. Appearing larger may be better.

In case you're forced into fighting sharks, we offer the following methods based on our experiences at sea in small vessels;

» **Be ready to use your knife or other sharp item:** Lash these on the end of a pole — if you're lucky enough to have one or find one floating in the debris. Use the weapon as a prod to discourage sharks that come near.

» **Deploy shark repellant:** Many life raft equipment kits contain shark repellent chemicals; but remember, it's a one-time-use-only solution that might only last an hour.

» **Strike aggressive sharks in their sensitive eyes or gills.** Use your fingers or any tool available. Many survivors have tried this with varying degrees of success.

» **Slap the water or scream underwater:** Sometimes this drives sharks away, but other times it seems to attract them. There are no guarantees, unfortunately.

Staying Warm as You Float with a Life Jacket

Floating with a life jacket seems straightforward, doesn't it? You just float there and the jacket does all the work. But you may be shocked: Floating *properly* can radically improve your survival time. Note that *very generally speaking*, most people can go about 8 to 10 hours in average-ocean temperatures (68°F or 20°C) before succumbing to hypothermia. This section gives some methods to extend that time.

What to do in the water

The first and greatest problem of floating in a life jacket is *hypothermia* — the slow draining of your body's core heat.

TIP

Entering cold water causes loss of muscle coordination and other symptoms leading to difficulty performing sophisticated tasks like removing things from bags or closing difficult zippers. Take care of such vital activities as setting up the survival raft, or rescuing other survivors, before you become incapacitated.

Once you have performed any necessary tasks, slow the onset of hypothermia with the following strategies:

>> **Remain still.** Contrary to popular belief, swimming, treading water, or generally moving around makes you colder because you are moving warmed water away from your body.

>> **Use the HELP body posture.** HELP, or the *Heat Escape Lessening Position,* is a body posture you use to close off your main heat leaks. Check out Figure 18-5, and remember to protect the following areas, which are some of the main places where your body leaks heat:

- **Armpits:** Hold your elbows near your sides to close the armpit area.

- **Crotch:** Squeeze your thighs together so that your crotch is insulated and protected.

FIGURE 18-5: The HELP heat-saving position

Staying warm in groups

If you're with a group, huddling for support and extra warmth is recommended by the U.S. Navy to increase survival times. Have everyone hold onto one another with their arms as seen in Figure 18-6.

FIGURE 18-6: Huddle together in groups to keep warm

Note that staying together in a group makes you a bigger target for search and rescue to see. For more on being seen, check out Chapter 12.

Floating without a Life Jacket

Though it's frightening to contemplate, many have survived floating in open water even without a life jacket. If you find yourself in this situation, the information in this section can improve your chances of survival.

TIP

If you have to abandon ship without a life jacket, remember that you may find one floating on the surface after a sinking; alternately, you may be able to cling to some floating object until help arrives.

Inflating your clothes

If you don't have a life jacket, you can create a provisional float from your own pants (though this doesn't work at all with shorts). The technique is simple (see Figure 18-7):

1. **Remove your pants and tie knots at the bottoms of each leg.**

    In our experience, tying each leg separately works best. Try to tie the knots just as close to the ends as you can, and tie them very tightly.

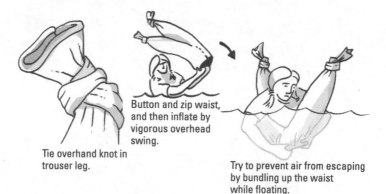

Tie overhand knot in trouser leg.

Button and zip waist, and then inflate by vigorous overhead swing.

Try to prevent air from escaping by bundling up the waist while floating.

FIGURE 18-7: Improvising a life jacket with a pair of pants

2. Hold the pants by the waistband and flip them up and behind your shoulders as though you were going to use them as a cape.

3. Using both hands, and in one swift motion, bring the pants over your head and end with the opening of the waist coming down flush on the water in front of you.

   The goal is to force air into the open waist area of the pants and trap it in the legs. Done right, the pants should make a hollow *whop!* when the opening smacks down on the surface.

   To increase the amount of air inside, exhale into the waist band to fill the legs.

4. Quickly cinch the waist closed with a belt, or if you don't have a belt, hold the waist closed with your hands.

You may need several tries before you get the hang of it (so practice before you set sail!), but it does work. You'll have to reinflate the pants anywhere from every 5 to 20 minutes, but done well, you can hold out for a long time this way.

Long-term floating

You can actually float for days — as long as you can remain conscious. But you need to think about conservation of energy. The position that uses the least amount of energy is called *drown-proofing* (by the U.S. Armed Services) or the less appetizing term, *dead-man's float*.

Essentially, *drown-proofing* requires you to take a deep breath while treading water vertically, hold the breath, and then (counterintuitively) settle your face down in the water. Because the lungs and buttocks tend to float high, your chest will support you and your rear will rise a little, suspending you with arms and legs hanging somewhat down from the surface. Maintaining takes very little energy and it's good for warmer-water scenarios. There are many cases of people who have used this position to stay afloat for several days. Of course, since your face is in the water in this posture, you must turn your head or raise it up occasionally to take a breath.

You should also look for search-and-rescue units when you take a breath. If you see them, get out of the dead-man's float posture so you can wave at rescuers.

Don't drown-proof in cold water. If you do, you end up with your head in the water, causing rapid onset of hypothermia. If you're in cold water and you have no flotation devices, tread water slowly and gently to keep the top of your head out of the water.

When floating long term in the ocean, maintain a sharp lookout for groups of jellyfish. Many of these animals are translucent, and unless you're really watching for them, you can drift right into the center of a group (we know — we've done it, and a close friend once wandered into a group and ended up sucking some of them down his snorkel!). If you feel a little sting, look around immediately. It's a lot better to swim around a group of jellyfish than to look up from your floating position and find yourself in the center — having to swim out!

Chapter **19**

The Great Drift: Aboard Life Rafts and Disabled Vessels

n most survival situations at sea, you end up on a drifting vessel, such as a raft or disabled boat (it happens on lakes and rivers, too).

Most large ships carry both l*ife rafts*, which are small inflatable vessels, and *lifeboats*, which are small rigid boats often equipped with motors. When the captain orders abandonment, the crew usually tries the lifeboats first because they're motorized. But if you're aboard a ship that begins to lean to one side, or *list*, your only chance of escape may be the rafts. As the ship leans, the crane-like arms (*davits*) that hold the lifeboats frequently can't launch them, so the life rafts are the only way off the ship.

This chapter covers the basics of how to deploy life rafts, how to keep them afloat, and other relevant info concerning a life raft at sea. We also explain what you can do if you're in a small vessel that loses power.

Getting from Ship to Life Raft

In this section, we give you the how-to on launching, inflating, and surviving in life rafts.

REMEMBER

Before going aboard any vessel, you need to know how to put on a life jacket; see Chapter 18.

Locating the life raft

Before you even leave port, make sure you know where the life raft is on your boat. Although life rafts usually come in containers, they may be hard to find, even buried in closets or under a lot of equipment. Ask the skipper where the raft(s) is before agreeing to depart.

Life rafts are packed into three main container types:

>> **The *valise*:** A large duffel bag with a carrying strap.

>> ***Cylindrical canisters*:** Barrel-like containers made of metal or fiberglass. They can be any color, but they're often white. Canisters sit in a *cradle,* or holder, like a large, sturdy bracket.

>> ***Flat canisters*:** These look like luggage racks found on the top of an automobile. They can be any color but are usually white, and they're usually strapped into a cradle.

All these containers should have a *painter*, the raft's main rope (*bow line*) — protruding from them. This line keeps the raft attached to the sinking ship or boat as you're launching, and it also activates the automatic inflator. The painter usually ends with a loop, which is called the *eye*. You inflate the raft by pulling the painter. See the section later in this chapter, "Inflate the raft in the water."

TIP

WHATEVER FLOATS YOUR BOAT: MAKING A DIY LIFE RAFT

If your sinking vessel doesn't have a life raft, you must act quickly. When boats sink, they almost always disgorge items that float, creating a *debris field* that can be scavenged for floating items to improvise a raft.

While afloat, always maintain a lookout for any floating objects; a lot of stuff is out there — Styrofoam, entire trees, and so on — and you can use any of these things to make or improve the buoyancy of a raft. Look for garbage patches and snarls of line and buoys. You can use plastic bottles if you find enough of them. It's not a bad idea to start collecting these bottles when you're in trouble. You need only about 25 to 50 plastic bottles, wrapped in a tarp, canvas, or netting, to make a raft that supports a human being.

When building your raft, anything goes, but here are a few structural ideas that may help you:

- You want to make a raft that is wide, not narrow. Oblong or rectangular rafts are more prone to capsize (turn over) than wide ones. An ideal survival raft is shaped like a square or a circle.

- The wider you spread out — in other words, the more stuff you tie on — the more stable your craft becomes.

- If you can rig rigid poles, such as bamboo canes, to floating flotsam, you can make a very stable raft.

Knowing when to abandon ship

Life rafts aren't pleasant, but they can keep you alive as a last resort. Basically, you deploy a life raft only if:

>> **The boat you're in is completely sinking.** If the boat sinks only partially, stay with the vessel. It's probably easier to see from the air, it has equipment that you can salvage, and it may float for a long time.

WARNING

A partially sunken vessel can sink suddenly, which could take your inflated (or *un*inflated) raft down with it. In case of a partially sunken boat, have the raft ready to inflate at a moment's notice and be ready to be cut free of the sinking boat.

>> **The ship's crew can't get you into a lifeboat.** Sometimes even a competent crew becomes overwhelmed, and you may have to deploy a life raft for yourself.

Launching a life raft

Letting the crew operate the safety equipment is always best. Launch the life raft yourself only as a last resort or you could end up with a disaster on your hands.

You must launch the life raft correctly. Prepare by getting acquainted with these steps *before* disaster strikes. Here's the basic procedure:

1. **If your raft isn't already in place, carry the raft to the side of the vessel.**

   If your raft is in a flat or cylindrical canister, it may have to be released from the cradle before it can be inflated. There are two main ways to free the canister from the cradle:

   - **Activate the *quick release*, normally a pin or button on the cradle or canister.** When you use the quick release, the canister may roll off into the water, or you may have to pick it up and move it to a safer place to launch; but at least it is now free.

   - **Wait for the automatic *hydrostatic release* to activate.** If you can't release the canister, let this device — which detects water and releases the raft if the boat sinks — do its job. In this option, you must wait for the ship to sink and then keep an eye out for the raft to rise to the surface.

2. **Make sure the painter (the raft's main line) is secured to something strong on the boat.**

3. **Throw the raft overboard.**

   No exceptions: You always hurl or push the raft into the water *before* you inflate it. If you inflate it aboard the boat, it can be punctured by sharp edges or wedged into the sinking vessel. This happens fast, and you can't stop inflation once it starts.

   Throw the raft *downwind* from the vessel if you can. If you throw it into the wind and it inflates, the wind just pushes it right back against the boat, where it deflates against the boat's sharp edges.

   Sometimes cradles are made so that when you release the canister, it just rolls right into the water. If the boat is leaning too far over, you may have to give the canister a good kick to get it to roll overboard.

4. Once in the water, inflate the raft.

Pulling sharply on the painter, often 20 to 60 feet (6 to 18 meters) in length, activates the raft's inflation device. Haul in any slack in the line, and when the slack stops coming, yank very sharply to begin inflation. Inflation normally takes between 30 and 90 seconds. The overhead canopy (see Figure 19-1) is the last part to inflate.

WARNING

When the raft inflates, it's a large, lightweight object easily carried away by wind. You may find that the painter is already secured to the *weak link*, which is a fitting designed to break if the boat has sunk and the raft has inflated underwater. These are usually made of lightweight wire or red plastic. If you think the painter is secured to a weak link, leave it alone. The weak link is strong enough to hold the raft near the boat while you get aboard. If the painter is not attached to a weak link, attach the painter to something solid, like a railing.

FIGURE 19-1: A typical modern life raft with a canopy (a), inflated bulwarks (b), and a boarding ladder (c)

Entering a life raft

Ideally, you enter the life raft directly from the sinking vessel — you never touch water. To board the life raft, try to climb down the side of the vessel and enter gently. You probably won't have access to a ladder to do this, so the process can be clumsy. Don't jump into a life raft; this can injure you and anyone already aboard and possibly damage the life raft.

If there's any chance that the life raft could come into contact with sharp edges from the sinking boat — any chance at all — you must keep the raft away and enter it from the water.

Entering a life raft from the water can be difficult. You must lift yourself over the raft's walls (see Figure 19-2), and you're usually hampered by fatigue, waves, and a life jacket. Keep the following ideas in mind:

>> **Get your upper torso on top of the walls of the raft.** If you can get your chest on top, or even just close, you can usually roll in or be pulled aboard by other survivors.

>> **If your raft has a submerged boarding ladder, step on the rungs (see Figure 19-2a), pull yourself up with your hands, drape your chest over the raft's opening, and start heaving yourself in.**

If you're almost there, throw your foot up to hook the opening, and then use the extra leverage to work your way in. Flight attendants practice this technique.

>> **Use the *boarding platform*.** This resembles an air mattress and floats right below the entrance; climb aboard the platform first and then pull yourself into the raft.

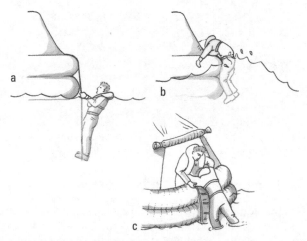

FIGURE 19-2: Using a boarding ladder (a), waves (b), or other people to help you get aboard a life raft

>> **Let wave action help you.** Watch how the waves rise to the raft entrance, and try to time one to correspond with your physical efforts to board (see Figure 19-2b). Momentum counts.

>> **Allow the strongest to go in first and then have them help the others into the raft.** The first person aboard should kneel on the floor of the raft and help to haul survivors aboard. If someone else is inside the raft, have them go to the other side to balance the weight and prevent capsize; also avoid bunching around the entrance, which can cause the raft to turn over. Grab the boarding survivors by the upper arms, or better, the armpits (see Figure 19-2c).

Adjusting to Life Afloat

When you're inside an inflated life raft, you're not out of danger. You and your fellow raft-mates have lots of work to do — which is good, because in a bad situation, staying busy is sometimes the best medicine. This section walks you through what you need to do while in a life raft and discusses possible scenarios.

The first ten minutes in a life raft

The first few minutes in a life raft are important for ensuring your safety. Locate the raft's knife immediately and be ready to cut the painter if the sinking boat goes down. The knife is usually in a pocket near the entrance. Knives in life rafts are squared-off, not pointed, to keep them from puncturing the raft. They have plastic handles that float, and they're usually orange in color.

WARNING

A sharp object can sink your only hope in seconds. Most modern inflatables are strong, but we've seen rafts, hard ones, sliced through like butter. Once aboard your raft, check everyone for sharp objects or protrusions such as purses with metal latches or ornaments, belt buckles, earrings, snaps with jagged edges, and even ballpoint pens. Gather these 'sharps' in some hard container. And make sure your pocketknife is folded.

Once everyone is aboard the raft, spread them out to distribute weight inside, and start assigning things for everyone to do. It's important for people to feel responsible for some survival task. Here's are the most important immediate survival tasks:

>> **Address immediate medical concerns.** We discuss first aid for problems such as cold shock response, hypothermia, and near-drowning in Chapter 22, and we cover general first aid in Chapter 13. Start by assessing everyone aboard for their health condition. Note that even a few inches of water can drown an unconscious person, so make sure nobody is lying face down in the bottom of the raft. As water accumulates in the raft as people board, assign someone to bail it out.

>> **If the boat you've abandoned has sunk completely, scavenge the debris field.** Grab any items floating nearby — containers, sheets of plastic, anything. You can tie these together and let them float outside if the raft is crowded, but do collect them; every floating object is a resource.

>> **Gather the raft's equipment (food and water supplies, flares, and so on) and tie it down, especially the inflation pump.** Rafts deflate a little over time, so you need this pump to maintain buoyancy.

>> **Check the pressure-escape valves and check the seams for leaks.** The escape valves normally hiss for a little while to release excess gas after inflation; this is normal. If you find leaky seams (listen for escaping gas), use the raft's repair kit, which should have instructions. If there is no repair kit, watch the leak carefully and try not to put undue stress or weight on or near it.

>> **Deploy the *drogue* when the raft is clear of the sinking vessel.** This is a small cone or parachute that drags in the water on a long line, keeping the raft headed into the waves (see Figure 19-3a). Some drogues have a *recovery float,* a piece of Styrofoam that connects to the drogue and makes it easier to haul out of the water (see Figure 19-3b). Some drogues automatically deploy, and some don't.

If you find a cone-shaped bag in the center of the raft, it's probably the drogue. Attach it to the outside of the raft at a location away from the entrance. The drogue is going to be under tremendous strain, so check the knot and the line periodically for wear and tear.

You want the drogue to float away from the raft on as long a line as possible. It should reach the trough between the waves when the raft is up on a peak of a wave. If you can get it to extend to two or three waves away, try it.

TIP

If the drogue seems to be damaging the raft by pulling too hard, try using a *sentinel,* a weight that you put on the drogue's line to make the line sink (Figure 19-3c) — this acts like an enormous shock-absorber. You can use anything you have handy as a sentinel, as long as you're not chafing the drogue line.

>> **Activate the *ballast bags* if necessary.** These are bags under the raft that fill with water to stabilize the craft (see Figure 19-3d). They should fill on their own.

>> **Inflate the raft's floor.** The automatic inflating cylinder normally doesn't inflate the floor. Look for the valve that accepts the nozzle of the hand pump. An inflated floor helps prevent hypothermia.

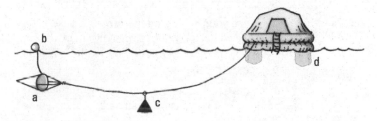

FIGURE 19-3: Deploying a drogue and sentinel to stabilize your life raft

Inside the raft: Giving order to the chaos

Being on a life raft can be quite a traumatic experience. Prepare for at least one emotional explosion from someone; sometimes it's panic, recrimination, blame, or indignation at being put in the situation. If someone does have a meltdown, let them blow off some steam in a benign way. For more on these problems, see Chapter 3.

In this section, we explain how you can organize your raft-mates to increase your chances of rescue, and we name a few ways you can keep everyone a little more comfortable while you're still adrift.

Organizing operations

Most rafts are small, so people are going to be crowded, which can cause injury. It also may be dark inside. Having a plan — and assigning specific functions that people can focus on — can help everyone stay relatively calm.

TIP

Take a look around. Who looks like they can function? They may not be the ones you expect. Begin discussing life raft operations with them rationally, just like you're operating any other piece of equipment. A few level heads working together rationally can have a tremendous positive effect on organizing the others.

Here's how to organize your crew, however small it is:

>> **Start a watch-keeping system immediately.** A *watch team* is a person or persons temporarily on guard. They look for ships, rescue aircraft, resources floating in the water (like plastic containers or rope), and tend the raft (bailing, for example) while others rest. Watch teams operate in scheduled shifts, adding order to the life raft existence.

>> **Organize your bailing operation.** Raft *bailers* (cup- or bowl-like containers) are notoriously small, so use a boot if you have one. Some raft equipment bags contain large sponges to dry the floor.

TIP

If you have two sponges, only use one for bailing. Keep the other clean for collecting fresh dew to drink later.

>> **Take stock of your equipment and how much food and water you have on hand.** Discuss each item thoroughly with your companions. For more on collecting and rationing food and water at sea, see Chapter 20.

>> **Prepare everyone for multiple capsizes.** If the waves are big and the wind is strong, you may have to get out of the raft and right it repeatedly. Familiarize everyone aboard with the procedure we discuss later in "The flip-out: Righting a raft."

>> **Make yourself visible.** Have your aerial flares, smoke, or mirrors ready to go (for more on signals, see Chapter 12). If other rafts are nearby, consider tying them to yours to make a bigger visual target. Don't do this in rough seas, though, because the rafts will beat against each other and cause damage.

>> **Watch for land (and search-and-rescue teams) and discuss navigation.** Start a *log*, a record of what is going on aboard; write down as much as you can right away, including your last known position. Then record weather and other events aboard (spotted ship headed West on the horizon) every day; this may be invaluable survival information later on. For more information on finding land, see Chapter 21.

Increasing your safety and comfort

Life in a raft is uncomfortable at best. Here are a few ways to keep everyone a little less cold, wet, and miserable:

>> **Dry off.** If you're in wet clothes, take them off and wring the water out, over the side, and then put them back on. Remember that cotton is a poor insulator; be especially vigilant about trying to dry out cotton clothes.

>> **If you're in cold conditions, or if you're trying to keep the seas out, close the canopy.** If you close it using ties, use bows (like tying shoelaces) so it can be opened easily, for example, if you hear a boat or helicopter.

>> **Stay with the raft.** If you have to leave the raft to do something, tie a tether to yourself.

>> **When someone starts to become seasick, anticipate vomiting.** Move the sick to the entrance; even a little vomit in the raft can make others ill.

>> **Know that sea creatures like to bump against life rafts.** These creatures include dorados (mahi-mahi), sharks, and turtles. This is largely harmless, but it can be annoying and unnerving.

>> **Treat sea-related ailments.** Be prepared for sunburn, seasickness, and the like; see Chapter 22.

The flip-out: Righting a raft

Life rafts are some of the lightest vessels in the world, used in the worst conditions including strong winds and big waves. That's why life rafts capsize all the time, especially right after inflation. Make sure you're ready to handle a capsized life raft. All life rafts have handles on the bottom to enable you to flip them right-side up. Use the handle and follow these instructions (see Figure 19-4):

1. **Swim to the downwind side.**

   This is the *lee* side, where you have a *wind shadow* — in other words, the raft is acting as a wind break.

2. **Brace your knees or feet against the raft and act like you're trying to climb up the handles.**

   When you start to pull on the handles, the other side will rise, catch the wind, and help you turn the raft over. This climbing force causes the raft to flip backward and on top of you — this works, and it doesn't usually cause injury.

3. **Board the raft (as we explain in the earlier section "Entering a life raft").** Inside will be a chaos of objects thrown around during the capsize and righting; get to work putting things back in order.

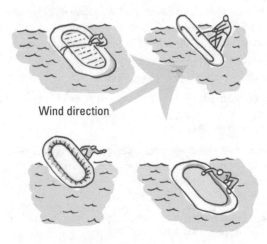

Wind direction

FIGURE 19-4: Righting a life raft

Controlling Drifting Vessels

If you find yourself aboard a small or medium-sized boat that has lost power, you must act fast to gain control of the vessel, otherwise you can enter the realm of the Lost Opportunity. Slow reaction time is the hallmark of many needless disasters. Most of the tips in this section also pertain to handling life rafts.

Taking action with depowered boats

Boats that have lost power are vulnerable to filling with water or capsizing because instead of driving through the waves, the waves overwhelm the boat. Even on a small lake, large boats can motor by and create waves big enough to sink a small disabled boat.

The moment your boat is disabled, take action immediately:

>> **Try to get some kind of propulsion going, quickly.** Organize a paddling operation immediately. Keep the boat pointed into (toward) the waves, and watch for unexpected waves. If you're with others, quickly explain why they need to paddle or row. Paddle with anything you can; even your hands will do in a pinch.

>> **Be ready to bail.** A wave can fill the boat halfway, and then shortly afterward, a second wave sinks the craft entirely. Bailing vigorously can keep this second wave from finishing you off. Organize your bailing operation before you need it.

>> **Balance the boat.** If the boat is tilted to one side, remove some weight to the other side. If the back end is squatting down, move some weight forward. If your motor is out of gas, take the motor off the back and stow it in the lowest part of the boat and as near to the center as you can.

>> **Consider throwing heavy equipment overboard.** If your boat is close to being overloaded and has lost power, you may have to heave something overboard to save your life.

WARNING

Only throw items overboard if your boat is so overloaded that it's in imminent danger of being swamped or flooded. Virtually everything aboard has some survival value, and your ability to survive is often based on your resources and resourcefulness. Outboard motors, for example, are very heavy, but they can be used to make spears, fishing equipment, signaling devices, and so on.

>> **If you're being blown in a way you don't want to go, employ a *drogue*.** A *drogue* is a weight that you stream off the vessel to slow you down. If you're near the shore and you're being taken out by the wind, try throwing out a drogue.

>> **If you're by yourself in an inflatable boat, sit on the front (bow) and paddle by pulling the water toward you (see Figure 19-5).** The process may seem clumsy at first, but you'll get the hang of it.

FIGURE 19-5: Paddling an inflatable boat by yourself

Traveling with current and sail

Beyond the use of paddles, the only other means of moving your disabled vessel or raft is to use the water's current or to use the wind. The key is to use one that's going the direction you want to travel.

TIP

To currents, you can simply put a paddle or a drogue into the water and let the water pull you. If the wind is blowing you in a direction you don't want to go but the current is flowing the way you want to go, drogues can many times pull you against the wind. Traveling against the wind in a raft is entirely possible if you can figure out the current. For more on using drogues, see "The first ten minutes in a life raft," earlier in this chapter.

You can erect a sail out of just about anything. A shirt stretched between two upright paddles will do. The higher your sail is, the better — just make sure you can handle the sail — when the wind really gets strong, be ready to take the sail down or it can easily be destroyed by wind force. Keep in mind that all life rafts travel in the direction of the wind, with or without a sail.

The wind generally cycles near land; during the day, it blows toward land, and at night, it blows away from land. But this is a generalization, not a rule. For more on winds and currents, see Chapter 21.

Restarting outboard motors

If your outboard motor won't run, you can take several simple actions that may get it running again:

» **Let it dry out.** A wet motor, or one flooded with gas, can often be restarted by removing the cover to let it dry out. Put the cover back on before sundown to prevent condensation from accumulating on the motor. Sometimes the drying process takes several days.

» **Make sure everything is clean.** The fuel or the fuel filter could be dirty and/or clogged.

» **Make sure debris hasn't fouled the propeller.** Examine below the water line. If anything is tangled, get down there and pull it out before restarting the motor.

Chapter **20**

Finding Food and Drink at Sea

Not surprisingly, the challenge of finding food and water becomes life-or-death business within just a day of being adrift in a life raft or lifeboat. It's a terrible irony that at sea you're surrounded by water you can't drink and by food you can't see. The good news is that you can find the food and water you need on the sea by using generous amounts of ingenuity and patience.

In this chapter, we show you the minimum needs you have to fulfill to survive on the ocean, and we look at your options for getting fresh water and food at sea.

On the (Drinking) Water Front: Surviving On the Salty Sea

To enhance your chances for survival at sea, attend the possibility of dehydration first, and take the following actions immediately:

» **Master disbelief.** Accept that the risk of dehydration is real and upon you, and go to work right away on your water plans.

>> **Expect water to be a problem even if you're within sight of land.** The ocean current can still take you out to sea within a matter of minutes.

>> **Concentrate on finding and taking any water you can from the sinking or disabled boat before it's lost.** Try to make sure the water containers you take with you have a little air inside them so they float well in the waves.

>> **Scan the *debris field*, the area around the sinking vessel, for important resources you can use later.** You may be able to find containers or sheets of plastic you can use for your water-storing needs. Though this may be hard to believe, it is nevertheless true: Your ability to survive long periods of time drifting on the open sea is largely dependent on your ability to store water. Containers are king.

>> **Take stock of the water you have and secure it.** Tie all your water containers to yourself or your life raft.

In addition to these immediate actions, you want to conserve and ration the water you do have. The following sections explain your body's needs and highlight what to do.

Understanding your body's dehydration limits

Without any liquid, the average human begins to lose consciousness after about three days on the sea and perishes after about six. We don't like these numbers any more than you do, but they provide the foundation for your hydration goals, so knowing and understanding them is key to your survival.

WARNING

If your body is in the water, death from hypothermia is a greater immediate threat than dehydration. Address your cold temperature first; for tips on staying warm at sea, flip to Chapter 18.

The first line of defense: Conserving your body's water

As soon as you realize that you may be entering a survival situation on the sea, begin conserving your body's water. The more you conserve, the less you'll need to consume to stay alive. Fresh water is always scarce on the open sea, so you have to cut your needs down accordingly.

TIP

Take the following steps to conserve your body's internal water supply:

>> Don't drink anything for the first 24 hours.

>> Don't drink diuretics, such as alcohol, soda, saltwater, or urine (which also contains toxins). For more on what not to drink, see Chapter 7.

>> Avoid perspiration; soak extra clothes in seawater and put them on your body to stay cool if it's hot.

>> Avoid excessive effort (tough to do in a survival situation) and breathe through your nose to add moisture to the air you're inhaling.

>> Try not to eat protein because doing so requires water to digest. Many types of seaweed are edible and are easier to digest. For more on marine foods, see the section later in this chapter, "Identifying Other Delicious Things to Eat in the Sea."

Chapter 7 discusses the importance of conserving your body's water in more depth.

Rationing your water

Controlling the amount of water you consume, or *rationing*, can improve your chances of survival at sea. A small amount of drinking water can last you a long time if you consume it efficiently. A human can survive for a short time on as little as 6 to 8 ounces of fresh water per day. That's a daily ration of about 1 cup, or 0.25 liters, or 3/4 the volume of a soda can. If fresh water is really scarce, you can get by for a short time, perhaps a week or longer, on this ration.

TIP

Inventory your water supplies and determine how much water you can afford to drink per day. Since you can't determine when you'll be rescued, think long-term, aiming for survival, not comfort or perfect health. Here are some rationing guidelines:

>> If you have little water, limit your intake to 1 cup (0.25 liters) a day. You may have to drink even less than that, but know that a ration of less than 1/2 cup (4 ounces, or 1/3 of a soda can in volume) usually doesn't extend survival time.

>> If you have an adequate water supply, you can afford to go on a larger ration. If your water inventory isn't so small, a ration of 2 cups (0.5 liters) per day can keep a person alive for many weeks.

>> If you find yourself sitting on a 50-gallon (190-liter) drum of beautiful drinking water, 1 quart per day (1 liter, or about the same as four soda cans) is ideal.

Keep in mind that this is a water ration *at sea*, and it doesn't apply to other environments, especially deserts.

Take your ration in several increments rather than all in one swallow; doing so relieves the agonies of dry mouth more often.

Before you begin a water-rationing program, talk to your companions. If you're the most knowledgeable, take a leadership role and explain how best to conserve water. Designate individuals to distribute water and to keep track of who has gotten a ration. Don't assume these positions yourself, because as leader you will be called on later to arbitrate any disagreements. This issue is sensitive, and the more you make it a group project, the better.

Avoiding salt water

Consuming salt water only causes you to further dehydrate, so don't do it. Drinking salt water increases your need for fresh water. If you drink 1 pint (0.5 liters or two soda cans' volume) of salt water, your body will drain at least 1 pint of fresh water from your tissues just to get rid of it. The net effect is to worsen your fluid balance.

Even worse, drinking saltwater is closely linked to delirium and hallucinations on the sea. The old warning that "salt water makes you mad" probably has some truth in it. There are so many case studies on the books that show castaways becoming mentally unbalanced after they drank large portions of saltwater that you can't ignore this danger.

No matter how thirsty you become at sea, don't drink even a little salt water, because after you start, you can't stop. People in survival situations often begin to drink salt water very slowly because they think that if they take just a few sips, it won't matter. It does matter, and you'll get into serious trouble.

REMEMBER

Drinking salt water only makes you thirstier. If you drink a few 'harmless' gulps of salt water, you feel satisfied for only about 10 minutes. When your thirst returns, it comes back with a vengeance. You'll be on a vicious cycle, needing to drink more each time.

WARNING

Don't consider mixing salt water with fresh water and drinking it. If you mix salt water with fresh, you'll most likely be creating a diuretic. You're better off concentrating on getting liquid in other ways rather than polluting what little good fresh water you have.

Making Fresh Water on the Ocean

All methods for acquiring fresh water at sea require patience and persistence. Some may give you only drops or a mouthful, but every little bit helps. The history books are filled with survivors who, after a little practice, were able to get enough liquid to keep them going.

Working with rainwater

Many showers and squalls at sea last only a few minutes, so before the first drop falls, be prepared to catch every drop you can. We cover rain collection in Chapter 7, but here are some notes on gathering rain-catching supplies:

>> Gather containers first. Scan the sinking site debris field and recover anything that can hold water.

>> After containers, sheets of plastic or fabric are of the highest priority. Hold onto any item that you can use as a rain-catching plane.

Shortly before a shower comes, make sure your rain-catching plane (discussed in Chapter 7) is fully extended, and then rinse off all the surfaces with seawater. The seawater rinse cuts through the salt crust that develops on all things within just a day or so on the sea.

TIP

If possible, designate a container to hold only the initial rainfall because most of what you collect in the first 20 to 30 seconds of a rain shower will be fouled by salt. Sample this water later to determine whether it's drinkable. If not, use it next time for rinsing collection surfaces.

The biggest problem in collecting rainwater at sea is keeping all the components in place. Violent flapping of the rain-catching plane in the wind can make it hard to collect the water. Develop a rain-catching plan that involves everyone, and use it as a team-building exercise.

TIP

Shade clear or translucent water containers from sunlight; it promotes algae and mold growth.

Collecting condensation

You can collect condensation from the surfaces of your vessel and use it for drinking purposes — but only if it's free of salt, which is rare. You can sometimes use a cloth or rag to soak up the moisture, but the results can be meager. Sponges (sometimes found in life raft equipment bags, one for bailing and one for fresh water collection) are better for this.

TIP

Maintain a close watch on all your water-collecting surfaces. You may have a surface that's relatively free of salt. You may be able to maximize the amount of water you collect if you act just as the condensation is forming during the night.

Using water makers

A *reverse osmosis* water maker is a small pump that forces water through a filter, making the water safe to consume (though not all are designed to remove salt from seawater, so check the capabilities of your device). The water maker looks like a small bicycle pump, and if you come across one in a life raft or abandon-ship bag, check immediately for a package of spare filters and put them in a dry, secure place. Most small cylindrical water makers require you to change their filters at regular intervals, although some use ceramic filters that must be cleaned.

REMEMBER

Always attach a cord to your water maker and then tie the other end to your body or to your vessel. As with all tools on the sea, the water maker has a good chance of slipping out of your hands and sinking to the bottom of the ocean or simply drifting away from you. Even if you have good hands and are conscientious, things slip. We can't stress this point enough. Why? Because we've lost a lot of good equipment to the deep blue!

If you have enough containers, draw water from the sea using a container and pour it into the pump while the pump is inside the boat or raft. This is vastly better than filling the pumping unit by dipping it into the sea because it reduces the risk of losing equipment overboard.

Setting up a still at sea

A *solar still* at sea is simply a clear container that uses the sun's rays to heat and evaporate water; the still then condenses the water vapor and collects the fresh water.

A variety of commercially manufactured models (see Figure 20-1a) are available, but they all work on the same principle: You pour salt water (or anything containing water) onto a piece of dark cloth or into a reservoir made of black plastic, and then you put the cloth or reservoir under a little tent of clear plastic. When you put the tent in the sun, the seawater evaporates — but it leaves the salt behind. Droplets of purified water soon form on the inside of the tent, and these trickle down into a receptacle at the bottom of the still.

Here's how to build a basic still using odds and ends at sea. (Remember the debris field you were in?) This still type is a variation on the land-based solar still (see Figure 20-1b):

1. **Fasten a container at the bottom of a medium-sized bucket.**

2. **Use a plastic sheet to form a dripper over the container.**

   The dripper is meant to sag above the container and drip water into it.

3. **Secure the plastic with string or a rubber band.**

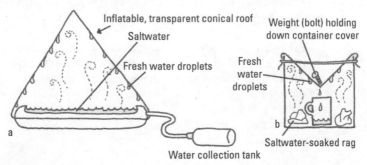

FIGURE 20-1: A commercially manufactured solar still (a) and an improvised design (b)

Using a solar still on the sea can try your patience to the breaking point because everything is in motion, and getting the little drops to fall into the right receptacle can be a nightmare. Once again, persistence and patience are key to survival.

Removing salt with desalination kits

Desalination kits use chemicals and filters to convert seawater into drinkable liquid. Even the largest ones only provide a few pints, but they can save you in a pinch. If you have one, use it as a supplement to other methods, rather than relying on it completely.

Drinking sea turtle blood

Many sea survivors have lived on the flesh and blood of sea turtles. These large, curious animals often approach life rafts and may be caught by hand, hooked with a barbed pole or snared with a rope. However they are brought aboard, they should be killed humanely. The blood may be drained from incisions at the neck; consume quickly, before it coagulates. Sea turtles are endangered and it is a pity to kill one, but we are talking about situations of human survival.

DRINKING THE JUICE OF FISH

The juices of many fish can be used to help stave off dehydration:

- **The spinal fluid:** For large fish, simply cut an incision along the spine and suck the fluid out; for smaller fish, cut the spine and turn the fish vertical to catch spinal fluids in a container.

- **The eyes:** You can chew or suck fish eyes for a bitter but life-sustaining drink.

But keep in mind: Some fish are toxic and you shouldn't consume them or drink their juices. For more info, check out "Knowing which fish aren't on the menu" later in this chapter.

Fishing at Sea

After you address your water needs, you can begin to take food from the sea. Fishing for survival at sea is a unique experience; it's done aboard a flimsy craft that's low in the water and subject to damage or destruction by large animals. So remember, you are not fishing at the local creek; you are now *hunting on the sea*.

Sea hunting basics

Keep the following pointers in mind when hunting at sea:

>> **Always use stealth when fishing.** Fish can see and often hear you, and many have a very strong sense of vibration. Try to be still and quiet.

>> **Keep a close watch on all your lines.** After you put them in the water, try to keep a hand on every line at all times. If you allow your vigilance to lapse, the fish will surely get away.

>> **Maintain a disciplined fishing time, just before dawn.** Get ready to fish every morning in the same way you'd get dressed for your job on land. Don't be late! Have all your gear in the water before dawn. Fish as long as you can every day, but especially in the morning, when oceanic fish like to feed near the surface.

The following sections focus on some specific fishing-related pointers if you're lost at sea. You can also check out Chapter 8 for more general fishing techniques.

Tackling hooks and lines

Fishing at sea, like fishing from land, requires hooks, line, and bait or lures. To learn how to improvise hooks and lines, see Chapter 8. The best substance for bait is freshly butchered fish meat or entrails (you might have to catch the first bait fish with nets or lures). Generally speaking, white or shiny lures work best.

Survival fishing at sea is normally done with *hand lines*, simply holding the fishing line in the hand rather than with a pole.

TIP

Fishing tackle can save your life on the open sea, but it's very hard to hold onto. Lines break and precious hooks are lost all the time, so take precautions to safeguard your equipment:

>> Stow your tackle in a container that's attached to the vessel.

>> Service your tackle — such as tying on new hooks — only when you have the boat's bottom below you, never over the side.

>> Fish with an assistant if possible. People lose gear or have other minor disasters usually because they're overwhelmed.

>> Maintain the lightest touch possible on a hooked fish. Never fight a fish on the sea if you can help it. Give the fish as much slack as it can handle and wait for it to tire.

Using a spear

Spearing a fish is well within the ability of even the most die-hard of landlubbers. Spears are immensely useful and can be good weapons for killing large and violent fish in the water (which is better than doing it in your raft or boat, because that can be a dangerous, clumsy and inhumane process). You can stab dorados (also called mahi-mahi or dolphinfish) in the spine to paralyze them or sharks in the eyes to produce the same affect.

Craft spears by sharpening wood that you find on the open sea or from metal (such as a rod from an outboard motor or the frame of a backpack). Make spear tips from odds and ends you find in your drifting boat, such as broken oar locks. Grind these metal parts on other metal until you form a point. You can attach the metal tip as seen in Chapter 8, or if you have access to wire (perhaps from dead electrical devices or outboard motors), you can simply bind the two together, wood and metal, as we show in Figure 20-2a.

WARNING

Misusing a spear can deflate your raft or cause injury in the blink of an eye! Never underestimate a spear; treat it like a loaded gun.

Remember that many fish on the open sea like to congregate. In the first few days you're adrift, you may see only the types of sea creatures that swim too fast to be speared. But after a few days, a community of fish will spring up, including the slower swimmers, such as the slow gray groupers, which are meaty and easily speared. Here's how you do it:

1. **Enter the water with a rope tied from the boat or raft to your waist or ankle.**

   Doing so helps you avoid getting separated. You also want to have a loop of string that goes from the spear to your wrist so you don't lose your new tool.

2. **Float quietly and wait for a slow fish to come near, or drift casually over to the fish without making any hurried movements.**

3. **Grasp the spear at the halfway point so that it's balanced in your hand; then cock your fist under your armpit (see Figure 20-2b).**

4. **When you think you're close enough, thrust straight out, from armpit to fish.**

   Because you're horizontal, this feels almost like you're pushing the spear directly over your head (see Figure 20-2c). This is the fastest motion your arm and the spear can develop underwater. No other way works. A forceful thrust from your armpit to the area directly in front of your face is the only way to propel a hand spear fast enough to kill a fish in the water.

5. **After you spear the fish, reach forward and hold the struggling animal with your other hand, and return to your raft or boat.**

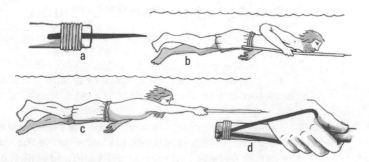

FIGURE 20-2: Fishing at sea with spears

You can construct a slightly more effective fishing spear, called a *Hawaiian sling,* by simply attaching a length of bungee cord, rubber tubing, or elastic to the butt end of your lightweight spear. Put your thumb through the loop of elastic, reach forward with the same hand, and grasp the spear about three-quarters of the way up, stretching the elastic so the weapon is ready to fire (check out Figure 20-2d). This weapon is very effective on small fish that congregate within a few feet of rafts.

Using nets to catch baitfish

You can use nets fashioned out of clothing and other fabric to capture small fish near your raft for use as bait. Submerge your net in an area where smaller fish may be schooling, wait a few minutes, then pull up sharply. This is an exercise in patience and quiet.

Advanced fishing for the hungry

Advanced survival ocean fishing methods include:

» **Get flying fish to jump in your boat.** These tasty fish may be attracted with a flashlight beam. They can be eaten or used as bait for larger fish.

» **Fish with a gaff, a pole with a *very* sharp hook on the end of it.** You can make hooks for this, but large, barbed fishhooks are the best. To fish with a gaff, drop your pole into the water, hook end down. When a fish swims over the hook, jerk the gaff sharply upward. Just be careful — this is a very effective way to puncture and sink your own raft!

Catching small sharks by hand

It sounds unlikely, but if well-organized, catching small sharks by hand is a viable way to get food and survive.

Use the barehanded method to catch only small sharks less than about 3 feet (0.9 meters) in length. To catch a small shark

1. Wait until the creature swims past the side of the raft and then swiftly reach into the water, grasp the thinnest part of its body just in front of its tail, and yank it out of the water smartly.

Don't grab a shark by the tail, grab a bit forward where the tail joins the body. Note the skin can be very abrasive. Also, never use both hands to grasp a shark; use one hand for the fish and the other hand to hold onto your vessel so you don't fall into the ocean.

2. **While on a reinforced area near the entrance of your raft, or on a cleared spot inside the raft, turn the shark upside down as soon as you can.**

3. **Throw something over its eyes, such as a shirt or towel.**

4. **Holding the shark by the tail, kill it by clubbing it in the head.**

Even the smallest of sharks is fantastically strong. They can buck and writhe violently for as long as 5 minutes and can still bite even after they seem dead.

Shark meat tastes of ammonia when first caught. To improve the flavor, let the whole shark sit out in the sun or overnight; eight hours should do.

THE BAILEYS' SHARK-CATCHING OPERATION

Hand-catching sharks may take you a couple of tries, but it's well within the physical abilities of most fit adults. Maralyn Bailey, a 98-pound (44-kilogram) tax accountant from Southampton, England, was frequently able to pull these animals aboard her dinghy during her famous 1973 survival voyage of 117 days, saving herself and her husband, Maurice, from starvation. During the operation, Maurice usually stood by with a towel to throw over the shark's head as soon as Maralyn pulled the animal out of the water. She was so good at it that Maurice eventually had to tell her to stop. We, your friendly authors, have used variations of this method to catch dozens of sharks during the voyage of the *Manteño II* without endangering ourselves in the slightest.

Bringing in Your Catch

Many fish have sharp points on their bodies that can deflate your raft or cause injury, so you must take precautions against this when bringing in your catch. Consider these strategies as well:

>> **Get organized.** Discuss thoroughly with your raftmates exactly how you plan to bring the fish aboard and keep it aboard.

>> **Estimate the pathway that the fish will take when you pull it from the sea and put it in your vessel.** Reinforce this area with anything you can, such as extra clothing or pieces of cardboard.

>> **Kill or stun large or aggressive fish while they're still in the water.** Stab the fish in the eye or just behind the head with a spear — grim business, but better than having a large animal thrashing around in a delicate life raft.

>> **Be ready to 'guard the exits' when the fish is aboard.** Get between the fish and the sea to help ensure that caught fish can't jump back into the water.

>> **Throw a piece of cloth or canvas over the fish's eyes.** This sometimes calms fish.

>> **Be ready to club the fish after it's aboard.** The fastest and most humane way to kill the fish is with forceful blows to the head.

Preparing and Eating Fish at Sea

After maybe a few false starts, we hope you're bringing in the catch. Now you have a new problem: How do you eat it? In this section, you find out how to prepare and dry raw fish. We also include some notes on identifying fish that aren't fit for consumption.

Setting up the sushi bar

After you've killed the fish (see the earlier section "Bringing in Your Catch"), you can fillet it if you're able, but many times it's easier simply to peel the skin back and then cut the meat into long strips for drying. This is especially true in the case of large fish such as dorado (mahi–mahi) and tuna. Here's how to prepare and dry large fish like these:

1. **Cut a large triangle in the fish's skin.**

   Start your triangle just behind the gill and narrow it down to a point at the tail fin.

   If you have no blade, you need to improvise. Any kind of sharp metal works; a close friend of ours once cut open the armor plating of a turtle with a sharpened tin can. Unfortunately — or fortunately, depending on how you look at it — you have lots of time on a raft.

   TIP

2. **Start at the point and peel the skin toward the gill.**
3. **After the meat is exposed, slice off long thin strips.**
4. **String a line from one side of your raft or boat to the other, and hang the strips over it to dry.**

Tuna is the only fish you shouldn't dry in this fashion. Tuna is easy to distinguish because of its shiny silver body and its very bloody meat. Consume this meat quickly, or it spoils within just a few hours. Save the entrails for bait.

TIP

Knowing which fish aren't on the menu

When you're fishing at sea, you need to know that not every fish you catch is edible. A few varieties of fish flesh can actually poison you. Most of these fish are found near reefs, although there's no guarantee that you won't catch them on the open sea. The following is a list of these toxic fish:

>> **Puffers:** Consider any fish that can expand its diaphragm, or puff up, or any fish covered by spines, to be toxic and inedible. These include

- Puffer fish (see Figure 20-3a)
- Porcupine fish (see Figure 20-3b)
- Cowfish (see Figure 20-3c)

>> **Barracuda:** Larger and older barracuda (see Figure 20-3d) carry the toxin that causes *ciguatera,* or seafood poisoning. This is especially true in Polynesia.

>> **Triggerfish:** Consider triggerfish (see Figure 20-3e) poisonous if found near reefs, but edible on the open sea. If you are uncertain, just use them as bait.

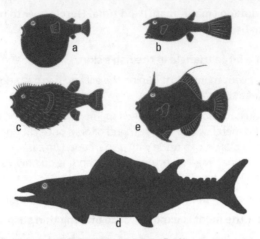

FIGURE 20-3: Fish with poisonous flesh

For more on fish with nasty spines and stings that can cause injuries at sea, check out Chapter 22.

Identifying Other Safe Things to Eat while at Sea

Beyond fish, you can find other creatures and plants to eat in sea. You can eat all these foods raw, like fish, although they're invariably more edible when dried in the sun. This section lists some of the more common foods you can eat at sea.

WARNING

If you're susceptible to deadly bouts of anaphylactic shock from seafood, abstain from eating, at least in the short term. You can try seaweed if faced with starvation, but perform the Universal Plant Edibility Test first (see Chapter 8). Note that tiny plankton can attach to the broad leaves of seaweed and cause a reaction, even if the seaweed itself doesn't.

Turtles

As mentioned earlier, turtles are among the easiest animals to catch in the sea because, like sharks, they frequently investigate small boats and life rafts. To catch a turtle, simply grasp its hind flippers and haul it aboard. But remember, they are strong and their sharp claws and beak can damage an inflatable raft.

If you can't pierce the turtle's hard shell, you can still cut out its forequarters and hindquarters. On large turtles, this can provide you with as much as 30 pounds (13.5 kilograms) of meat. Cut and dry turtle flesh to preserve it.

Birds

You can catch the sea birds that inevitably land on your life raft or boat, many times by hand. We've had many birds land on our rafts (though we haven't had to eat them), as have many castaways. All bird flesh is edible, though without the ability to cook over a fire, they are more likely to sicken you than fish meat.

Once caught, a humane way to kill a bird is to wring the neck with a sharp, forceful action. Birds do not have to be plucked before butchery, but plucking makes butchery less messy.

WARNING

Sea birds can administer nasty bites that can become infected almost immediately. Put on gloves, if you have them, when catching birds, or improvise something to protect your hands.

Barnacles

Barnacles, which begin to grow almost overnight on any hull, are the little brown creatures that cling to the undersides of boats or rafts. They appear as long brown tubes, usually with white shells at one end. These critters are crustaceans, related to lobsters and crabs, but they aren't nearly as appetizing. We can tell you here that the good news and the bad news are the same: They're completely edible. You can eat them raw, so feel free to pull them off with a satisfying snap. *Bon appétit!*

Seaweed

Seaweed is unappetizing but edible. Generally speaking, you're looking for seaweed with broad, flat leaves. Kelp is good, and it contains carbohydrates and fiber, which are hard to come by on the sea. You can find many other broad-leaf species floating in the open ocean. To see what the edible types of seaweed look like, go to Chapter 8.

WARNING

Thin, threadlike seaweed can be acidic and irritating to the stomach. Also, keep in mind that eating too much seaweed (rarely a problem) can cause diarrhea and dehydration. You should use seaweed to supplement your diet, not as a main staple.

Dry seaweed in the sun before eating it. Rinsing it in fresh water helps tremendously if you have that luxury. Avoid eating salty seaweed that will dehydrate you.

Chapter **21**

Emergency Travel and Navigation at Sea

Regardless of what circumstances you find yourself in — whether floating, swimming, drifting in a disabled boat, or castaway in a raft — a few good decisions can help get you back to land. We hope to show how a little wily observation combined with some decisive action can help you walk on the shore again — drenched, to be sure, but alive and well.

In this chapter, we discuss how to size up your situation at sea and what signs to look out for — just in case you're in the mood for some dry land. We also give you a few pointers on how to make your landing a little smoother.

Swimming Back to Land

When you're in the water, getting back to land (or just back to the safety of a good vessel) becomes your most important goal. And you don't need us to tell you that it's a heck of a lot harder than people think. But if you can measure a few things — if you can use some knowledge and techniques to eliminate chance — you can, like so many survivors before you, give yourself that little edge.

In this section, we talk about getting your bearings, considering a current's direction and speed, and measuring distances when you're in the water. We also tell you how to decide whether to swim or float and give you advice on getting out of a rip current.

Measuring distance to shore

Estimating the distance you must travel to get back to land can be tricky. Land has a nasty habit of always appearing to be a lot closer than it really is. This is especially true when sunlight shines on large landforms, such as large rocks, peninsulas, or mountains near shore. When the sunlight is shining on these types of landforms, expect them to be much farther than you initially estimate. (For more on the funny business of estimating distances, see Chapter 9.)

TIP

When you're in the water (either in a life raft or bobbing in a life vest), your ability to see land is diminished because the water interferes with your line of sight. Nevertheless, here are some general guidelines for estimating distances to land:

>> **Within a mile (1.6 kilometers) of shore:** You can clearly distinguish the limbs on humans or the individual branches on trees.

>> **Roughly 2 miles (3.2 kilometers) out:** You can distinguish individual windows on houses or buildings.

>> **More than 3 miles (4.8 kilometers) out:** You can't distinguish exactly where the surf strikes the land.

REMEMBER

This last distinction is probably the most important, because if you're in the water and you're more than 3 miles out, you should try getting to land by drifting, not swimming. We talk about the decision of whether to swim or drift later in this chapter.

Figuring out where the current is taking you

You can do a lot of things in life, but you can't swim against an ocean current — at least not for long. You have to work with the current, and that takes patience and faith. Regardless of your predicament, you save a lot of energy and frustration by knowing which way the water is moving before you start making swimming plans.

Debunking some myths about ocean currents

To really understand how currents affect you, consider these truths:

>> **The current isn't necessarily going with the waves or swells.** So even though you may feel as though you're being pushed one way, you may be drifting another.

>> **Tides aren't currents (usually).** Generally speaking, when the tide is flooding onto the land or ebbing away from it, the current actually flows parallel to the shoreline. This isn't always true, but it helps to point out that the current isn't necessarily rushing toward the beach or hurtling out to sea during the tides — it may be just running down the coast.

Determining the direction and speed of a current

So which way is the current really going? Here's one way to be sure: If you can see land, you can use a range. A *range* is simply an imaginary line drawn through two objects on land (see Figure 21-1). Using a range is an exceptionally accurate way of determining which way you're moving — vastly more accurate than using the waves as a measurement.

FIGURE 21-1: Using a range to tell which way you're drifting

When you're in the water, take a look at the lights or landmarks on land and try to find two that are in line with each other — such as two large trees, or perhaps the glow from a village and the hill behind it. The line through these two landmarks is your *range.* In a few minutes, you should be able to detect that the linear relationship between the two landmarks has changed. *Remember:* You're moving in the *opposite* direction of the closest landmark.

Another way to figure out the current's direction is to look at a buoy. Most river mouths and bays have large navigation buoys anchored to the riverbed. If you're near a river mouth or a bay inlet, you can simply observe which way the buoy is leaning — that's the direction the water is headed. A buoy that's leaning at a 20-degree angle indicates a pretty strong current.

Whenever two large rivers converge, or whenever a powerful river emerges into the ocean, the water is pushed up so that you get very dangerous, turbulent seas. These large, standing waves can cause havoc for you when swimming. When making your way back to land, avoid these places at all costs.

Also, beware of *riptides*, or rip currents, that lead back out to sea. This current exists very close to the shoreline and causes a lot of drowning. For info on handling this special type of current, see "Swimming out of a rip current," later in this chapter.

Moving in the water: Float or swim

When you're in the water, you have a decision to make: float or swim. Either mode of transport can get you where you need to go — you just need to know which is better in your situation. In all but a very few cases, it's better to float or drift with the current. Because the current is doing all the work, you may be able to travel as much as five or ten times as far by drifting than by actively swimming.

In this section, we cover floating and swimming as a means of travel toward land. Before you do any type of swimming, either for travel or just to escape from a burning vessel, you should take a look at Chapter 18 on staying afloat.

Letting yourself float

Many floating survivors have been picked up or have reached a distant shore that was well beyond their swimming abilities. If you're without a life jacket, using the *dead-man's float*, or *drown-proofing*, may give you the ability to float for as long as two days. For more on floating, see Chapter 18.

Do not drown-proof in cold water, because floating like this makes your head go under, which makes you lose too much heat.

Swimming slowly

The most critical factor when swimming back to land is *conservation of energy.* In practical terms, that means that you need to relax and take your time. Swim more slowly than you want to — much more slowly because that keeps your heart rate down, which does more to prevent fatigue than just about anything else. Swimming slowly can try your patience and make you feel as though what you're doing is futile, but it's the best way.

If you don't have a life jacket on, keep in mind that the more you fatigue, the less efficiently you swim. One way to cut down on fatigue is to use a variety of strokes, sometimes referred to as *relief strokes.* The three strokes usually recommended for swimming long distances are a lazy backstroke, the breast stroke, and the sidestroke. Alternating among these three is your best bet.

You swim best when your body is horizontal, with your legs more or less behind you instead of below you, where they create drag (check out Figure 21-2). One way to avoid this is to take your time and try to relax; another is to use the backstroke, where you're lying flat on your back.

FIGURE 21-2: Swimming failure

If you feel yourself becoming fatigued, you should float rather than swim. When you're fatigued, swimming starts to become counterproductive. You can also check to see whether you're moving toward the coast or away from it. If currents are moving you away, stop wasting your energy. Many people have survived by floating until they were picked up. Also, after you've floated awhile, your strength may come back.

Swimming out of a rip current

Anywhere near shore, watch out for a *rip current*, an area near the surf line where the water is flowing quickly out to sea. This normally appears as a calm stream or creek flowing between the breakers, perpendicular to the beach. This is dangerous to small boats as well as swimmers.

To get out of a rip current, wait until it has taken you past the breakers, then swim at a right angle to the flow of the water (therefore, parallel to the beach). Don't panic — just realize you're in a rip current, swim to the edge when you're somewhat past the breakers, then get back to shore with the breakers to either side of the rip current.

Improvised Open-Sea Navigation for Life Rafts

What happens if you're out on the ocean and you can't actually see the land? In this section, we talk about long-term navigation, such as the type you have to perform when you're in a life raft, lifeboat, or aboard a disabled boat, adrift on the open sea. (For info on actually steering or propelling your vessel, flip to Chapter 19.)

TIP

If you're out of sight of land, start writing down as much information as you can (if you haven't already started), such as estimated rate of travel, sightings of ships or signs of land, and so on. This is your log, and it's one of the best safety devices you can have because it helps you put all the pieces of the navigational puzzle together. Even if you're lucky enough to have a GPS unit, you quickly realize that navigation is best when it's the product of a combination of many factors.

Getting your bearings

If you can get your bearings at sea, you can estimate where land lies. Even if you don't have a map, you still usually know where the world's continents lie, and you may have a good idea of where a large island is. So developing a sense of direction can help you guide your craft to safety, or at least help you to know how long you may be drifting, which helps when figuring out what your food and water rationing program should be.

The following sections discuss improvised navigation methods that are unique to the sea. For a basic course on navigation, including instructions for correcting compass errors, see Chapter 9. For info on finding directions by using the sun and stars, see Chapter 10.

Finding direction with compasses and charts

When you're at sea, the most common instruments for navigation are compasses and nautical charts. If you have access to a compass, take a moment to see whether any metal or electronic device may be influencing it — simply move the compass around and watch the needle carefully. Metal items can cause errors by pulling the needle toward them. The best thing you can do is to try to locate the interference and move as far away as you can.

The compasses found in virtually all cellphones will work at sea. You don't need to have reception or access to GPS because the phone has a magnetometer, a sensor that detects Earth's magnetic field. Cellphone compasses usually have an error in them just like conventional compasses. For more on cellphone and GPS navigation, see Chapter 9.

If you have access to a nautical chart, the compass-error info is called *magnetic variation* — not *declination,* as it's called on land maps. These two terms mean precisely the same thing — that your compass will always be in error by a certain amount in the area of the chart. If your chart says *VAR 10 W,* the needle is always pointing 10° west of the true direction. If it says *VAR 10 E,* the needle points 10° east of the true direction.

REMEMBER

Whenever you measure any distance on a nautical chart, you must use the latitude scale on the side of the chart. This scale may be delineated in minutes. A *minute* is equal to 1 nautical mile, which is about 15 percent longer than a terrestrial (statute) mile.

TIP

If you think you're located somewhere in the middle of the nautical chart, simply go to the latitude scale nearest your position, take a piece of string, and measure out a minute (a nautical mile). You can use the string as a scale to measure how far you must go from your position to get to land. If the latitude scale nearest you is in degrees, keep in mind that there are 60 minutes (60 nautical miles) in a degree.

For more on correcting compass error and using latitude and longitude, see Chapter 9.

Determining direction with waves

If you don't have a compass or any other type of navigational instrument, you can use the direction of the waves (and swells) as a rough guide to help you steer your boat or raft throughout the day. At dawn, when you know the sun is rising in the east, study the prevailing direction of the waves. This can give you a general sense of direction throughout the day — until late in the afternoon, that is, when the sun is obviously pointing west, and you'll have to measure the waves' direction again.

REMEMBER

This method of orienting with the waves is only useful if you understand that at least two wave systems are usually around you:

>> **Swells:** These are the largest masses of sea and are usually very constant. In other words, if at dawn you see that the swells are moving to the southwest, you can be pretty certain they'll continue to do so all day. These are the best to follow, because they're so constant.

>> **Waves:** Usually, waves aren't exactly in sync with the swells — they're smaller masses of sea that come along a little faster than swells. Sometimes the waves can be in sync with the swells, though watching swells is almost always better.

You need only about an hour of careful observation to see which is a swell and which is a wave, and the direction each is moving. Give it a try. If you combine this method with the navigation method of using the sun and stars that we describe in Chapter 10, you should be able to figure out which way you're moving without too much trouble.

Estimating current at sea

If you're far out to sea (you can't see land), it's virtually impossible to establish the current's direction and speed unless you have navigation instruments such as a GPS or sextant. If you use these instruments, study their manuals carefully so that you don't have false confidence or expectations about them.

Generally, you can assume that most of the world's ocean currents move at a speed of between 0.5 and 0.75 miles (0.8 and 1.2 kilometers) per hour. While many currents move much faster or slower, it's important to keep in mind that a current is likely moving you every hour of the day, even if there's no wind and it feels like you're not moving at all!

Understanding signs of land

With heightened awareness, you can find your way to land — even if you can't see it and you don't have a compass or nautical chart. Land gives all kinds of clues, but many of them are subtle, so you have to pay close enough attention.

REMEMBER

At sea, the height of your eye or your antenna or your signal means everything. So when you're looking for land, try to get in as high a position as you can — just standing up for a few minutes in a raft can make all the difference in the world.

Signs of civilization

Some signs point you not only to land but sometimes even to civilization:

>> **City glow:** This can be more subtle than you think. Many times a city's glow shows up as a very light gray dome way out on the horizon.

>> **Navigation lights shining from land:** Many are very hard to see, especially because they often blink only about once a minute — and then only in red!

>> **The courses of small airplanes, helicopters, and small boats:** Watch which way small boats are traveling — if you see a civilian helicopter moving in the same direction, an offshore platform may be nearby.

>> **Nautical bells and horns sounding from shore:** Nautical bells are rarely bells at all; they're long, heavy bass tones. They can be heard at night from immense distances, but you have to be on guard — you can easily miss them if you're not paying attention.

We hate to tell you this, but many times foghorns are deactivated because someone finds them annoying or because they need repairs. This is a common problem. If a foghorn is listed on your nautical chart but you can't hear it, that doesn't necessarily mean it's not there.

If you're out to sea or in heavy fog, you can use an AM radio to find land. This is an easy and reliable technique:

1. **Open the antenna and point it toward the horizon.**

2. **Tune the radio to any station you can, no matter how poor the reception.**

   You're not trying to hear what they're saying on the station — you're just trying to pick up a signal.

3. **Slowly pivot your body while keeping the antenna pointed at the horizon.**

4. **When the station disappears completely, you've hit the** *null* **— the quiet spot where the station suddenly goes silent or gets very faint.**

   When this happens, you're pointing directly at the transmitting tower — and land!

If you have an AM radio with an internal antenna, you have to take the housing off and find out which way the antenna is pointing. The antenna is simply a metal rod with a lot of wires coiled around it. When you find the antenna, point it toward the horizon and start your pivoting procedure.

Taking hints from the birds

Sometimes the flight paths of seabirds can point you toward land. The general rule when using birds to find land revolves around understanding what they're doing out at sea. Each day at dawn, they leave the land and fly offshore to hunt for fish. Then, in the afternoon, after they've eaten their fill, they begin steadily gaining altitude. When they reach a certain height and spot land, they tend to immediately fly in a straight line, and often in a V formation, to their home.

Watch for groups of birds coming out to sea at dawn and then leaving in the afternoon or at dusk. If you see birds behave in this manner, especially in groups, that's a pretty good indication that the direction of their flight leads to land.

The idea that all birds must eventually return to land is a myth. For some unknown reason, this idea still persists today, even among some serious mariners. This is false. Many birds stay out and sleep on the ocean — often thousands of miles out to sea.

The problem with identifying birds is that so many varieties exist, so it's easy to mistake land birds for those that sleep on the sea. The most reliable land-returning birds are the following:

>> **Boobies and gannets:** Boobies and gannets have two important distinguishing characteristics: long, thin wings and tails like arrowheads. Their tails aren't split, blunt, or flat-edged — they look just like a sharp triangle or a spear-head. If dusk is coming and you see a group of these birds, watch carefully to see which way they fly away.

>> **Frigate birds:** Identify these birds by their split tails, which are long, thin, and forked, like swallow tails. Frigate birds return to land at dusk.

Other land signs from the water, wind, and air

TIP

There are other signs of land, ones that the great Polynesian navigators have used for centuries. Now, you can't master all of these overnight, but you'd be shocked at what you can see if only you pay attention:

>> **Sea breeze/land breeze:** On many shorelines around the world, the wind's direction frequently changes with the time of day. Here's the standard pattern: The wind blows toward the land from about noon until sundown, and then it reverses, blowing out from the land from early evening until just before dawn. If you record these types of wind changes in your log, they're probably coming from land. Land will most likely be in the direction from which the night breeze is coming.

>> **Smells, pollen, or brown or gray air:** Land has a very distinctive smell, especially at night, when the wind tends to blow offshore toward the sea. If you have allergies and your nose starts to run just after the wind switches direction, the wind is probably coming from land. Also keep in mind that off the coasts of North Africa, Chile, and even Southern California, when the winds get things stirred up, the sky turns brown with dust from the desert.

>> **A stationary cloud:** Most islands — even islands that aren't in the tropics — tend to develop puffy cumulus clouds over them during the day (see Figure 21-3a). If you see a single,

puffy cumulus cloud that stays in the same spot while all the others are drifting by, this is almost always a dead giveaway that an island is underneath.

>> **Discoloration of flat-bottomed clouds:** Low-lying, flat-bottomed clouds reflect whatever is directly under them. If these types of clouds are over an island, they appear distinctly green underneath.

>> **Long, curved waves:** If you see long lines of straight, parallel waves moving in the general direction of the wind and then you suddenly notice a distinct curve in the waves (a long bend that extends from one horizon to the other), an island is probably near the middle of the arc of these waves. The island is bending the waves, and you're seeing the first sign of it.

>> **A sudden, confused wave pattern:** When ocean waves hit islands or ricochet in and out of gulfs and large bays, they develop a distinctive crosshatch pattern (see Figure 21-3b). The sea suddenly becomes exceedingly turbulent — which means the waves have been hitting something solid and reflecting. You're close to land. Unfortunately, this cross-hatch pattern usually means you've already passed the island — although you may still be able to navigate toward it.

FIGURE 21-3: Stationary clouds (a) and wave patterns (b) indicating land

>> **Walls of white mist on the horizon:** Some very low shores — like many of the beaches around the Gulf of Mexico — are so low that they're hard to see, but you can see the mist that their multiple lines of heavy breakers kick up. Look for a wall of mist on the horizon that doesn't evaporate as the day gets hot. You may hear this before seeing it.

>> **Water color:** Generally, deep water is blue and shallow water is green or turquoise, although there are exceptions. This is another reason to keep your log — if you can combine clues, you can put together a pretty good picture of what's going on around you.

>> **Increase of flotsam:** Random debris floating on the surface (such as tree trunks, coconuts, garbage, and so on) usually indicates the presence of land nearby — especially if the wood or vegetation is still fresh.

>> **Butterflies and other insects:** There are no insects on the sea, so unless they've stowed away on your raft, they're coming from land.

We hope that all these indicators help you find your way back to land. Just know that when you get there, you still have some surviving to do.

Coming Ashore: A Dangerous Ordeal

Make no mistake about it: As good as land seems after you've spent a perilous time at sea, coming ashore can be dangerous, involving heavy surf, coral, rocks, and vicious currents, all of which can drown you and your companions. Stay vigilant!

Basic landing principles

Before landing, consider the following facts, which can mean the difference between life and death:

>> **If you have stormy conditions, stay offshore and wait until things calm down.** The closer you get to land during heavy weather, the more violent the waves become. If you have a sea anchor, a drogue, or the ability to paddle, deploy these defensive measures to hold your position until things calm down.

>> **If it's dark out, try to wait until dawn to land.** Going ashore in the dark is excessively dangerous. Waiting for dawn takes a lot of discipline, but this alone can save your life. (We know. We can remember nights when we really wanted to come in to land but didn't — because it was suicide!)

>> **If you know the tide cycle, try to land when the tide is coming in.** When the tide is going out and opposing incoming waves, the seas peak more sharply, making a landing more dangerous.

>> **Try to land on the leeward side of an island or peninsula or near a headland or jetty that breaks up the waves.** The *leeward* side is the area of land located in the wind's shadow; it's where the wind is *not* directly blowing on shore. A *headland* is a bulge of land, and a *jetty* is a finger of land, and they both protrude from the main shoreline. Usually, neither of these landforms has as violent a surf as a beach.

>> **Try to avoid any area where you can hear the breakers *before* you can see them — especially if you see a high wall of mist over the breaker line.** These are signs of violent waves.

>> **Look for a lagoon, bay, or sandy beach that has less wave energy.**

- **Lagoons on volcanic islands:** Generally speaking, lagoons on volcanic islands have inlets that face the wind. This would be the only time you'd want to approach land on the shore where the wind is blowing. Ideally, you'd like to sail and paddle through the inlet and into the lagoon.

- **Lagoons on coral islands:** Generally speaking, lagoons on these types of islands are on the leeward side. If you're on the approach to a low-lying tropical island — especially if you can hear the surf and see a veil of mist around the surf line — you must do everything you can to navigate around it and come in for your landing on the back side.

Procedures for landing

We hope you manage to get to land, and we hope that your landing does nothing more than give you a fine old war story, but the truth is that landings are usually not romantic or fun at all. So get ready:

>> **When you know you're going to land, heavily reinforce your paddles and bailers.** These are the most important objects in your raft, and they're most likely to break just when you need them. Use tape or rope or anything you have to do this.

>> **Dress yourself in every piece of clothing you have for protection against the landing.** Use anything you have handy as extra protection. If you're barefoot, tape cardboard, wood, or metal to your feet. If you have duct tape, now's the time to use it all.

>> **Tie down all objects inside the boat, and tie important electronics, wrapped in waterproof plastic, to your body.** You still need to be able to swim, no doubt, but if you land on an uninhabited coast; you want to land with a stripped-down collection of your best gear, intact and functioning.

>> **Deflate the overhead canopy of the life raft.** That way, you won't be trapped below during capsize.

TIP

>> **If you're in a small, rigid boat, consider backing in.** Simply tie a line to something heavy (such as a big battery or a tire) and hurl it over the front (bow) of the boat. This gives you a drogue that keeps the front of the boat pointed toward the surf while you're landing. The surf has more than enough power to slowly push you — backward — onto the land. This is a safe, common method used by mariners throughout the world.

>> **On approach to any shoreline that has steep land nearby, such as a cliff or a mountain, be ready for the wind to die.** High cliffs frequently block the wind and cause a vacuum near the shore. If you're using sails to guide your craft to safety, these areas can mean serious trouble. Be ready with your paddles and have the paddling chores already assigned.

WARNING

>> **Be ready for multiple lines of breakers.** Many times it looks like you have to get through only one line of big waves. Watch out — you may face two or more.

>> **Stay with the raft or disabled boat for as long as you can.** You'll most likely get stuck — hung up on a rock or some kind of coral. Try to stay with the vessel; the ocean has the nasty habit of hammering boats, and hopefully, it will hammer you ashore. Don't get caught between the boat and a rock or shore.

» **Cut your drogue or sea anchor only as a very last resort.**
If you stall and you're still far offshore, you may have to cut
it free.

Ideally, you want to wash up on shore and quite literally crawl out
onto the sand. That may sound crazy, but that's a safe landing!

Chapter **22**
First Aid on the Water

ven just a little knowledge and ability can make a big difference when you're trying to survive emergencies offshore. Knowing the danger signs — and some of those signs are only visible if you know exactly what to look for — can save lives, including your own.

In this chapter, we show you how to respond to cold water immersion and near drowning, how to handle medical problems common in life-raft situations, and how to treat bites and stings from sea creatures.

Responding to Water Casualties

In any survival situation on the water, you face four major threats. Most people know about *drowning*, but you should know that anytime you go into the water — especially when you go into cold water — you're also at risk for the following:

» Hypothermia

» Cold shock response

» Near drowning

In this section, we first tell you how to get people out of the water so you can treat them, and then we show you how to deal with these dangers separately.

Getting someone out of the water

When rescuing people from the water, always try to *reach* or *throw* something to them so you can haul them in. This is almost invariably better than going into the water yourself, unless you're trained in lifesaving, because the weight and movement of the person in peril can easily overwhelm you. Resist the impulse to get in the water; instead, start by reaching or throwing a flotation device. Here's how to get to someone out of the water:

>> **Reaching:** Plant yourself firmly. Use one hand to hold onto the vessel and one hand to extend a long stick, pole, or rope — any long object — to the person in the water. Expect a heavy tug when the person grabs on.

>> **Throwing:** The best thing to throw is a coil of line or a *life ring,* a circular flotation device found on practically every vessel. When throwing, remember to use a long, swinging forehand (don't throw it like a Frisbee), and always hold on to the vessel with your other hand. Throw the ring past the person in the water and then pull it towards you so they have time to grab it.

>> **Getting in water:** If you must get into the water, tie a tether from the vessel to your body so you can get back safely.

For pointers on how to help someone into a life raft, see Chapter 19.

Grasping the gradual nature of hypothermia

Hypothermia is the progressive cooling of the human body, which leads to mental and physical impairment and later, death. Hypothermia occurs faster in water than on land because water conducts away body heat over 20 times faster than air. It is also particularly lethal in water because it can cause you to go limp, allowing the mouth to dip into the water, causing drowning.

Hypothermia can occur even if you're in tropical waters. It can sometimes take days, whereas it can take only minutes in frigid seas, but enough heat can eventually leave your body to cause hypothermia.

Anytime you've been exposed to a water environment, be on guard for one or more of the symptoms of hypothermia:

>> Extreme shivering

>> Bluish coloring in the lips or skin

>> Apathy and the desire to lie down or give up

>> Dizziness, disorientation, slurred speech

>> A stop in shivering (very dangerous)

If you or one of your companions exhibits the symptoms in the preceding bulleted list, treat for hypothermia. Here are the main points of treatment:

>> **Try to keep the subject from over-exertion.** Climbing out of the water can put an enormous strain on a person with hypothermia. Assist the subject as much as possible.

>> **Try to keep the subject's body horizontal, even when pulling them out of the water.** After the person has cleared the water, elevate the feet slightly, and, if possible, roll them onto their side and place them in the recovery position (find complete instructions in Chapter 13).

>> **Warm the subject slowly, especially if they have been in the water for a long time.** Warm the torso and neck first. Use blankets or other insulation to keep the person warm. In dire circumstances you may have to hold the subject close to your body to transfer heat; be careful that this doesn't cool you to the point of hypothermia as well.

>> **Monitor the airway closely, and don't allow the person to inhale vomit.**

>> **Be prepared for *afterdrop*, which is a continued decline of central body temperature after the rewarming process has begun.**

Turn to Chapter 13 for a detailed explanation of how to treat hypothermia, the deadliest of conditions.

Treating cold shock response

Cold shock response is a sudden incapacitation of the human body due to cold water immersion. It can incapacitate you so suddenly that you can't swim, inflate a life vest, or climb into a life raft. Signs of cold shock response include the following:

>> Accelerated heartbeat

>> Dizziness and disorientation

>> Hyperventilation

>> Motor skill impairment

WARNING

Anyone immersed in water that's less than 50°F (10°C) is considered at risk for cold shock response.

When subjects perish from cold shock response, their core temperatures aren't at the level necessary to cause death from hypothermia. Cold shock deaths usually come from the inability to move (the muscles don't respond) or sometimes cardiac arrest, either of which may lead to drowning.

Treat cold shock response the same way you treat hypothermia, which we discuss in the preceding section. If you're with someone who's at risk of cold shock response, monitor the person closely (don't leave the person unattended) and be ready to perform CPR.

REMEMBER

Studies have demonstrated that humans, if exposed to cold water often enough, can build up a tolerance to cold shock. If you're accustomed to crossing cold rivers or swimming in cold seas but you're with someone who isn't, be ready for the possibility that your companion will go into cold shock response, even though you don't feel any effects yourself.

Handling near drowning

Drowning is death due to asphyxiation from fluid in the lungs. Unfortunately, you can't do anything for those who've expired. But many times people inhale enough fluid simply to lose consciousness, become incapacitated, or have difficulty breathing. This condition is called *partial drowning* or *near drowning*.

Reviving near-drowning subjects

You can revive some near-drowning subjects through resuscitation. Treatment involves performing CPR and allowing gravity to withdraw as much fluid out of the lungs as possible. Follow these steps:

1. **Remove the subject from the water, trying to keep the head, especially the mouth, lower than the rest of the body.**

This prevents the accidental inhalation of water that may be in the throat.

2. **Lay the subject down on the ground and check their circulation, airway, and breathing, in that order; perform CPR if the subject isn't breathing or has no pulse.**

Continue CPR until you're exhausted. The only good thing we can say about long-term cold water immersion is that sometimes it slows the body's functions down to such an extent that people survive for a very long time, even after they've lost consciousness.

3. **If the subject is breathing and has a pulse, place them on their side in the recovery position, and make sure the mouth is free of obstructions.**

Water and vomit should be able to drain freely from the airway.

4. **Monitor the subject (as we explain in the next section).**

For more on CPR and the recovery position, flip to Chapter 13.

Monitoring someone after near drowning

WARNING

Even just a small amount of inhaled water can cause the lungs to become swollen and congested in minutes or hours. Death often occurs after the subject has been pulled from the water and seems to be recovering. Watch near-drowning subjects for the following signs:

» Incessant coughing

» Coughing up water, froth, or bubbles

>> Shortness of breath

>> Lightheadedness and disorientation

Treat these symptoms by putting the subject in the recovery position and consider another bout of CPR (see Chapter 13).

Treating Common Ailments while Afloat

Most of the problems we talk about in this section aren't deadly by themselves, but they can become deadly when they're combined with other conditions, fatigue, or demoralization.

REMEMBER

Dehydration is a serious concern on salt water; go to Chapter 20 for information.

Seasickness

Seasickness, or simply *motion sickness,* occurs when a vessel's bobbing and rolling motions on water irritate your sense of balance. Symptoms include yawning, headache, nausea, and vomiting. Seasickness usually lasts no more than three days, although in severe cases it can be persistent.

You can take medications to prevent seasickness, but generally speaking, you must take it before going afloat. The most common over-the-counter medicine is dimenhydrinate (Dramamine), which is sometimes in first aid kits. One effective prescription treatment is the *transdermal patch* of scopolamine, a dime-size adhesive gauze that sticks to your skin and releases medication into your body over a period of days.

TIP

Prevention and treatment are basically the same thing when dealing with seasickness. Your goal is to try to relieve the irritation as much as you can. The following list includes the most reliable methods for preventing and treating seasickness — experiment with each method until you find one that works for you:

>> **Look at the distant horizon.** The distant horizon is a stable 'landmark,' and looking at it can prevent your sense of balance from being irritated.

>> **Try not to sit down.** Sitting only makes seasickness worse. When you stand, you allow your body to compensate a little

for the boat's motion. If you can't stand, even kneeling upright can help.

>> **Stay active.** Give yourself something to do to take your mind off of being seasick.

>> **Change the motion of the vessel.** This may be impossible to do in a life raft, but if you're in a vessel you can steer, try turning to a new course so the vessel has a different motion in the waves. Some rolling motions are easier to take than others.

>> **Change your location on the boat or raft.** You may be in a position where you're getting a bad motion, one that's making you sick.

>> **Get some rest, or even better, some sleep.** Seasickness and fatigue are buddies — wherever you find one, you usually find the other. When resting, lie on your back with your face up and your eyes closed.

>> **Eat ginger.** Take ginger capsules the moment you feel the symptoms. If the symptoms are advanced, and especially if you're about to vomit, try nibbling on sugar-coated ginger pieces. Some consider ginger to be ineffective, but we've used it with great success.

>> **Drink something.** If you're vomiting, you're dehydrating, and that weakens you. If you're not dehydrated, consider a clear soda, if you have access to it, to settle your stomach.

Sunburn and heat maladies

Sunburn is a serious threat on open water. Combined with other problems, it can cause you to go into shock. Do everything you can to shield yourself from the sun, and remember that the sun's reflection on the water can burn you, too. Try to keep every inch of your skin covered. Use sunblock if you have it, or try making improvised sunblock from mud, charcoal, or used motor oil.

Exposed to the sun on open water, you are also subject to heat exhaustion and heat stroke. These result from hyperthermia, or the overheating of the body. For symptoms and treatments, go to Chapter 17.

Saltwater chafe

Of all the unheroic injuries, *skin chafe* must be the most painful. When skin rubs continuously on any surface in a saltwater environment, you're going to have a problem. If your skin is rubbing on a surface like the side of the raft, try to change your body's position or try to protect the skin.

If left unattended, saltwater chafe quickly degenerates into *saltwater sores*. These inflammations start out as pea-size ulcers, but they can widen to become dime-size or larger.

To treat saltwater sores, scrupulously clean every break in your skin with soap and water if possible. Bathing in fresh water helps, but if none is available, clean gently with saltwater.

Treating Bites and Stings at Sea

We wish we could tell you just to avoid the dangerous animals of the sea, but unfortunately, the sea has a way of throwing them in your way, regardless of what you do. This section tells you how to treat injuries from these creatures of the sea.

Jellyfish

Jellyfish stings occur when you brush against the animal's membranes and it releases venom into your skin. All stings are painful, and some are fatal. The white, translucent *box jellyfish*, which inhabits the waters north of Australia, is probably the deadliest. An animal that looks like a jellyfish, but is actually a colony of small animals, is the clear, purple *Portuguese man-o'-war*, which is present in all the world's oceans. Reactions to serious stings include nausea, vomiting, shock, and cardiac arrest. In a survival situation stay clear of all jellyfish.

To treat jellyfish stings, follow these procedures:

1. **If you have access to vinegar, pour it on the tentacles; otherwise, use seawater.**

    This neutralizes the stinging mechanism. There is no truth to the urban legend that urine or meat tenderizer relieve jellyfish stings.

2. **Remove the tentacles using a hard plastic card, tweezers, sticks, or gloves.**

   Don't touch the tentacles with your hands.

3. **Apply shaving cream, soapy water, baking soda, or even mud to soothe the wound, and then shave the area with a razor or a knife.**

4. **Apply more water or vinegar (or seawater) to the wound to dilute the poison.**

   If the tentacles have gotten in the eyes, irrigate liberally with fresh water. If in the mouth, rinse with a solution of one part vinegar to three parts water.

5. **Treat the wound like a sprain and use the RICES procedure (see Chapter 13).**

WARNING

Severe jellyfish injuries may demand CPR — see Chapter 13.

Sea snakes

Sea snakes normally don't envenomate the subject enough to cause serious harm; however in a survival situation, you should consider all sea snakes as lethal. The first sign of envenomation is usually a headache and aching muscles.

Treat a sea snake bite like you treat other snakebites: Start by keeping the bite lower than the subject's heart at all times. Check out Chapter 13 for more details.

Stinging fish and stingrays

Fish stings can damage large portions of tissue and be exceedingly painful — the pain can sometimes last for days or even weeks.

WARNING

Never try to handle any fish that has spines, points, spikes, or bristles. Never handle a fish that's spotted, that looks like a stone or a rock, or that has zebra stripes or tiger stripes. And never wade near a reef barefoot.

Anytime you believe stingrays may be nearby, keep your bare feet off the seabed. Stingrays swim across the seabed, and if they feel threatened, they may sting you with the barb on the end of their tail, which is sometimes fatal. If you hook a stingray while fishing, consider cutting the line rather than boarding the ray.

If you get stung, wash the wound immediately with soap and water if possible. If you have access to hot water, immerse the wound in the warmest water you can handle without being scalded. Repeated immersions in hot water should help. Be prepared to treat for shock and administer CPR. See Chapter 13 to get the details on performing CPR.

Cone shells and terebra shells

Cone shells are small gastropods that look like miniature, brightly colored pinecones, between 1 and 4 inches (2.5 and 10 centimeters) in length. You can find them in the Indian and Pacific Oceans, and they frequently travel across the seabed, usually at night.

Terebra shells also live in the Indian and Pacific Oceans. They're thin and usually 4 to 6 inches (10 to 15 centimeters) in length. Like the cone shell, the terebra shell has a stinging barb and should be considered very dangerous, although the stings are rarely fatal.

Like ray stings, you treat shell stings by immersing the wound in the hottest water the person can stand without scalding.

5
The Part of Tens

Chapter **23**
Ten Ways to Practice Wilderness Survival Skills

Practicing the skills presented in this book even just once will help a lot if you ever have to use them in the wild. Practice makes these techniques familiar and teaches you how persistent and resourceful you must be to survive.

This chapter covers important skills including fire building, toolmaking, direction finding, and performing CPR.

WARNING
When practicing fire building, have a garden hose or other fire extinguisher ready, don't build next to anything flammable, and check out local regulations regarding *campfires* or *open fires* before you start!

Start a Fire with Two Matches

The ability to start a fire can save your life in a survival situation. See if you can get a fire going with just two matches. This will teach you to build the fire structure very carefully, using plenty of the three fire fuel types described in Chapter 5: tinder, kindling, and fuel.

Light a Fire with a Magnifying Glass or Eyeglasses

Any magnifying glass should work to start a fire; see Chapter 5 for instructions. As for eyeglasses, only those for farsighted people work.

Fire Up the Flames with a Bow

Using a bow to rapidly spin a spindle and create fire by friction is a super survival skill, but it takes time and persistence to learn how (check out Chapter 5). Practicing will teach you:

>> What kind of cordage does — and doesn't — work for the bowstring (try bootlaces, parachute cord, and others)

>> How to select a branch to make the bow

>> The speed and pressure you need to maintain on the spindle to get an ember

>> How fiddly the whole operation can be!

Turn Your Pants into a Flotation Device

A couple hours in a swimming pool can teach you a lot about making a life preserver from a pair of trousers (see Chapter 18). This is a very realistic simulation, and it's one of the best survival practice sessions you can do.

Start in chest-deep water to learn the inflation process. Then do it in the deeper end of the pool, where you have to take your pants off while floating and/or treading water. You will have to learn to float and very gingerly slip off shoes and trousers.

WARNING

If you're not a good swimmer, obviously the deep-end practice session can be lethal, because you may get tangled in your clothes and drown.

Find North with Help from the Sky

Finding North day or night is usually easy, and once you face north, east is on your right, west is on your left, and south is behind you. Chapter 10 discusses both day-time and night-time methods to find North; practice some of these while out on a walk, day and night, and you will feel much more confident in the wild.

Build a Tripod

A tripod of stout poles is useful to hang a pot over a fire and as a rack for drying clothes or food. In the wilderness, you'd make a tripod from three saplings, stripped of bark and each about 1 to 2 inches (3 to 6 centimeters) in diameter. At home, simulate these with broomsticks or other similar poles.

Practice teaches you how much tension you need to lash the tripod together, and what kinds of cordage is good for the job (see Chapter 14).

Download and Experiment with a Plant Identification App

There are many apps for identifying all sorts of vegetation. Some specialize in certain regions, like urban areas or wilderness areas, and some specialize in types of plants, such as mushrooms. If you plan on taking a smartphone into the wilderness, test some of these apps first. Respected apps include PictureThis, which identifies plants that you photograph, (about 100,000 species are available for comparison) and WildEdibles (less than $10), which focuses on edible wild plant foods.

Use a Transpiration Bag to Collect Water

Water is a major concern in any survival situation, and you should know several places to find it outdoors and several ways to extract it from wilderness resources (such as plants). Chapter 7 shows how to make a *transpiration bag,* which is simply a large bag (preferably plastic) that you wrap around the bushy end of a tree or bush limb. The resulting assembly, about the size of a beach ball, is then fitted with a drinking hose. As water naturally evaporates from the plant tissues, it collects inside the bag. Attaching a drinking tube that doesn't leak is the main challenge.

Don't cover more than 20 percent of a plant's leaves when using a transpiration bag; that could kill it.

Use a Reflective Surface to Practice Signaling

You can practice signaling for help with reflective surfaces, such as a CD or a shiny smartphone, in a park, with a friend. Without blinding anyone, try to use the reflective surface to flash the sun at your friend from across the park. Aiming is the hardest part; see the Cheat Sheet at www.dummies.com for a good method.

To make the exercise more fun, start by having your friend stand still, and then see how fast you can get at spotting them, picking the reflective item off the ground and signaling successfully. Or try a moving target: signal your friend while they walk along at a normal pace. Don't try to signal actual airplanes; that's dangerous and can get you in trouble!

Practice CPR

You can practice *cardiopulmonary resuscitation* (CPR) simply by going through the motions of finding the right place to press on the chest, lacing your fingers in the right way to do the compressions, and getting accustomed to the rhythm of compressions and breaths (see Chapter 13). This builds memories that you can refer to if you end up in a bad spot. Taking a course from the Red Cross is the best way to practice CPR, and it's inexpensive.

When practicing CPR, don't actually do the compressions or breaths; just practice the motions and the rhythm.

Chapter 24
Ten Quick Escapes

W hen you get home, you can tell everyone how you cob-bled together a shelter, built a fire, and finally flagged down your rescuers. The most dramatic part of your story, however, usually comes when you have to tell how you made your great escape. In this chapter, we tell you how to get out of ten high-adrenaline situations.

Getting Out of a Sinking Car

Here's how to escape if your car ends up in water:

1. **Roll the windows down and unlock the doors before water disables the electrical system.**

2. **If water is NOT coming through the window, unbuckle your seatbelt and climb out.**

3. **If water IS coming through the window, stay buckled up and wait.**

   Water rushing into the car can overwhelm you and push you around in the car. Also, as the car floods, it could roll, and staying in the seat helps to keep you oriented.

TIP

4. When the water level reaches your chin, unbuckle your seat belt, take a deep breath, and swim out an open window.

5. If the window is up, use a heavy object to break the window, take a deep breath, and swim out the broken window.

TIP

Don't try to break the windshield — it's too strong. Many companies manufacture survival tools specifically made to both cut seatbelts and knock out a window to escape a car in danger. Every car should have one convenient to reach, and everyone should know how to use it.

6. When you are out of the vehicle, follow bubbles up toward the water's surface.

In a sinking-car situation you must wait until the car floods before trying to open a door. Even then the door will feel heavy and it will be hard to open, but adrenaline will help you do it!

Escaping a Small Plane Upside Down in Water

Many small planes flip forward and land upside down when they ditch in the water, so you're most likely to find yourself inverted, with the cabin filling with water. Here are the steps to get out, once the plane has stopped moving:

1. Place one hand on the nearest exit (a door or window) and keep it there.

2. Release your seat belt and pull yourself out through the exit.

3. Follow bubbles to the water's surface.

Deal with stubborn windows with a heavy tool, like a fire extinguisher, or by kicking with your legs (which are much stronger than your arms).

Surviving a Small Boat or Canoe Capsize

Small boats and canoes are easy to *capsize* or tip over if you're not careful. If you're alone and not far from shore, you can probably just climb on top or hang on the side and paddle to safety, because many small boats and canoes have integral flotation devices for just this purpose. If you don't have that option, here's what to do if your vessel turns over.

For small sailboats:

1. Stand on the *daggerboard* (also known as a *centerboard*), which sticks down from the underside of the boat.

2. Let your weight roll the boat upright.

TIP

If the boat has turned all the way over, you may have to climb up on the overturned hull, grasp the daggerboard with your hands, and lean back to slowly turn the boat on its side.

If you were in a canoe and you have a friend with you:

1. With your lifejackets still on, go under the overturned boat.

2. When you're both underneath and ready, count to three and then, together in one fluid motion, push the canoe up out of the water a few inches and then throw it over to one side, flipping it right side up in the process.

Many times, this maneuver requires the two of you to kick with your legs at the same time to give yourself just enough buoyancy to lift and flip the boat.

TIP

If you have two canoes, one capsized and the other upright, you can lift the inverted canoe out of the water and slide it crosswise across the floating canoe; then turn it over and launch it back into the water.

Escaping a Forest Fire

Forest fires can move quickly and wipe out almost anything in their path. For humans, the main dangers are *suffocation* (the fire consumes so much oxygen that there's literally nothing to breathe), choking (breathing in ash or dense smoke), and of course, burning. Here's how to escape a forest fire:

1. **Make a mask from a bandana or other material and use it to cover your mouth and nose tightly to protect yourself from smoke inhalation.**

2. **Try to get downhill and into a clearing where there is little or no fuel to burn.**

   Fire moves upward fastest, so going downhill buys you time. Sandy areas like dry riverbeds are good places to go. A forest clearing is better than a fully vegetated forest. If you find a lake or river, get in and wait for the fire to pass. The main thing is to find and go toward an area that has less fuel (vegetation) to burn.

3. **If you can't find cover and a fire is coming close, dig a ditch, get in, and cover yourself with as much sand or dirt as you can.**

4. **When the fire has passed, stay in the areas that are burnt off and begin efforts to signal for help.**

   With nothing left to burn, the fire can't come back.

Evading a Bee Swarm

Here's how you can evade a bee swarm attack:

- » Run as fast as you can toward dense vegetation; they may lose your trail there.

- » If you have a campfire going, run to it and throw some wet vegetation on it to make dense smoke, which deters bees.

- » If you have a blanket or tarp, wrap yourself in it tightly and wait them out.

- » If you can find a body of water, try to lay in it on your back, breathing with just your lips out of the water or using a reed to breathe (a fun thing to practice on a hot afternoon).

WARNING

Try not to crush bees; their dead bodies emit an alarm to others.

Surviving a Bear Encounter

Bears are common in many wilderness regions. In bear country, it's best to let them know you're coming in the first place. Some people wear a bell while hiking, or yell, "Hey bear!" periodically, and/or hit trees or rocks with sticks. These sounds often frighten bears away so there's no encounter at all. For more on deterring bears, see Chapter 15.

TIP

Although bears are unpredictable, some general advice has proven valuable if you actually encounter a bear:

» **If a bear spots you:** Don't run or make eye contact. Hold your ground for a moment and then back away slowly. You can try speaking in a calm, monotone voice to reassure the bear. If you're between a mother and a cub, get away quickly but without making jerky, panicky moves.

» **If the bear rushes you:** Hold your ground. This is important but hard to do. Often bears will make a bluff charge and turn away from a person who holds their ground.

» **If a bear attacks you:** Don't fight back. A bear is much stronger than you are. Play dead by curling up in a ball and protecting your neck and skull with your hands. The only time to fight back is if the bear doesn't leave you alone after you've played dead for a while; then, it has decided to eat you, and you might as well fight. Go for the eyes!

TIP

Many people venturing into bear country carry *bear spray*, a canister containing chemical deterrents much like mace. Sometimes it deters bears, other times it doesn't, and sometimes it backfires when the wind blows the spray back into the human's face! Still, it's a good idea to carry bear spray and learn how to use it.

Encountering a Mountain Lion

Mountain lions (also known as *cougars, pumas,* or *panthers*) are big cats that can weigh as much as adult people. They rarely attack people, but they are opportunistic predators, looking for the easiest thing to eat.

If a mountain lion confronts you, do not run. Also, do not crouch, limp, or act infirm; the cat knows the difference between strong and weak prey. Instead, you want to convince the mountain lion that you're the *hardest* thing in the world to eat, so make yourself larger by opening your jacket and spreading it out to the sides, or by lifting your backpack over your head. You can also try holding up tree branches or large boards — anything that makes you appear to be a very large animal.

If the animal attacks, it usually goes for the neck or head. Many people have fought off mountain lions. A sharp blow to the bridge of the nose or to the eyes with your fist or better yet a large stone or the blunt end of an ax communicates to the animal that you're not easy prey.

Surviving an Avalanche

Avalanches are sudden landslides of ice and snow that can bury and suffocate you in the blink of an eye. The best policy is to avoid avalanche terrain altogether (see Chapter 16). However, if you are caught in an avalanche, follow these steps:

1. **Ditch anything attached to your body.**

   Skis, snowshoes, backpacks and ski poles all tend to drag you down into the snow (if crossing avalanche terrain it is good to loosen these before you start).

2. **Use a swimming motion to try to stay on the surface.**

   Swim in an overhand, freestyle motion. Some survivors say being in an avalanche is like being caught in a raging river.

3. **As you slow down, fold your arms across your face to help create a breathing space as the snow settles around you.**

4. **After you stop moving, try to dig for the surface or make sounds to help rescuers locate you.**

   This is a good reason to carry a whistle on a cord around your neck in snowy country.

   If you're not sure which way is up, let some drool slide out of your mouth — it heads downward, so you want to dig in the opposite direction.

TIP

Waiting Out a Whiteout

A *whiteout* is a thick mist or blizzard that reduces visibility to just a few feet. If you don't know exactly where you are, you may find yourself stepping off a cliff, so traveling in a whiteout is a bad idea in survival situations.

To wait out a whiteout:

1. Get your hat on to save body heat.
2. Make a snow shelter (refer to Chapter 16).
3. Sit on your backpack or vegetation so you are not in direct contact with the cold snow.
4. Use candles, space blankets, huddling with another person — whatever you need to stay warm overnight.

Getting Out of Quicksand

Quicksand forms when water wells up from an underground spring and "liquefies" sand or mud to the consistency of gelatin. It's most often found near riverbanks and beaches, especially at low tide.

If you find yourself in quicksand, don't panic — your body is denser than quicksand, and you are unlikely to sink. In most cases you know when you are in quicksand because one leg goes in deep and does not want to come out (a good reason to use a walking stick when on wet ground). Don't panic; instead follow these instructions:

1. Push your walking stick down the length of your leg and work it back and forth to break the suction and allow you to pull your leg out.
2. If Step 1 does not work, try to sit or lay flat on the surface to spread out your weight.
3. Using your arms, try to crawl or swim towards firm ground.

Index

carotid artery, 219

cars. *See* vehicles

car seat covers, 58

catchment plane, 102

caterpillars, 283

cattail, 265

caves
   checking for animals in, 87–88
   as shelters, 87–88

CB radios, 206

CDs as reflectors, 201

cellphones
   battery discipline, 209
   caution on overreliance, 14
   conserving battery, 209
   importance of, 209
   light, 205
   protecting before abandoning ship, 343
   sending texts, 211–212
   signaling with
      charged phoned without reception, 210–211
      charged phone with reception, 210
      noncharged (dead) cellphone, 212
   temperature, 209–210
   using in the wild, 167

centerboard, 419

Centers for Disease Control (CDC), 284

centipedes, 324–325

charcoal as sunblock, 313

Cheat Sheet, 3, 416

chert, 259–260

cholera, 275

circles, 152

circulation, checking, 13, 219

city glow, 393

civilization signs
   detecting when at sea, 393
   detecting when lost, 185–186

clay as sunblock, 313

cliffs
   drop-offs, 329
   glissading caution, 303
   potential falls, 14

topographic contour lines of, 152

whiteout caution, 423

wind updrafts/downdrafts, 21

closed fractures, 229–230

clothes drag, 218

clothing
   animal skins in, 59–60
   for cold weather or environments, 9–10, 53–61, 306
   colors and fit, 64
   for hot environments, 62–64, 312–313
   improvised layers for, 58–59
   improvising cold-weather clothing, 55–61
   inadequate, 14
   inflating when you don't have life jacket, 348–349, 414
   insulating, 9, 306
   for jungle environment, 277–278
   layering for temperature control, 53–55, 64
   as protection for landing, 399
   sewing kits, 32, 57
   for thermoregulation, 9–10
   ventilation, 64
   wetting for evaporative cooling, 64

clouds, 21–22, 326, 395–396. *See also* weather

clove hitch knots, 250–251

clubs, 132

coconuts, 106

cold, defined, 287

cold environments. *See* snow- or ice-bound environments

cold shock, 299

cold shock response, 344, 404

cold sweat, avoiding, 54

cold therapy, 232

cold trap, 290

cold-weather clothing
   animal skins in, 59–60
   improvised layers for, 58–59
   items of, 55–56
   sewing, 57

collapsible water containers, 25

collisions involving vessels, 338–340

comfort, 38

compasses
   carrying, 25
   checking when disoriented, 180
   declination (or variation), 157–158
   deviation, 158
   finding direction with charts and, 391
   importance of, 155
   improvising, 163
   orienteering, 30, 156
   stick and shadow method, 171–172
   trusting, 148
   types, 155
   using
      boxing the needle, 160, 161
      correcting for potential errors, 156–158, 161, 175, 180, 391
      establishing field bearings, 159–160
      with map, 159–162
      orienting maps, 160–162
      setting course from map bearing, 162

compression bandage, 232

condensation, collecting, 372
   gathering dew, 103
   solar still, 104–105
   transpiration bag, 103–104

cone shells, 410

contour intervals, 151

contour lines, 151–152

cooking
   fish, 140, 142
   mammal foods, 141–142
   plant foods, 141

cooling off, 311. *See also* thermoregulation

coordinates, 153–154

coral islands, 398

cordage. *See also* knots
   improvising, 57
   making own, 255–259

sea birds, 383
  seaweed, 369, 383–384
  turtles, 382–383
fish, 134–140
insects and invertebrates, 142
mammal foods, 141–142
managing supplies, 122
plants and fruits, 115–123
poisonous plants and animals,
    avoiding, 12
preparing, 140–143
preserving, 114
rationing, 114
smoking, 142–144
staying nourished, 11–12
in survival kits, 33
footbed, 304
footgear
  boot wraps, 306
  in cold environments, 60–61,
    288, 302–306
  for deep snow, 52
  gaiters, 306
  for hot environments, 313
  importance of, 60–61
  insulating, 61
  for jungle environment, 270
  layers inside of, 60
  loosening, 288
  snowshoes, 305–306
ford, 190
forepeak, 342
forest fires, escaping, 419–420
forests in desert areas (gallery
    forests), 21
forests in temperate climates
  camps and shelters, 281–282
  dangerous wildlife
    bears, 270–271
    mountain lions, 271–272
    snakes, 272
    spiders and ticks, 272–273
  diseases
    from contaminated water or
      food, 274–275
    from insect and animal
      bites, 276–277
    preventing, 274
  edible plants, 118–119

foxes, 322
fractures
  closed, 229–230
  defined, 229
  open, 230–231
  padding and bandaging, 231
  splints for, 229–230
  traction for, 230
  treating, 229–231
frap, 253
freeboard, 336
frigate birds, 395
fruits, edible, 116, 141
frustration, 45
fuel for fire
  gathering, 67
  in snowy places, 294–295
  types, 67

G

gaiters, 52, 306, 324
gallery forests, 331. See also
    deserts
game trails, 101, 124
game-trail snare, 126
gannets, 395
garbage bags, 29, 58
gathering and hunting. See food
giardia, 275
Giesbrecht, Gordon (doctor),
    299
ginger capsules, 4–7
glacial cracks (crevasses), 302
glaciers, 302. See also snow- or
    ice-bound environments
glass, sharpened, 130
glissading., 302–303
gloves, 33
goggles, 52, 307–308, 312
GPS (global positioning system)
    receivers. See also
    navigation
  caution on overreliance, 14
  datum, 165
  displaying location, 164
  how they work, 164–165
  position format, 166
  settings, 165–166

in survival kits, 25
  tracking feature, 166–167
  unit format, 166
  waypoint feature, 148, 166
granola bars, 33
grasshoppers, 142, 321
Great Lakes weather forecast
    services, 18
green wood, 66
grommets, 90
ground-to-air emergency code
    (patterns), 198–199
ground vehicles, 182
ground water, 101
group
  decision-making, 41
  falling behind, 16
  getting separated from, 16
gunwale, 336

H

hammerstone, 251, 260
ham radios, 207
handhold, 78. See also bow fire
hand lines, 375
handrail, 148–149
hands, keeping warm, 60, 288
handwear, 59, 60
hatch failure, 341
hats. See head coverings
Hawaiian sling, 378
hawks, 101
head coverings
  in cold environments, 60
  in hot environment, 63–64,
    312
  in jungle environment,
    277–278
  in water, 343
headlamp, 23
headland, 398
headwear, 60
heat exhaustion, 310
heat maladies, 407
heat stroke, 52, 310–311
heat therapy, 236
heel (boat), 337

About the Authors

John Haslett is a veteran expedition leader and adventure writer. He is the author of various adventure books, magazine articles, and academic papers, and his work has been featured in *National Geographic Adventure, Archaeology, QST,* and other magazines. In the 1990s, with the help of an isolated community of Ecuadorian mariners, he built four 30,000-pound wooden rafts and then voyaged on the Pacific Ocean aboard those primitive vessels for hundreds of days. His memoir of that extraordinary time is called *The Lost Raft* (Great Adventures Press).

Cameron M. Smith's mountaineering, sailing, archaeological, and icecap expeditions have taken him around the world. In 2004, he made the first solo winter ski crossing of Iceland's storm-lashed Vatnajökull icecap, an expedition televised on the *National Geographic International* and documented in his book *Where Survival Is a Palace* (Great Adventures Press). Cameron's writing has appeared in many magazines and the anthologies *The Best Travel Writing* (2008, 2009) and *They Lived to Tell the Tale* (Explorers Club Books). A Life Fellow of the Royal Geographical Society and past member of the Explorers Club and the Society for Human Performance in Extreme Environments, Cameron is currently exploring the lower stratosphere with his hot air and hydrogen balloons, flying in his home-built pressurized suits; you can find out more at www.cameronmsmith.com.

Dedication

John Haslett: This book is dedicated to Annie Biggs, Cameron Smith, Alejandro Martinez, Cesar Alarcon, and Dower Medina — five extraordinary people who know a thing or two about surviving in bad conditions.

And to the boys and men of Troop 100, BSA, wherever you are . . .

Cameron M. Smith: Like John, I dedicate this book to my companions in climbing, flying, diving, and ice-trekking; thanks, all, for throwing your dice with me! I also dedicate this book to the indigenous people across the globe — the Samburu of East Africa, the fisher-folk of West Ecuador, and the Inupiat of Alaska — who taught me how to survive in places where suburbanites like me would otherwise just vanish.

Authors' Acknowledgments

John Haslett: Thanks to my wife, Annie Biggs, for her editing, proofing, scheduling, strategizing, and solid-backboned, fighting spirit. I am lucky. I would also like to acknowledge Cameron McPherson Smith, PhD, my coauthor. Not only did he write roughly half of this book, but he also hand-drew some 120 technical illustrations at the same time. Thanks to our agent, Matt Wagner, at Fresh Books, Inc., who has proved to be a first-rate literary rep. I'd like to thank the original editor of this book, Chad Sievers, who was great to work with. The editor of this revised edition, Alissa Schwipps, deserves recognition for her positive attitude in guiding some pretty significant changes. Search and Rescue veterans Gary Cascio and Rick Goodman, both of New Mexico, should be thanked for their sound advice on the finer points of signaling for rescue.

Cameron M. Smith: I thank John Haslett for inviting me aboard one of his extraordinary raft expeditions and for his rock-solid friendship over more than twenty years, and I thank John's wife, Annie Biggs, for supporting John's expeditions. I thank our agent, Matt Wagner, for suggesting this project and everyone at Wiley who have guided us through now the second edition. I thank my friends and mentors from Boy Scout Troop 616, among whose company I first learned the rewards of an outdoor life. Thanks also to my high school buddy, Idaho Falls Fire Chief Jeff Parsons, for his technical comments, and, of course, my parents, professors Donald E. and Margit J. Posluschny Smith, for granting me the freedom to weave reality from my dreams. There is no greater gift, and I know that the price — their worry while I'm on expedition — is real.

Publisher's Acknowledgments

Executive Editor: Lindsay Berg

Development Editor: Alissa Schwipps

Copy Editor: Jennifer Connolly

Technical Editor: Megan Hine

Senior Managing Editor: Kristie Pyles

Production Editor: Mohammed Zafar Ali

Cover Image: © Galashevsky Yakow/ Shutterstock